C000048100

Girls, Assassins & Other Bad Ideas

A Memoir

Mae Wagner

Burning Soul Press

Girls, Assassins & Other Bad Ideas
A Memoir

Copyright © 2022 by Mae Wagner

All rights reserved.

No part of this book may be reproduced in any form or by any electronic or mechanical means, including information storage and retrieval systems, without written permission from the author, except for the use of brief quotations in a book review.

Cover Design by Dee Dee Book Covers

ISBNs:

978-1-950476-54-1 (hardcover)

978-1-950476-51-0 (paperback)

978-1-950476-50-3 (eBook)

Published by:

burning soul press

Contents

For the goodest girls, and boy, ever ... Betsy, Makaila, Paisley, Knightley, Emma, and Elenor ... the love of a dog is the truest, most faithful form of love we'll ever know. They never let us down, but sometimes they pee on the carpet.

Introduction

The music would consume me, this is what I remember. I would belt out the lyrics—or more likely, what I believed them to be—while dancing and twirling.

Freedom.

My feet were everywhere, only landing on scorched asphalt long enough to push me into the air again.

I felt alive!

My heartbeat aligned itself to the rhythm coming from the local pop station as I lived out my best life on those Saturday nights in my grandmother's driveway. Dinner dishes done, she would ask me to go out and close the gate. Little antenna radio tucked beneath my arm, I'd spend the better part of two hours dreaming I was a student in *Fame*, or at a raging high school party just like the ones in the John Hughes movies I loved. My grandmother's dusty New Mexico driveway set the stage as I stepped into my own world. The only thing jolting me from my imaginary paradise of pulsating music was when the local DJ would interrupt for a song "going out to" someone. In those moments I would freeze, waiting.

Would he ever say my name?

Those minutes were the lowest because of course he never did. Despite my sneaking phone calls to dedicate songs to my mom (Nora was a tried-and-true country and western fan and therefore would never have heard them), my best friend Melanie (always "Girls Just Want to Have Fun" or "True Blue." Always.), or to some other random person of the moment.

I lived for those Saturday nights all week.

Now in my midforties, I look back and wonder what my grandmother's neighbors thought of that ridiculous little white girl losing herself in the driveway. There was no landscape coverage. These poor people had complete access to the *Misty Mae Show*, terrible vocals and all.

For what it's worth, they were always so kind to me, even after the magic of the driveway could no longer save me. Even if it was pity that replaced their neighborly charm, they still smiled in kindness when they said my name.

I'll never forget that. Also, I miss that girl. I miss her unabashed love and the freedom she dove straight into, not caring who was watching. I miss that girl who, brokenhearted that no one felt songs for her, still recovered in time to dance her heart out.

These pages are for her.

Dear Friend, these pages are also for you.

I needed to begin this book with a letter to you. At its core, this book is a collection of letters. Letters to others, letters to myself, letters of equal parts vulnerability and gratitude because of a unique compilation of moments, people, and experiences. The beating heart of this work is about connection and humanity, growth, failure, resilience, and love.

Always, always it is about love.

This is the story of a girl turned woman who lost only to find, who hid in darkness only to one day reach for the courage to chase the light. This is the story about a girl who ached to be wanted, to be loved.

This is my story—the journey of how I learned to finally love myself, and the lights along the path that lit my way.

I am so grateful you are here, walking through this journey with me.

In case no one has told you lately:

You are beautiful!

You are made up of value.

You are meant to be a dragon slayer, just like that brave little girl ...

~ M

The Anthill

{To the girl who would: "I of the Storm" by Of Monsters and Men}

One of my earliest memories is sitting at the edge of my front yard, in a yellow jumper, screaming. I was sitting on an anthill, and the ants were biting me. The memory of those hot tears on my face and the sound of my deep, wailing sobs feels like yesterday. My mother stands, smoking, on the front step of our gold and white single-wide, telling me to "figure it out" myself. I can still feel the deepest feelings my little two-year-old self had ever felt. Those powerful truths being stitched into my tiny soul told me that I was not worth saving; I knew I deserved the pain. I could not imagine how to move past the pain to get off the hill; the ants just kept coming and I was done. For the first time ever, I knew what it meant to give up.

As a woman, now in my forties, I will accept that over time I probably projected feelings and thoughts into that memory. It isn't likely that a toddler could process such big things, and yet ...

And yet, they feel so true to the moment when I recall it.

At some point, as I sit there accepting my end, another character enters the scene. She is a teenage girl who spends a fair amount of time with my mom and me. Her name is Amy and I love her. She swoops in, picks me up from the anthill, and this is where the thin veil of a memory stops.

Over the years I would ask my mother about this memory, and of course she would deny it ever happened. For a long time, this left me feeling like I might be crazy. How could I know so many details, from every thread of that jumper to the exact hues in the vast New Mexico sky? How could I recall something so vividly overwhelming and painful if it never happened?

One day late in my thirties, Amy and I reconnected via Facebook. There were many things said because there were big things that she'd sat on the sidelines for, powerless. I did ask her about the anthill, but only because she'd been there. Did it really happen? It was so traumatizing. Could she solve the mystery?

Amy did not remember saving me from the anthill.

I was crushed, but I didn't tell her that. In fact, I had downplayed the memory, there in that one-dimensional font conversation, as though it were a funny little moment that *may have* happened. Barely a minute passed before she continued, "I'm not saying it didn't happen, just that I don't remember it. I also feel like I should point out that this sounds like the sort of thing that *would* have happened. It fits in with a lot of the types of things I saw."

This book is my anthill, of sorts. It hurts at times. It is a retelling of love, which saves me again and again. Love from others, love from myself. Love. Like the anthill of my toddlerhood, however, it is important to note that there will be opinions that offer different perspectives than mine. Even so, this is how I remember it.

I also remember hundreds of summer hours at the public pool. There were endless swimming lessons where I took pride in my ability to hold the side of the pool while kicking. There was the complacency that I eventually settled into, where I did not see the point in finishing the dull swimming lessons when it was much more fun to stay in the three- to four-foot part of the pool with my friends. We could play mermaids, we could sit cross-legged on the bottom having underwater, imaginary tea parties. We could play games and laugh and pass the best parts of sun-kissed summer days.

Eventually, those same friends began gravitating over to the diving board and deeper parts. I would look longingly from my side of the blue bobbing divider. Sure, my side of the pool was still pretty full. There were little kids everywhere. Little kids and *me*. Even so, I came to the pool excited. I inhaled the chlorine, grabbed my swim basket, and optimistically bounded through the entrance before reality crashed in around me.

Every. Single. Day.

Despite often feeling alone, I found comfort and solace in that water before I understood what that even meant. I knew it was sad and lonely, but also vital somehow.

One summer day in particular, even as my friends moved on to the deep end and I was stuck with the little kids, I marched into that pool with so much confidence. For the first time ever, my mom had allowed me to choose my own swimsuit from the Sears catalog, and it was definitely the cutest suit I had ever seen. I knew then, at eight years old, that I would finally be the envy of someone. That some boy would think I was pretty and smile at me, or some popular girl would see my suit and decide we should be *best friends*. Smelling of cocoa butter and slipping my way from that swim locker, I knew that this was about to be the best day of my life.

It wasn't.

I held the side of the shallow end and I kicked, wishing someone would notice me, wishing some kid there would care that I had come to the pool in the first place.

One day, my mom said she was no longer willing to pay for lessons. I was OK with her decision because I was unwilling to take swim lessons with babies and little kids. Instead, I continued holding the edge of the pool and kicking, showing off the highest level of my swim achievements to the cute middle school and high school boys who walked by. I began to notice girls around me who'd developed more, were prettier, and had boys flirting with them. I started comparing—I was fatter than this one girl, and that other girl's hair was way prettier than mine. I did not like how my poolside observations made me feel, so I began to daydream about dates with this one boy or slumber parties with those popular girls, laying out on towels and laughing. I escaped into a place in my mind where reality was not invited.

Eventually, I stopped wanting to go. I could easily daydream at home alone without my mom's complaints about driving me.

I did not want to try to swim. I was content never to know how to do more than kick on the side. My mother would not set foot near a pool—she was terrified of the water. I had, with my mediocre effort, surpassed anything she had done, so I grew complacently satisfied. I spent many summer breaks in Phoenix with my aunt, and though they had a sparkling, kidney-shaped pool, they mostly paddled around in tubes. It seemed I was a girl in a family of non-swimmers, so I accepted I had no reason to know how to swim.

One summer I was hanging out in my aunt's Phoenix back yard, doing my favorite pastime: singing and dancing around, enacting scenes from my very favorite movie, *Grease 2*. (Yep, the Michelle Pfeiffer one. I longed to one day be Stephanie, in love with my very own Michael, singing songs about life and love. *This* would be my future; I just knew it!) I was belting out "Cool Rider," knowing all the words by heart, while dancing my way around the pool. In my mind, I was a million miles away in a prop warehouse after a rehearsal for the winter talent show. In one careless-yet-confident move, my foot touched the edge of the pool and—

I realize, *wow, this sounds like I almost drown.*

I don't.

I woke up. I woke up to the reality of the scorching afternoon summer sun. I woke up to the fact that I wasn't in a warehouse at all, but rather a backyard. I woke up to the truth, that I was not Stephanie Zinone, but rather plain, ugly Misty Mae Moore from Lordsburg, New Mexico. I was a loser in all meanings of the word I understood at nine years of age. Standing beneath that sweltering Arizona sun, I looked at the diamond-like pool, shimmering and calling my name. Suddenly I craved the comfort and solace I'd once found in my public pool days. I knew we would probably spend time floating in the pool that evening, but this was little consolation for the sweaty, overwhelmed way I felt in that moment.

For the first time, I was filled with a need to do something.

I thought then about my swimming lessons. How I had just given up. I called myself stupid and then, *then* I told myself, *If everyone else can swim* ... (OK, maybe no one in my immediate family, but all the cool kids at the pool) ... *there is no reason that you can't. Just swim.* And then, in my summer outfit that was likely very retro-80s and awesome, I climbed onto the diving board and jumped in.

And I did not drown.

There was life in the way that water felt, the relief of its coolness against my sun-pricked skin—the way being in the water reconnected me to a piece of myself I had lost somewhere. Everything went silent as my body was gliding toward the bottom. In my memory, that kidney-shaped pool may as well have been twenty feet deep. I doubt it was more than five or six feet. There are so many great elements to this very childish thing I did. Like how terrifying (and a little funny, in hindsight) it must have been for my aunt. I mean, who would jump in and save me? See, it's funny now. It's also over thirty years later.

Somewhere deep inside, I woke up from the coping mechanism I'd grown accustomed to: retreating to a fanta-syland in an effort to avoid reality. It might be unrealistic to think a nine-year-old grasped all of that, and maybe I did a little, but I see the milestone of a shift now.

I can still feel the water that day. Thousands of feelings and sensations—and a brief moment of complete peace and connection to something that made me feel whole and relevant. On a whim, I dove (well, jumped) into a knowledge that I could take care of myself, and I should allow myself to let go and embrace the effort.

Spring

A Beginning

{To Nora and her baby girl: "Bright" by the
Gardiner Sisters}

Two years before the anthill incident, I made my way
into this world. Tiny, pink baby me was born to Nora Jane
Dugan. She was a twenty-eight-year-old waitress, about to
be five-times divorced, living in small-town New Mexico. Nora was the youngest of four—three girls and one
boy—though her brother had been killed in Vietnam a
few years before. The year was 1976, and the month was
March. A friend drove her the forty-five-minute trip up the
mountains because she was craving a cheeseburger and a
milkshake. I've been told that this was a big deal because
she had survived her entire pregnancy on Coca Cola and
Payday bars. So when she craved something substantial,
people made it happen. Shortly after the meal, she was
delivering me. No one really knew if I came early or not
because times were different. Testing was less accurate, and
my mother hadn't even realized she was pregnant until she
was more than six months along.

I've heard so many stories about Nora before she became
a mother. During her happier moods, she loved to regale

me with tales of the many men who'd pursued her and the fun antics she'd get into. My favorite story was the one where her best friend John had proposed to her for the twentieth time, and she turned him down. In one smooth motion, John picked her up and laid her on the pool table of their favorite bar. Once she was speechless from the shock of it, he diapered her with a T-shirt and an entire tub of baby powder, right there on the felt of that table with the whole bar cheering him on. "Nora, you'll always be my baby, but if you want to keep acting like a child and turning me down, I'm going to treat you like a child."

Always a rebel at heart, Nora had been jailed in Missouri, married to a man with mob affiliations, and developed a reputation of nefarious sorts. Her closest friends were male. She was certain each one of them was madly in love with her (except for her gay friend Roy), and she took pleasure in stringing them along.

Were they in love with her? Maybe. Nora wasn't the kind of person you could advise. She knew what she believed was fact, and there was no changing her mind. Stubborn, opinionated, vulgar, and habitually flirtatious, men loved spending time with her.

Girlfriends, on the other hand, were few and far between. It seemed she often felt in competition with other women and teetered on viewing them jealously or believing they were envious of her.

Nora was prone to migraines, and ever since her brother Ben died, they had become nearly constant. She had been told, many years before I came along, that she couldn't have children. Her "tipped uterus" had given her the freedom she needed to chase love with whoever was willing to give it. The different people in Nora's life may have known varying versions of her, but everyone in her gravity knew she'd never been happy. Whenever things didn't go the way she believed they should, she allowed resentments to fester. She burned bridges, ended relationships—impulsive and drastic was a speed she frequented. Perhaps it was the stress of all of this which increased her migraines as she grew older. Since she was unable to get pregnant, it is likely the doctor had given her medications dangerous for an expectant mother. During those first six months of her pregnancy, my mom was in "the worst migraine of [her] life. [She] thought about killing [herself] often." So, when I came out tiny nearly three months later, no one seemed surprised.

Nora had been so sure she was having a boy. *Surprise!* Having always loved things like squirmy puppies, baby animals, and little dolls, she seemed happy to have a baby. I don't know if she had been sad to learn she couldn't have children some years before, though I did grow up with the story about how I was a miracle, followed closely by the implications that maybe I was a big mistake.

In addition to the unexpected blizzard debilitating southern New Mexico that day, no one knew what to name me. My mom was so distressed after pushing a baby through her vagina only to learn it was a girl that she tossed the responsibility over to my grandmother. My grandmother liked the movie *Play Misty for Me*, and chose her own middle name, so there I was, little Misty Mae.

Between my grand entrance and the afternoon of the dreaded anthill, a lot happened. My mother married an abusive alcoholic named Jerry, who took me to a bar and got me drunk to celebrate my second birthday. Shortly thereafter, we moved to Las Vegas with my mom's older sister to hide from him. Eventually we made our way back to Lordsburg, where a diagnosis of uterine cancer led to a full hysterectomy for Nora. She was unable to do much, and while family members have memories of taking care of me during that time, I recall a lot of moments where it was just my mom and me. This was when, feeling so thirsty, I learned how to move a stool over the sink to fill up my own Mickey Mouse cup. This, I think, is my first actual memory. There are snippets of things like a plane ride to Oklahoma and choking on water in Vegas, but nothing as solid as the sound of that stool scooting across the linoleum floor toward the sink or that terrifying feeling of mounting it to do such grown-up things.

I was my mom's shadow. These aren't defining moments, just the knowledge that she wore me like an accessory. The cute little baby (and *I WAS*) she loved dressing in the tiny outfits and aprons she sewed. She always said she pierced my ears so everyone would stop calling me a boy in the supermarket. This was more a defining memory for her than me because she mentioned it often as I was growing up. I used to wonder who all these strangers were in our tiny little town where everyone knew everyone. To hear her talk, she could not leave the house without the boyish assumptions raining down on her, as though these baby boy seekers were camped outside like paparazzi.

When I was little, I wanted to be loved and adored, like my mom was, when I grew up. Everywhere we went someone came over to talk with her. People loved to make Nora laugh, and her laughter was infectious. For the whole of Nora's life, she had a collection of superficial relationships. She needed to know she was popular, even when she herself liked very few people, and the ones who seemed to adore her barely knew the real her.

Papa & Misty Mae March 1976

Mommy & Misty Mae March 1976

Misty Mae Moore 3 months

*Anjanette & Joseph at
Misty's 1st birthday 1977*

The Fence

{To Melanie: "Seven" by Taylor Swift}

When I was a little girl, I knew what love was. I resigned myself to the fact that I may always crave a love from my mother, which she seemed unwilling to give. I knew there was a safe comfort with my grandparents, my Aunt Gloria and Uncle Phil, and older cousins, Terry and Perry. In the early days I was lucky to be with my extended family a lot. It was in the silly nicknames, the giggles, and daily routines that I knew I belonged there. Summers with my cousins tasted of bubble gum ice cream and watermelon as we had seed spitting contests in the back yard. They were several years older, so I did a lot of tagging along on their dates or lip syncing to Journey in the mirror while Terry got ready for work (I preferred the curling iron for my microphone but usually got stuck with the hair dryer). Back home, when Papa wasn't at work, I was his buddy, tagging along for whatever task he had that day. With them, I knew that I belonged. Children should know that feeling.

My very first best friend, Melanie, was born almost a year after I was. We shared the honor of three M initials, lived next door to one another, and had interweaving early childhoods. This is the one thing I am most grateful for. But there is photographic proof I knew Melanie's older brother, Joseph, and her sister, Anjanette, before that beautiful March day when she was born. While I have no recollection of being an infant and imagining myself as the bride of her brother, Joseph, I can say with complete certainty that I do not remember a time (in my childhood) when I was not in love with the boy next door.

There was a fence between our homes—the cheap, wiry kind you buy in rolls at the garden store. Growing up, I would sit alone and watch their house across that fence. With what I knew, mixed with imagination, I could envision the home inside. There would be teasing, inside jokes in Spanish, disappointed tones, and unconditional parental love. From my bedroom window, I could see as they came and went. I would see when the parents would leave. I knew when they were outside and chatting with neighbors or family members who dropped by. I could see when Melanie, Joseph, or Anjanette were out to play.

I wasn't always on the outside of that home. As much as it sounds like the intro to a creepy horror movie, with the eerie, silent child watching this family's every move, the truth is that much of my childhood was spent inside with them, embraced as a bonus member of their family. When I was in my own house, though, I was usually stuck in my room alone with only that tin-framed window to connect me to the world outside.

It was easy in my early childhood years to keep track of Joseph. He was six years older than me, and in those days, I was so sure he did not even know I existed. I grew up questioning a lot of big things that I should not have had to ponder, but the one solid certainty I knew was my love for Joseph Martinez.

Their parents, Ray and Lorrie, never tried to take my mom's place. Living just across the fence, they were privy to many of the things that happened on my side. They knew of the countless days when I was locked out of the house but unable to leave my small yard. They knew of the verbal abuses, manipulations, and other questionable things. They suspected worse and darker things, too, but didn't mention them. This isn't their fault. In those days, no one ever talked about stuff like that. Instead, they invited me for before-school-bus breakfasts, dinners, sleepovers, entire weekends, afternoons—pretty much anything and everything that my mom would allow. Sometimes she couldn't stand the sight of me and so I felt as though I lived with them. Other times, she still couldn't stand the sight of me, but she also wanted to hurt me, so I wouldn't be allowed to so much as look in their direction for fear of her wrath raining down.

Whenever and however they could, they opened their hearts and home so seamlessly to me that I don't really know what life would have been like without them.

Before I was born, my grandparents had owned the entire block that my childhood home sat on. While my mom and I lived in a trailer, the rest of the homes were houses. Ray had done some odd jobs for my grandfather when he offered to sell Ray and his bride their home. My grandfather made them a fair offer, his intent simply to help them out and be supportive. This, of course, was years before Melanie and I came along.

While Joseph was the love of my single-digit life and Melanie was my BFF, their sister, Anjanette, played the role of villain. She was the mean older sister of my best friend, so naturally I was terrified of her. I adore Anjanette now, but life on the other side of that fence was *real*. It wasn't some grass-is-greener escape. There was a bully. She picked on Melanie and, adjacently, her pasty little white friend, who happened to be me. No blood was shed, and no psychological trauma occurred. To a small only child, she was terrifying. But I'm so grateful she gave me the real experience of a "big sister."

I was a minority white kid in a small New Mexico town. My best friend was a little brown-skinned girl with the biggest smile, and the sight of her face was my very favorite thing. Yes, her family would joke about the color of my skin, and no, it was never mean. They also called themselves Mexicans, spoke Spanish, and tried to teach me, though I couldn't grasp it. (I had that accent down like a CHAMP though.)

In the decades since 88045 was my home zip code, this small, almost border town has become a home for many different people, but my class photos featured mostly a sea of Hispanic children, speckled minimally with bright white faces like mine. It wasn't until I was several years into school when I realized what racism was. I knew, as I climbed the grade school ladder, there were kids who called me *gringo* or made comments about my skin, but honestly it never resonated as relevant. Then, one Halloween, my mom dressed me in my terrible plastic-masked costume and took me to a diner to sit beside her while she chatted with friends. I was a tangled mess of sadness because I wanted to be Rainbow Brite, but my mom made a big deal about wearing my old Casper costume again. (If you think Halloween costumes have gotten scarier, I encourage you to google "1980s costumes." My Casper the Friendly Ghost mask looks far more like *Casper is going to eat your children and steal your soul.*) With disappointment heavy, I cheered myself up with the thought of trick-or-treating. Once the realization began to sink in that I would not be going door-to-door to beg for candy, something shifted in me. Sitting there picking at the gross jelly donut in front of me, I began to understand the things the adults at the counter were saying. Words like "those damn Mexicans," "wetbacks," and "nasty spics" slapped my little ears over and over again. I felt my small, plastic-cloak-clad body stiffen in defense of people I loved. There were so many I had never identified as Mexican before, yet now I knew they were. In an instant, the divide between us felt much larger than a few playground insults. I took in the number of Hispanic people filling up the other diner seats, and I shrank in embarrassment for the words flowing from the mouths of these people I was with, including my mother's. The most perplexing thing to me, though, was that if the others heard the hate being spoken (no discretion was being used—my mother operated at an obnoxious volume), no one seemed to care. As a child of six or so, the injustice of this consumed me.

That night met me with a fitful sleep as I lay dreaming dreams heavy with grief. I knew I had lost my next-door family. They would surely be aware now that I was a little white girl, and even worse, I was a little white girl with a mother who was a racist. I did not have the word yet to describe that level of hatred, but I knew in my heart what it was.

I avoided Melanie and her family as best I could. It felt like an eternity, but it was maybe days, a morning, or even only an hour. What I do recall was playing in my front yard because my mom had banished me from the house and dashing to hide when Ray came out his front door. He gave a little wave and that smile (a smile which has lived at the top of my *favorite things* list for my entire life). "Melanie, Misty is outside!" And before I could stop and think about anything that was happening, my sweet friend was bounding down her front steps, and we were talking over the fence like normal.

They didn't care that I was white or that my mother could be terrible.

As an adult who now understands the cost of things and the value of sleep, I cannot imagine a child like me being a beloved neighbor. While I had always been an early riser, my favorite next-door family was not. They had a large family, and their back yard was often the spot for late-night gatherings filled with music, food, and laughter. I was lucky enough to attend a few of those nights, and I loved them until Melanie's cousin was mean to me and told me she hated me. I was aware of all that was stacked against me and knew that my place with this family was hanging by a thread, so whenever the Tucson cousin was in town, I disappeared. I could not allow whatever covert knowledge this cousin had to ruin my life.

When they were not hosting the weekend and summertime night life, they were still a family who enjoyed late nights. I won't lie—this was something I cherished when I slept over. My mom, as you may have guessed, did not love having me around. When I was home, my bedtime was well before the streetlights came on. This also meant that I was up before, or with, the sun. If it was a Saturday, my favorite cartoons ended pretty early, or I simply tired of the television and wanted to be out in the sunshine. Whatever it was that took me outdoors, my routine was to grab my ball and bounce it off the wall of the house next door.

Their house.

Ray and Lorrie's bedroom wall, actually.

No one, to my recollection, ever came outside to yell at me. Little joking comments would flavor banter when I saw them later in the day, with a loving smile and a twinkle of the eye. (Lorrie's twinkle is right up there on the list with Ray's smile.)

Once Melanie would finally close the eternally long morning and make her way outside, we would commence routine number two. She on her side of the fence and me on mine, we would begin to softly slam our bodies against the fence, smacking stomachs as we did. It sounds absolutely ridiculous, and how this ever became *a thing* I don't know. My grandfather would drop by my house and tease us for a moment or two, then Ray and Papa would catch up while Melanie and I bounced. We talked and bounced for hours after Papa died. This fence had become the one place where I could talk about the hard things, the dream things, anything, really.

It was there, bouncing on that fence at twelve years old, I told my oldest friend about the horrors happening in my house and begged her not to tell her parents. The fence had brought the truth out of me, as it always did, but that constant fear that this confession could be the one thing that could finally sever the connection between her family and me loomed thick.

It was also there at that fence where I encouraged her to stay away from my house. I knew I was leaving, and I needed her to stay safe. We were each such fixtures in each other's homes that I didn't realize that with me gone, she'd have no reason to visit mine anymore. It was this same conversation, in our safe space, when she confessed she had told her parents because she was scared, and she knew they could help. I forgave her. Of course, I did. I understood she had been protecting me. Looking back, I realize the only reason I had not wanted them to know was because I had wanted them to still like me. I had placed an unbearable burden on an eleven-year-old little girl.

By the time I left Zinc Street in August of 1988, a terrified and weather-worn girl of twelve, the fence between our homes was a chain-link, sagging mess. It was stretched and worn, unstable from years of life lived and the abuse we had brought it. I loved that fence.

It is funny, looking back, because I struggle to pull out significant moments with their family. I feel like I need to record them here as proof to the validity of my heart for them or the evidence of their love and acceptance. Instead, all I can find are flashes of normalcy woven so intricately into the DNA of my childhood. Lorrie cooking tortillas, stirring dinner, cooking eggs with chorizo for breakfast; Ray laughing, telling jokes; Joseph there and never knowing I existed; Joseph not there because he went into the military. The exact details of Joseph never seemed to matter much beyond the butterflies that wiggled in my core whenever he (or even just the mention of his name) appeared. Their home always smelled of cumin mingling with other spices. Looking back on the moments spent within, their house always seemed bright and airy, radiant with natural light, where memories of my own home always seemed to be filtered through clouds of cigarette smoke and blackout curtains. Their dinner table always seemed filled with people and voices, smiles and platefuls of delicious food. Quite the contrast to the generic white bread and bologna most nights at home held.

I spent so much of my life wishing for "normal." A normal family, a normal adolescence, and experiences like everyone else was having. While I desperately craved a family life that looked something like the Seavers on TV, it felt like every single moment was ripped from some offbeat dark comedy or perversion. It wasn't until I was an adult looking back that I realized my time living next door to the Martinez family was the part of my story that was equal parts miracle and average. Average because my best friend was the girl next door. Both born in March, one year apart, our childhoods ebbed and flowed in sync in every average American television show way. I grew up with a blushing crush on her older brother, scared of her comically mean older sister. Her dad told dad jokes, and I loved him for that and so much more. When I didn't know what a real father was like, I only had to look across the fence to Ray and see that he loved me as if I was one of his own. This is the only element of my life that could have been written for family viewing, prime-time TV, and it blended in with everything else that was on. I would not trade this for anything because I needed a ribbon of stability to be woven throughout my everyday chaos, and God knew that this family was the perfect choice.

They were there, arms and front door always open, regardless of the color of my skin, the instability of my mother, my mooning over their son, or my early morning ball-bouncing wake-up. Therein lies the miracle: I needed them, and they showed up.

I always knew of their relationship with my grandparents. The very amicable love, trust, and respect between Ray and Lorrie and Mommy and Papa was *huge*. Tears unexpectedly warm my eyes as I sit here now, writing these words. Perhaps this is the reason why their lives were open for me and they became my soft place to land, time and again. It doesn't matter because that very admiration, gratitude, and respect that Ray and Lorrie displayed for my grandparents, Perry and Bertha Mae Dugan, is the only living example I have for my own heart toward them.

Our fence

Kindergarten graduation

Melanie &
Misty
1990

Misty & Mel 2011

Ray & Lorrie 2011

Matriarch

{To Mommy: "In Case You Don't Live Forever"
by Ben Platt}

My grandmother was a member of the small, yellow church, tucked into the heart of our dusty New Mexico town. I loved that church building, with its faded mural baptistry and its deep red, velvety carpet. I knew every secret hiding nook, and potluck Sundays were my key to adventure and exploration. To a little girl, there was no end to the mystery and magic within the rooms which led to more rooms, each containing a felt story board complete with every figure imaginable. I could create tales for days with those little figures and animals. Being that I was one of the few kids my age, this gave me free rein while grown-ups caught up over mustard potato salad and chocolate cake. Even as an adult, when my eyes take that building in, my heart sighs with the sort of deep relief one feels as they arrive home after a long, hard day. I have had large spans of time pass between my visits to that little yellow church, and yet when I walk in, it still smells exactly the same. Because my grandmother is no longer living, I don't know who leads the church, or who is even left that I might know. The last time I set foot in that church was my grandmother's funeral.

Even more than the key to freedom that faded sunlight-colored building awarded me, I loved it because she did. And though, like most women her age, she did have strong opinions about what should happen within the walls of that building (and *with* the walls, the floors, and the very pews inside), she also had a fierce love for the people who called this church "home."

I had the privilege of growing up with a strong, independent woman who lived the way a believer should live. If someone needed something, my grandmother was always the first to volunteer. She would not simply raise her hand; this tiny, spirited woman would barge in with dinner in one hand, baked goods in another, and get to work. Was it a ride? Cleaning? Something needing repaired? To many people in our small tumbleweed town, my grandmother was the woman who could do anything—at least until she couldn't.

Every June, my grandmother would spend days baking loaves upon loaves of zucchini or banana nut bread. After the Father's Day Sunday service, she would stand at the back with the pastor and hand the loaves of bread to the fathers as they left. She prepared the same way for Mother's Day, only without the food. She would make a small sewn, crocheted, or plastic canvas craft that usually accompanied a fresh flower. The afternoons of these holidays often contained a box or bag in the backseat with which we would drive around and make deliveries to other fathers and mothers she knew. It wasn't just these holidays, either. There were baked treats and homemade chocolates at Christmas, canned goods in the summer, gifts for Valentine's Day, and similar things for other holidays. For as much as my Depression-era grandmother downplayed the size of her bank account and hoarded the oddest things, she was so giving. My grandmother sent birthday cards signed with words of encouragement to every person who'd ever set foot in that church, along with every distant cousin and neighbor she'd ever known. Her faithful thirty-seven-cent stamp and card did not depend on how regularly one had sat in those beloved church pews. None of these things were notable to me growing up. *This* was normal for me. *This* is the example I had of what women do. She showed me that a woman's place was in the kitchen, but it was abundantly clear that this was only appropriate when that woman loved being in the kitchen. My aunt did not love to cook and was a woman working within the corporate world. She had a love for restaurants, shopping, and expensive beauty appointments, and this was acceptable too. In my family, women did exactly what the men did; there was no limit to what girls could do. It was my grandmother's example, however, when I saw this the most. No one sat me down and said, "Misty, you need to model this behavior." But in many ways, it was so foundationally ingrained in me, I just did.

On the Sundays when she didn't hand out gifts at the back of the church, there was always someone to invite to Sunday dinner or someone for whom she'd prepared a meal to deliver. In a once-thriving, now-dying small town, Bertha Mae saw herself the caretaker of the sick and the elderly. I love that I can say that my grandmother loved the world in this way. You might picture her as a gentle and loving lady. Nope. My grandmother, God bless her, was a hard woman. She was weathered in all the ways a rough life, loss, love, and tragedy can weather a woman. She buried parents, siblings, a son, and her husband, all before she was ready to do such things. She started a family, also before she was ready. She had learned the lessons about doing what needs to be done, and she mastered life this way.

When my grandmother met my husband (then boyfriend), he was certain she hated him. She wasn't kind. She did not receive his extended kindness well. She wasn't mean, but there was a definite chill. To our surprise, a few months later she sent him a crocheted blanket for Christmas that she'd begun making for him just after she met him. He wasn't the first boyfriend she had met, and she was not thrilled that I was neglecting my education. But she was intuitive, and the moment she met him, she knew we were going to get married. She had known, in her core, he was the one.

My grandmother had an antique jadeite mixing bowl that was the thing I saw most in her hand when I was growing up. Sunday mornings had her mixing Jiffy muffins. Late-night arrivals of out-of-town guests had her whipping up cobbler. Fruit salads were prepared in that bowl for potlucks. If she knew you, she knew what you loved to eat. If she knew you were coming to town, it was guaranteed that Bertha Mae would be preparing those favorite things, that blessed bowl tight in her hand.

This is just who she was—the sort of woman who loved people by feeding them and sacrificing herself to make them a handmade gift or to help them with a task. She wasn't the frilly, fancy-bow gift giver, but instead the one to get down on her knees and help you scrub your floor while she told you all about the mistakes you were making and what you needed to do differently. She wasn't always right, but that didn't matter. Whether you were in a high or a low season of your life, my grandmother was exactly the right person to have in your corner. She didn't have these opinions for any reason other than she cared. If she was telling you your business, it was a major compliment because it meant she loved you and wanted so much for you.

I wish I had realized all of this when she was still alive. I wish I had grasped how special it was that she went to such lengths for anyone who needed it. She wasn't a saint, and I am sure the world has an array of people who knew her and suspected she hated them, but she didn't. She was just gruff. But that tiny woman LOVED FIERCELY. An *I love you* wasn't nearly as comfortable for her as handing you a bowl of fresh collard greens and a hunk of cake (from scratch) because she knew you were coming by.

Our family was beyond lucky to have a woman like my grandmother at the helm of it. We were a family of mostly women, and maybe everyone else realized what an amazing matriarch she was, but I didn't wake up to this until she was gone. It was not long after she died, though, that I began to see her in a more genuine light. In all fairness, I had a mother who was incapable of loving her own mother. From my earliest memories, I was poisoned against the possibility that this mousy-gray-haired woman could be coming from a good place. I saw beyond the images my mother painted on the outside, but subconsciously, I suspect my childhood was weaving a wicked grandmother element to the story. As a teen, whenever someone would ask me what my birth family was like, I would reference the evil grandmothers in many V.C. Andrews novels and say, "That's my grandma." It couldn't have been further from the truth, but the foundation of my perception had been laid with so many conflicted contributions, it would take a lifetime to sort it out.

My grandmother saw things. She saw the death of her son in Vietnam, roughly the instant he died. (This was well before the Internet and text messages, so it's a little complicated to imagine.) The military vehicle did not arrive to tell her of her only son's death until an entire day after she watched it pull up from her kitchen window. There was no way that she could have known, and yet she had already informed her family, all together for the Fourth of July, and was preparing for the chaplain's visit. She was a woman who listened to her gut, took in her intuitions, and treated them as gospel. Bertha Mae knew things. There was the middle-of-the-night conversation with a brother who appeared, told her he'd died, and asked her to phone his wife first thing in the morning to help her take care of an issue. After the interaction, she drifted right back to sleep. The next morning, she woke and did as he'd asked. No one on the Tucson end of that phone call questioned how Bertha Mae knew he'd died because this was just the way things happened. When she warned that something may happen a certain way, it was probably a good idea to prepare, just in case. She was also incredibly stubborn and opinionated. Her reprimands and warnings did not always feel like the gifts that hindsight may reveal.

This woman did not let a day pass without reading her Bible. She devoutly read from the free *Our Daily Bread* devotionals stacked on the small, wooden table at the back of the yellow church. She wrote notes in the margins, underlined words, and wrote prayer notes wherever there was space. When Bertha Mae said she was praying for you, she was. I'd grown up seeing it. This woman's quiet time with Jesus took the hours of a part-time job, and if she had company, she simply woke earlier in order to have this solitary time undisturbed before going in and making a full breakfast. *Love.*

My grandmother often had someone visiting her. She had two guest rooms, always clean and ready. She knew when someone was coming, and she would prepare a feast.

You always knew, coming to my grandmother's home, that there would be plenty to eat, accompanied by the best sorts of conversation and games of dominoes or Yahtzee.

She never grew lazy. She never stopped working hard, while making it look effortless. Whether it was out-of-town guests or a neighbor from across the street, Bertha Mae always made the time to talk. As an adult, when I look back on all that her days held, I am exhausted. This superhuman powerhouse must have derived an energy straight from the heart of God because it just does not feel possible. This woman woke up every single day and did what needed to be done, with what she had. She was known to carry her own gravel, mix and pour her own concrete, and grow her own food. Granted, toward the end, her arthritis made many things more painful. Toward the end she wore a sweater when it was 100 degrees out and moved a bit slower, but she still showed up every day.

I was pretty young when I began spending Saturday nights at her house. My afternoons were spent playing in the shed out back, which was far more playhouse than storage. Early evenings were spent in her driveway, dancing and singing to the local request hour. Best of all, though, was the prebedtime routine. Either she or my grandfather would go to their bar and make them each a vodka seven. Then, he in his La-Z-Boy and she in her rocker, we would watch something on TV while talking. I would be included in the conversation, even when it was clearly over my head, and was allowed a sip of one of their cocktails. They never dumbed down their topics for me. Formed from harsher generations, they talked about politics, religion, pop culture, and the news, fielded my childish questions, and allowed me to come to my own conclusions. (*As* a child I was a devout socialist. Things like rich and poor were dumb. Abolish money, I believed. It was beside them during the campaigning of Ronald Reagan when I shouted, "No more money! Make everyone have the same of everything. Be fair!" I'm not sure I hold the same views as my five-year-old self, but I'll admit I still see her passion in me.) Once their glasses were empty and washed, it was time to get ready for bed. My grandparents slept in twin beds, and I would snuggle down in a foldaway cot at the foot of theirs. We would pray out loud, and I would sleep the best of all sleeps. From a very early age, in my own bed, I struggled with sleep. I was known to watch the clock tick away hours before drifting off. On Saturdays, though, I slept like a baby. I fell fast asleep to the rhythmic breathing of the grandparents I adored, and I seldom rose early.

I called my grandmother *Mommy*. I have heard so many stories about how this began, including my mother's very hate-filled ones. Some said I couldn't pronounce *grandma*, while others said my grandmother had told me to call her *Mommy*. It wasn't until well into adulthood that it occurred to me how strange it was.

When my grandparents were out of town for my grandfather's cancer treatments, I desperately missed those normal Saturday nights. There were afternoons at their house toward the end of my grandfather's life, but always with other family members also present, and I wasn't allowed to stay the night. I had no idea my grandfather would die, or what that even meant. I was seven. I understood sick, and where sick was concerned, I also understood getting well.

He did not get well.

Eventually, Saturday night sleepovers resumed. There would always be a hole left due to the death of my grandfather, but in time, my grandmother and I developed a new normal. There were no more vodka sevens, but my grandma did develop a liking for Orville Redenbacher flavored microwave popcorn. There was cheese or sour cream and onion. She'd pop our snack, and we'd settle in front of the TV. On Saturday evenings in those days, all the good shows were on. We'd watch *The Facts of Life*, *227*, and *The Golden Girls*. Then at nine o'clock, she'd watch *Hunter*. During the sitting, post-popcorn snacking, she would give us each a manicure and paint our nails, readying them for church in the morning. When our shows were over, she would switch the channel, and we'd watch a thirty-minute program recapping all the top music videos of the week because she knew I loved music. These were precious times—Madonna or Samantha Fox grinding and singing about sex, nearly naked male models inappropriately involved somehow. This Jesus-loving, fairly judgmental, four-foot-something firehouse never said a word. There was no negativity, she just sat right there beside me, letting me do the things all the other kids my age were doing.

My grandmother passed away of a stroke-triggered brain aneurysm rupture in August of 2006. I was exactly thirty years old. We had known of the aneurysm for years. So many of her siblings had passed from them, and she knew that would be how she'd go too. In some ways it was a ticking time bomb. In the years leading to that fated afternoon, there had been gatherings to say goodbye when her time wasn't even close. To clarify, *she* never said her time was near. She hinted at being tired and ready, but it was life, doctors, and our own family fears that dictated the reunions. The Sunday before she died, she called me. I was living all the way up in Michigan, the mom of a busy young girl and always operating in overwhelm. People weren't quite texting yet, but I had already grown frustrated with long, leisurely phone calls. While I don't think I was rude, I also know I didn't give that call (or any of her calls, if I'm being honest) the undivided attention that I would soon wish I had. She told me she loved me and that she hoped I knew that. She spoke frankly and emotionally in ways that weren't normal for her. I am sad I didn't realize this was her goodbye. I was distracted by Sunday afternoon life and not completely present. I failed to cling tight to a beautiful moment, and the regret of that walked with me from that day on.

I know my grandmother enough to know, while she wouldn't encourage such regret, she also would be OK with me using it to be more aware should that sort of thing happen again.

My grandmother passed away after a beautiful day with my mother. Toward the end, they had a lot of those—something my grandmother likely ached for, and my mom always ignored. Being a major penny pincher, she had a soft spot for meal deals. KFC had a lunch special on Tuesdays that she got really excited about. (This and the sporadic return of the McRib. She loved those sandwiches so much that when McDonalds would bring them back, she would stockpile a portion in her freezer so that she could pull one out and warm it up. Don't worry if that gagged you a little—me too. I guess that's what the Depression did to people. She was resourceful and could eat just about anything. When my mom was young, my grandmother made a meal of sautéed tumbleweed, and the family loved it. Mom goals right there!)

That last Tuesday, they had their special KFC lunch. Before they'd made it the few blocks to my grandmother's house, she had a stroke in the car. My mother was there when her own mother died.

Bertha Mae Dugan lived a hard life. She grew up fast, worked hard, and was never given the privilege to chase a dream or develop a passion. She wasn't perfect, but she did her best. She lived out her days in a house far too big for her, with a life that was sometimes lonelier than she deserved. Her most consistent company was the bipolar daughter who often treated her like a chore. Not being one to verbalize her heart, she stuck around far longer than anyone expected, we all suspect because of my mom. It was after this stroke, which triggered the aneurysm, when my very emotionally unstable mother, sobbing, told my grandmother to let go.

"I'll be OK, Mom."

And she let go.

Her funeral packed the little yellow church. Her body lay at the front of the small sanctuary, and I sat there teary and memory-flooded by the hymns we sang the countless Sundays we walked through those doors and the life we lived within those walls, *together*. As loved ones gathered in the social room to talk over potato salad and chocolate cake one last time, her absence was felt. Laughter, tears, and stories filled the room, but I felt struck by the way her name was being used in the past tense. I snuck away, exploring those quiet, tiny rooms, running fingertips across felt boards. It was all so much smaller: the rooms, that church, me.

I flew home a few weeks later, that jadeite bowl safely in my bag. In the years that followed, my own muffins, cakes, and cobblers were mixed in it, just as hers were. When my palm wrapped around its handle, I felt closer to her. Last year, as I reached high on the shelf for that precious bowl, I miscalculated, and it fell on my head and then shattered on the floor. I grieved then, less restrained than I had been the years before, for the woman I finally knew. For the knowledge of the incredible woman I had been fortunate to have and deeply wounded to lose.

It has been nearly two decades since I last stepped into that church, and I cannot hear the words of most hymns without hearing my grandmother in my left ear, somberly singing along. The way she loved, the way she loved me, and the way my grandmother showed me *how* to love was defining.

Telling Time

{To Papa: "And Then You" by Greg Laswell}

While anyone who knows me can attest to my love of old photos, there is one in particular that holds my heart. It is one of my birthday parties—I believe it was my sixth or seventh. My grandfather is standing in front of the kitchen window, behind the cake table. I am standing on one side of him, and Melanie is standing on the other. He is radiant and his warm smile consumes the photo. There in that picture, I get to celebrate the passing of another year with the things that compose my entire world: my best friend and my grandfather. (And also cake. I love cake, but that isn't what this chapter is about.) To a stranger looking at the photo, perhaps his smile wouldn't seem so encompassing. But for those of us who knew him, it was.

In every single snapshot.

For most of my life, my grandfather has been this ghost of a man. I knew that I loved him more than anyone else in the world, and I also knew that a large part of this was because there was no question that he loved me and would keep me safe. He was the source of life for little-girl me. Then his own light was gone, and I was left in an unfamiliar darkness.

To be fair, the man behind the fragmented memories and the warm feeling of security I've attached to him is one constructed mostly of other people's stories. My mother told hundreds of stories about what an amazing father he was, what a saint of a man he was, while my grandmother was practically the devil herself. Every recollection of my grandfather, from her lips, involved him as the hero of some sordid tale. My cousins had known him longer, since they were older than me, and I found this a bit unfair. He was the constant in my everyday life, and then he was lifeless in a coffin and no longer there at all.

After he passed, there was a period of time when a counselor said that I needed to see no photos of him because I was not coping well. The pictures were all put away, and I felt him ripped from me once again. Before cancer stole him from me, we did everything together. I spent many days at my grandparents' home. Before his retirement, he'd driven a short-haul truck. Sometimes I got to go with him, and sometimes I waited with my grandmother. She'd make me breakfasts of bread and gravy or cinnamon pie crusts, and we'd sit together and watch *The Price Is Right*. The day would go on in normal ways, I guess, because I don't remember how the time would pass beyond these things. One minute we'd be eating and watching Bob Barker, and then memory tells me it's much later and Papa is coming through the door. He'd take a seat, and I would crawl into his lap. He always had a Twix bar in the pocket of his snap-up shirt after those workdays, and when I found it, he would hand me one half while claiming the other for himself. "Twix are meant to be shared!" he'd chuckle, and we'd eat our candy, wide-eyed and raving over how delicious it was.

Twix is still my favorite. Like so many other pieces of my early childhood, this insignificant detail probed itself deep into my foundation being formed. I'll choose Twix out of the candy bar lineup every single time. I'd also prefer to share it, though most of my adult Twix splurges have been eaten alone. It's kind of poetic, really. Twix is meant to be shared, but so is life—even more so—and yet there is this threaded theme within my lifetime DNA that suggests perhaps mine wasn't.

Also, since I'm being completely honest, I'd much rather have some of my grandma's cast iron skillet gravy and fresh white bread, or her delicate pie crust baked with butter and sugar. Those things supersede a prepackaged candy bar, but the loyalist in me would still probably choose the Twix on principle.

Perry Dugan was a good man. He was a kind and a generous man. He laid the path for families to catch breaks. He was a faithful friend, a dependable father, and one of the most respected men in our small town. After so many years of hearing everyone rave about my grandfather, filling in the gaps of my fragmented memories with their air and imagery, it is hard for me to imagine him as a flawed man. For me, he was the other half of the most delicious candy bar. To me, he was the driver of a Datsun pickup, always saving the passenger seat for me. On one of our excursions, I watched him climb from the truck and instinctually sever the head from a rattlesnake with a garden hoe in one move. Long before people told me what an amazing man he was, this snake-slaying act solidified him as a superhero in my book. On another pickup drive, we rescued a puppy. My grandfather named him Beauregard and I loved him instantly. My grandmother, however, did not adore the puppy and wouldn't let us keep him. (This was the very first time that I buried a personal resentment against my grandmother, which validated my mother's hate-filled stories.)

Beyond those drives, it is the memory of weird trivial things ...

The small rake, shovel, and hoe that were my size so I could "work" alongside him.

The slow, rotating silver exhaust fan that created a surreal glow from the rays of twirling sunlight in his workshop.

The smell of his breath after he used the gross brown mouthwash.

The calluses of his hands as he held mine.

The lighting of army tank fireworks on his birthday, which also happened to be the Fourth of July.

His smile. Not just the smile in the photos, but his real one. The one that came in after a long day and greeted me, pre-chocolate treat.

He was always Santa, and I was always his elf as we passed out gifts to the family. Everyone was happy because everything was perfect.

A less than happy memory was my sixth December, when my grandparents called me to their house and gave me an early Christmas present. The two of them made a big show of it, and I was so excited because I was six and Christmas presents were magical. Inside the foil paper was a Strawberry Shortcake watch. While I loved Strawberry Shortcake, I was disappointed in the gift, and it showed. Many of my friends had digital watches, which made it easy to tell time, but this watch had little gold numbers on its face. It was too hard to determine the time, and I must have reacted a bit spoiled. There were words spoken about the gift of time itself, and I dismissed them. I was six. I was so overwhelmed by my disappointment and one more way that I would be different from all the other kids at school. *Didn't anyone care that I just wanted to be liked and loved, to fit in with everyone else?* I don't know if I hurt my grandparents' feelings that evening. The magic of the hushed phone call earlier in the evening and getting to go to their house after dinner on a school night had faded. I distinctly remember falling asleep to my embittered disappointment that night. My memory is very aware of how I felt, but I'll admit that in the hazy blur of memories that don't exist from my childhood, this seems an odd one to stick out. As I look back, I have to wonder if this is the night I was told about my grandfather's cancer. The watch symbolized something real, and the conversation—so far beyond my emotional capabilities—was perhaps meant to wake me up and encourage me to savor the time we had left. I wish I had.

Beyond this small list of mental snapshots of a childhood faded are the sharper and more distinct moments of his absence—the gaping hole, in spurts, of a man going to hospitals and enduring chemotherapy. I knew of all these things, but I had no idea what they meant beyond medicine. I knew he was sick, but I also knew that someday he wouldn't be, and that was the part that mattered.

As a six-turning-seven-year-old, I had no concept of time. There was Papa before cancer and Papa during cancer. There were gentler hugs and phone calls. There were presents brought home from gift shops and sometimes the occasional Twix to share. Sleepovers ceased, and his twin bed was replaced with a hospital bed. Those days I was only going to my grandparents' house with my mom or when other family was in town. Quiet, teary conversations happened on this side of his closed bedroom door. It felt like a dark cloud had appeared out of nowhere and was suffocating our perfect life. I wanted to be on the other side of that heavy brown bedroom door with Papa. Sometimes I was allowed, but only ever with someone else, and only for a few hushed moments. Conversations were made in whispers, and I was only able to gently caress his chest or hand. His smile still beamed, though less brightly. Those days seemed to last for decades, though looking back, I think they were maybe weeks at most.

Beyond the superhero God gave me in my grandfather and my perfect little dark-hair pigtailed best friend, the thing I loved most in the entire world was movies. Our small town had a beautiful old theater with a balcony, and whenever an evening called for a trip to the movies, I knew I was living my best life. Movies released much less frequently in the 1980s, so it was a rare and special treat to go. When my mom would take me, we'd buy a giant bag of her favorite popcorn from the gas station across the tracks to sneak into the theater. She made it such a fun game that the popcorn runs made a bigger impact than the movies themselves. When my aunt would come to town, we'd almost always do two things: visit Dairy Queen and go to the movies. Going to the movies was a tradition of the happiest times.

While cancer ravaged my grandfather's body, there weren't many happy times. Even so, a little movie came out that he somehow managed to take me to see. I snuggled into the crook of his arm as Gertie and Elliot formed an unlikely friendship with the peculiar little alien known as E.T. I don't remember who else was with us, but it didn't matter. I was there with my favorite human in the whole world, taking in the magic of the movies. This was the turning point assuring me that everything would be OK.

On one of his many hospital trips, my grandparents returned with an amazing E.T. night-light. I say amazing, but it was actually pretty horrific. For me, it was perfect. The comfort of E.T.'s lights when I slept got me through the darkest chapters that lay ahead. For my birthday, they also gave me a wall clock made from a glass E.T. plate. I grew in my ability to tell time, watching the wide-awake hours of the late nights tick by, illuminated by the glow of that night-light.

Because my family knew that my grandfather was not long for this world, they threw my grandparents a forty-eighth wedding anniversary party. The preparations for this silver and powder-blue celebration created the opportunity for very needed celebration and happiness. The bustle of planning had people eager again, and light seemed to break its way through that heavy cloud we had all been living under. Family was coming from all over the country. Even as a seven-year-old, I could feel the electric charge. For a long time, things had been hard and heavy, but suddenly there was something to look forward to. My mom sewed matching dresses for the two of us to wear, and with so many guests arriving, I was filled with excitement for the party.

I have had a lifetime of looking at the photos taken during that event. Hundreds of family shots. My grandfather frail and seated, my grandmother beside him, their oldest daughter to the left, and my Aunt Gloria to their right. Gloria's kids made it into some of the pictures too. I, in my lace and powder-blue dress, exist in none of the photos. We had gone that day, my mom and I, to the beauty shop. We'd had our hair done. My mom's boyfriend took a Polaroid of us before we left for the big event, the two of us in our matching dresses, corsages pinned just over our hearts. I have that photo too—the only way I know my memory of it all is true.

This party happened while my grandfather was still able (though barely, I'm told) so he could have a beautiful evening of celebration with his entire family. It was to be that sort of thing which many people on their deathbeds wish they'd had. We made it to the party, and it was filled to the brim with so many smiling people. I was mesmerized by the weeks of planning that came together to form such magic there before our eyes! It was the biggest event I had ever been to. There were so many people happy to see us, celebrating, when we walked into the Elks lodge. I can still see my grandparents, dressed so beautifully.

And then we turned around and left.

My mother shouted and wailed in the car about how we were kicked out, that everyone else in the family was loved, but we weren't wanted. I had no idea what had happened, I only heard my grandfather quietly beg my mother to at least let me stay. "Over my dead body!" she'd raged.

We went to the movies, though we skipped Nora's traditional popcorn run. We sat in that theater in our fancy dresses, watching *E.T.* My mother made it very clear we were only there because of me, because I loved that *dumb movie*. I spent the entire time thinking about how, finally, Papa had seemed like himself again, and she'd taken me away. I loved E.T. because of him. It was the first time I ever remember feeling hate for her. I knew there was more, I knew she was to blame, and I knew she'd never see it that way.

Perry Dugan passed away not long after that. It was a September day, and there were several of us at my grandparents' home. I sat on the gold, 1950s art deco sofa beside my mother as the ambulance arrived and carried him out. There was a pastel pink balloon tied to his gurney, and through a labored breath, he told me he loved me and to be good. The next time I saw him, he lay still and waxy in the coffin. We walked as a family to view the body before everyone else arrived. The funeral home put us in a room off to the side, tucked away.

I believe there was a giant window through which we watched the funeral. I also remember that he smelled funny and didn't look much like himself at all.

During the funeral, Nora screamed and cried; I did not. I handed her tissues, caressed her back, and stayed beside her, her palm in mine. I knew that I existed, in that moment, to bring my mother comfort.

Between the pink balloon and the funeral, something happened.

While I slept the night the ambulance had taken Papa, I dreamed. In this dream, I was playing in the shed at my grandparents' home, like I always had before cancer ruined things. Two men walked into the room, one in overalls and one in jeans and a white T-shirt. I couldn't see their faces, or if I could, I don't remember them. I do remember the feel of the wood floor beneath my feet and the smell of dust in the storage room where I was playing. Every ounce of the room felt familiar and real, as though I'd been teleported there. The two details that were out of place were the absence of Papa's twin bed (having been stored once the hospital bed arrived) and the addition of the *Just Married* car sign with crepe paper flowers from the anniversary party. (It had never been out there when I had played before.) Without any introduction, the men came in and sat down, and the overalls man urged me to climb into his lap, which I did. I knew this man was God and that the other man was his son.

God proceeded to tell me that Papa was very special and had been sick for a very long time. He told me that it was time for him to take Papa to heaven to be with them. This overalls-wearing God-man was so loving when he spoke, and though I was very sad about having to say goodbye to the most important person in my world, the way God spoke to me made it OK. As they stood to leave the room, God told me I would need to be strong for my mom. He told me she was broken, and he loved her very much, but she needed extra help sometimes. Then his son hugged me and told me to go carry that hug to my mom, right now.

I woke instantly. At seven, we don't need the type of analyzing and process time that we do as adults when strange things happen. Part of the magic of childhood is that we simply believe. It had been a dream, but also, I knew that it hadn't. My bare feet carried me down the hall toward the dim light of the kitchen. There my mom sat, tearstained and smoking. The second she saw me, she reacted with anger that I was out of bed. Unfazed, I continued toward her, placed my arm around her, and said, "Papa is going to heaven tonight. It's very sad, but he will be OK."

She was livid. She hurled hatred at me, but nothing she said could reach beyond the warmth I felt inside. As she shouted and I stood planted there with my arm tight around her, the phone rang. Her face morphed from anger to an expression of blanched horror. After a few moments she cradled the receiver, demanding to know how I had known. So I told her.

It was years later when I realized the pink balloon on his gurney, which seemed ill-placed and never made sense to me, was actually an IV bag. Had he really said those words to me as he left his earthly house for the last time, or did my childhood perception give him E.T.'s dialogue of goodbye? I don't know. I hope he did, but no one who was there can remember.

Did God really come to me? I believe that he did. Something kept me strong for my mother. Something far bigger made me forgive her for ruining the night of the party for everyone and hurting so many. Was there really a giant window between our room and the one where Papa's body lay? Maybe. It seems strange, but sometimes strange things are true. Somehow, the same little girl who had cried herself to sleep over a stupid watch was able to observe and shoulder the grief of countless people who loved her grandfather.

Perry Dugan, father to Wanda, Gloria, Ben, and Nora, beloved and faithful husband to Bertha Mae, left a gaping chasm where his life had been. The world was changed for so many because he had impacted so many with his life.

Perry Dugan was an amazing, generous, and kind man. He believed in people, he believed in love, and he lived as he believed until the day he died. He was my Papa, and though I didn't get to know this man as everyone else did, the hole was there for me too.

Christmas 1976

Always Papa's Girl!

Papa's Last Christmas 1982

Chosen

{To little Misty and her mama: "Broken Lady"
by The Gatlin Brothers}

She married the love of her life well before I came along.
She called him Roger, though that technically wasn't his
name. She had met him in Las Vegas, at a skating rink.
He was in the military. These are the only facts I know. I
am not here to share her story, but how her story deeply
impacted mine. Roger was not her first husband, and he
certainly wouldn't be her last. My father played the brief
role of husband number four. His name was Robert, also
a soldier. He'd been a childhood friend to both Nora and
her brother Ben. How he came to be her groom, I've never
been clear. He married a woman unable to have children,
and he brought into their union a boy and a girl of his
own. My mom added to their complicated family a very
high-maintenance poodle named Princess.

In the long string of men that trailed my mother, I've
always looked for commonalities. If she had a type, these
men couldn't have been from a broader spectrum. Tall,
redheaded, and abusive; pudgy, dark haired, connected
to a major crime family ... Maybe she was always looking

for something different. Her marriage to my father lasted about fifteen minutes. She couldn't handle having kids
around; he (and his kids) wasn't thrilled with coming in
second to Princess and her spoiled needs. They were well
on their way to divorce court before my mom realized she
was pregnant, and who could blame my father for doubting
the baby was his? My mother loved men and had a wild
reputation, which she proudly wore pinned to her lapel.

Her fifth and final marriage happened before I was two.
He was the redheaded gem of a fellow I already mentioned—the abusive alcoholic who celebrated my second
year by gifting me my own inebriation. We fled New Mexico for the solace of Las Vegas until that husband was long
gone. My mom's oldest sister, Wanda, lived in Vegas. This
was how we wound up there, in the safety of Sin City. I was
young and don't remember a lot. Wherever we slept was
filled with hordes of stuffed animals and a red scarf spread
over the lamp shade, giving the room a horror vibe. One
morning I was watching cartoons in the comfort of a thick
shag carpet when I made the brave decision to conserve
my energy by lying down to drink a cup of water instead of
sitting up. Bloodred gauzy toys and nearly drowning myself
in front of Bugs Bunny pretty much sum up my collection
of Las Vegas memories. I have wondered, though, as an
adult, if that was the only reason we headed toward the
famous strip. Roger lived in Vegas. Roger still lives in Vegas.
(Facebook told me so.) Did she see him? Did she wish she
could work up the courage to see him? Did she perhaps try
but find he was already remarried? I will never know. The
only thing I know about Roger is that he was the love of her
life.

While some children grow up with stories of their parents' distant childhood adventures, I grew up fatherless,
with a mom who regaled me with tales of her collection

of husbands. As a young adult, I became privy to more details of these mystery men, and one could speculate that either my mom's love life inspired the genre of movies that make up the average Hallmark and Lifetime lineups, or my mother's memory of her love life expanded after years of consuming said average TV movie lineups. In her defense, others have told stories that substantiate hers, mostly. The tragic ending between her and Roger seems to be the one with the biggest conflicting accounts, and honestly that isn't surprising.

Anyone who has watched Hallmark or Lifetime movies will have questioned how odd this analogy is because the plotlines could not be more different.

This rings true because Nora was bipolar.

My mother was bipolar before bipolar was commonly acknowledged. Back in those days, there were other diagnoses tossed around. Once, she was diagnosed with multiple personality disorder, other times, severe depression. Considering the time frame, it's a wonder she never had electroshock therapy.

Looking back, I doubt a week of my childhood passed without me hearing about Roger (the love of her life, in case you forgot) and how amazing he was, how much she loved him, and how deeply he had hurt her. She'd be sewing at her machine, justifying why she had to divorce him and how it had *broken her*, while I sat playing at her feet. Roger was to blame for her inability to ever marry again, even though she'd been married after him. Roger took the blame for my fatherlessness, even though Roger was not my father, and she'd married my father well after Roger was out of the picture. I grew up with this image in my head of the dreamiest hunk of a man who was also a coldhearted monster and the biggest reason why my mom's inability to be alone led us down the worst path of all.

I have already alluded to the fact that I was sexually abused. I don't want to attempt some big theatrical reveal of this very traumatic thing which is neither the point of this book nor the focus of this chapter. Even so, in many ways, it is woven through each of these chapters because that is how sexual abuse works. Innocence lives within a person, and then suddenly sexual abuse infiltrates all the crevices and empty spaces. I know this because I have lived it, and I know this because of my mom.

Nora was the headstrong sort, quick to rush into love, especially if it gave her a way out of something. "Romance sort of saved me," she once said, and every time she'd tell tales of past relationships, I'd see how that once-uttered sentiment applied. Most instances were with unsavory men. There were a couple of raging, abusive alcoholics, a man evading the FBI for mob affiliation, and a variety of other unfortunate traits. For a while it seemed she'd take the mistreatment—maybe even believing she deserved it—but then something might set her off, and headstrong, impulsive Nora would return.

Between her divorce from husband number five and my third birthday, my mom met her last real relationship. His name isn't important. If you're in my family, you know both him and his name well. If you aren't, the name is irrelevant. For clarity, I'll refer to him as her boyfriend because he may be the only guy she dated but did not marry. (That's probably not true, but honestly, I don't know.) The other reason why it isn't necessary to name him within the pages of this book is twofold: one, he is still alive, and I feel the need to protect him. Two, to anyone reading this who has been equally abused, we know an abuser's name has nothing to do with the abuse itself.

At this point, I'm also going to confront the bomb you may feel I just dropped—yes, I said *protect him.*

I hope, before you rush to judgment, you'll read these pages with an open mind. Some of you may have heard me speak about this, but in case you have not, the chapters of my life story involving my mom's boyfriend are complicated. This book is filled with beautiful names, like the tributes that are the prettiest aspects of my life. It is filled with the names of the people who gave me life, taught me love, and shaped me. His name has no place within its pages, but also, I do not hate him. This book exists to share the good with the bad. It exists to show the gray between the black and white. It is not being poured out of me to exact a revenge. Most abusive situations are not black and white, as much as we may want them to be.

I disliked my mom's boyfriend the moment I met him. I didn't know why. I loved my grandfather, I adored my male cousin, and I was close with my Aunt Gloria's husband Phil, so it was not a fear of men. Perhaps it was the fact that the psycho husband number five hadn't been gone too long. My mom loved men, and even by this stage in my two and a half years, I was no stranger to men in our home. Her best friend John was always around. Her other best friend Roy, who lived in Utah, visited often. Then there was her other very good friend George, who lived in Las Vegas and came to visit on his motorcycle, making the whole world shine a bit brighter. I loved these men who loved my mom. As if this infusion of regular testosterone in our small, single-wide trailer wasn't enough, the railroad was thriving in our little town. Railroad workers (dubbed *rails*) made up a huge portion of the men frequenting our shops, bars, and restaurants. My mom was a waitress, and a flirty one at that, so many a night she brought a rail home.

With the boyfriend, though, it was different. A huge deal was made the first time I let him pick me up and hug me. The enthusiasm from the room of faceless people still crowds my memory. It was as though I had completed some extraordinary task, but to this day I still remember that I felt all cringey inside. I must have adapted to the situation in time, but it was clear that the rest of my tight-knit family did not. I found myself walking the confusing tightrope of being protective of him and my mom, while also wishing he were gone.

The boyfriend wasn't going anywhere. Somewhere along the line I began to call him *Daddy*. Daddy was an engineer with Union Pacific, making him a rail. Like all the other regular rails, he would travel from his home city into Lordsburg. Usually he became "rested," meaning he'd been in town for at least twelve hours, but sometimes several days. Other times he was "deadheaded" back home after just a quick meal. Making plans as a family was difficult, so from around my third birthday on, my mother lived by his train schedule. When he was headed toward us, she'd bathe, dress, put on makeup, clean the house, and cook. On the days that gapped in between, she was a depressed mess, chain-smoking in front of the TV. The window shades were pulled tight, and the entire trailer became a dark cloud, air thick with nicotine.

There was no middle. Happy mom meant the train was coming, unhappy mom meant it was not. These were the 1980s—they wrote each other long letters. She would give them to him or put them in his grip box before he left, and he would pen long letters to her (at her insistence) while he sat for hours on the train. I have a box of them. I've read them. They paint a picture much different from the one always told to me. He'd tell my mom she needed to break away from her mean and selfish parents. (PARENTS, not *mother*.) She'd complain about me and what a hassle I was, how I'd been sick, or how her father was a dictator. The letters both filled in gaps and created even more questions, questions I know that I will never have answers to.

The worst days were the ones when he was en route and she was dolled up and waiting, and he'd get word to her that the train was stuck, had derailed, or was turning back and heading home. These days caused her to die a little bit inside, and these were the times when I paid the steepest prices.

My mother hated me. She never went around telling me she hated me, but she showed it. I do not remember many moments after the two of them got together when she was genuinely kind to me. Of the few, I do not remember any that happened when it was just the two of us. The only exception to this was when she was manic. Of course, I didn't know that she was manic, or even what manic was. What I did know was that there were these magical moments when my mom would emerge from this deep place within, and she was radiant with happy fun. We would go for long, late-night drives where she'd belt out all the fun music on the radio and dance in the car. These were the nights when she'd pull me from my bed to dance and twirl to Sha Na Na records, while we made 2:00 a.m. banana milkshakes. This was not the same woman who begrudgingly sat across from me to color in my Porky Pig coloring book, only to tell me that pigs aren't purple, that it was the ugliest picture she'd ever seen, and that I had done a terrible job, so I should never color again. The moment feels as though it happened earlier today. I was so excited my mom was actually coloring with me that I made the pig her favorite color so she would know that I loved her.

The coloring book mom. That's the one I got to spend the most time with.

Every time it came on TV, she'd sit me down four feet from the tube and force me to watch the Sally Field movie

Sybil. She would comment on every scene with parallels to her own traumatic childhood and her own abusive mother.

Though she wasn't one to hit, she did love using me as a pawn so that everyone involved sustained injuries. When I was in the fourth grade, I wasn't allowed to talk to my grandmother for ten months because she recommended that my mom and I go to counseling. My mom agreed because she knew that I was the problem, and this would validate her. When the counselor gently told my mom that she was mentally abusive and that she could help her change some of her tendencies, my mom pulled us out of counseling. She threatened to sue the practice for "programming" me, despite my never having been in a session without her. The idea had originated with my grandmother, so my mom concluded that my grandmother had conspired with the therapist, and I was no longer allowed to see her. She lived two blocks away, and her home had been my safe place.

Another time, she decided I couldn't see or talk to Melanie or her family. We lived next door with a flimsy fence in between. This wasn't possible, which was why she chose it. She knew she could hurt me, so she did. (When I was younger, she would stop me from seeing family or take things and people away from me because I was such a "bad girl.") At some point, I realized I was the key to changing these scenarios, so I outsmarted her and took control of the situation. I faked sick one day at school when I knew my mother was unavailable. The school had no choice but to call my grandmother. Once that happened, I got back into my Saturday sleepovers with her. The situation with Melanie was handled similarly, and things went back to normal. I won, and Nora gave up, just like I knew she would. For a while, things felt manageable, but then one day she started telling anyone who would listen terrible things about me.

Things like ...

I held her at gunpoint.

I beat her.

I threatened to stab her.

While Nora was doing her best to depict me as a monster, she was the one demonstrating her cruelty. When I would kiss her goodnight (at her insistence—always kisses and never hugs), she would blow smoke in my face or sneak a thumbtack into the back of my nightgown so I'd roll onto it in my sleep.

She had her boyfriend install locks on their bedroom door so that she could "feel safe" from me while he was gone.

None of the things she said had happened. I was a little girl. I did steal two hundred dollars from her once when I was nine. I went snooping in their dresser because I wanted to find some money to take to the bus stop. We had a market by our bus stop, and all the kids would buy treats before school. I'd ask my mom and she always said no. This had become one more way I didn't fit in—I just wanted to be *normal*.

In my search for a few dollars, I was about to give up when I saw the corner of some money sticking out from under a small jewelry tray. It was two one-hundred-dollar bills. I snatched them and headed out the door.

I had absolutely no concept of how much money that was.

At the shop the next morning, I pulled the bills to pay for a Coke and a honey pie. The man who owned the store sweetly told me he didn't want me to lose my money at school (or worse, get robbed), so he put it on my "account." Two hours later, my mother raged into my third-grade classroom and pulled me out. She drove like a maniac the few blocks to the police station, where she "pressed charges," and they put me in jail.

The jail cell I was held in had a man in it. He asked me what I was in for, and I told him. He gave me five dollars and told me it was wrong to steal from my mom. When the big scary lesson was over, I was released. While my mom lit up a cigarette as we walked to the car, smugness consuming her face, she asked me what I had learned.

I am not sure what my answer was, but I know I didn't tell her about my five dollars. I didn't point out she had only technically lost seventy-five cents, since Mr. Hernandez called her and returned the money. She could call me the worst of things all across town, but I still saw this as a small victory.

A week later, I came home crying for the third day in a row. I had started getting headaches and there was a bully in school who would grab one of my pigtails and yank it as hard as he could so my head would hurt worse. When I shared with my mom, mid-headache nausea, that it happened again, she feigned love and promised she'd take care of it. She enveloped me in a rare hug. Through my throbbing head, I inhaled the smell of her. Just as my body was releasing into a deep sigh, she cut my pigtails off with the jagged kitchen scissors that had been sitting on the counter next to us. I lived with the ugliest, uneven cut for weeks, until my grandmother took pity on me and booked an appointment to get it fixed.

The message was received loud and clear—my mother would always have the upper hand because she would always be my weakness. I was beginning to learn that every time I needed her, she'd open her arms wide and then crush me once my head rested upon her chest.

Girls

{To third-grade Misty Mae: "I See You" by
Missio}

In third grade, a scandal broke out in our small, dusty town. As with most small towns, we weren't without our share of scandals. As a child, though, they all seemed detached from my reality, at least until the *Third-Grade Incident* ...

All these years later, the biggest detail to stand out is my mother's silence on the matter. My mom had passionate opinions about literally everything. Whether it concerned her or not, she had a strong opinion. She also had the superhero skill of jumping to conclusions and opinions at light speed. Yet, on this, I recall nothing from her.

There was another white girl at my school named Erica. While she was tough, unfriendly (to me), and popular, I was none of those things. We weren't friends, and though she was sort of a bully to me, I can't recall any one specific thing that she did. Most of what I remember is being scared of her and jealous that the other kids seemed to love her.

One day in the middle of the week, the police came to the school with a social worker and pulled Erica from class. By recess, the news had traveled around most of the students that Erica's mother had been selling her to truckers at the local truck stop and had been arrested.

I was barely nine years old and had no idea what any of that meant, but I knew it was terrible. I didn't like Erica, but I was deeply sad that something horrible had happened to her.

Sometime later, Erica ended up back at school. She wouldn't talk about it and was pretty much left to herself. It is weird how the politics of elementary school seemed to unfold. It wasn't that she was an outcast as much as the cool kids had gone on without her, and she was more than happy to keep her head down, staying out of everyone's way.

It was around this time when Erica walked into our little yellow church with *her* grandmother. My initial reaction was irritation, of course. *What was* she *doing here? This was my place!* My grandmother quickly set me straight. My grandmother invited them to join us for lunch and, just like that, life changed.

Over the summer, I spent many nights and most of my days at Erica's home. She was living with her grandmother just outside of town. We did all the normal things and had all the normal conversations that girls our age were supposed to be having. We walked the fine line of giggling over crushes, playing like little kids, and being too old to play. Over that summer we became close. This wasn't like my friendship with Melanie. Something tethered us there, something invisible.

Erica never talked about what had happened with her mother or why she couldn't see her anymore. She never needed to. Somehow, I understood it was bigger than me, and I loved her fiercely despite it. Once school started, we still hung out in different small-town social circles, but passing one another in the hall now held random smiles, high fives, and notes about adolescent nonsense.

My mother neither questioned my sudden friendship with Erica nor denied my requests to spend time at Erica's house. In some unspoken way, Erica became a boundary my mother could neither accept nor forbid. Erica remained a constant in my life for the next few years. She was a safe haven where, when things in my life imploded three years after hers, we never had to talk about them. We connected in unexplained ways far beyond our years.

Family Photos

{To the illusions and the moments we believed them: "Light Years" by The National}

A traveling photographer set up shop in our little tumbleweed town. He was able to produce all the fancy techniques one could want, ranging from shadow portraits to the image of a couple gazing at one another from within a wine glass. In the 1980s, these were the must-haves in any portrait package. It's fun to look back and realize just how much of an expense these packages were, only to become meme fodder today.

Residents scheduled their appointments, and families dressed in their best to line up at the Western Auto, waiting for their turn. By the time I was aware of things like feeling awkward or embarrassed, the relationship between my mom and her boyfriend was widely accepted. Everyone understood that he had a wife and kids back in El Paso, and my mom and I were his second family in our town. It just *was*, and it was all I knew, so I didn't know to feel less because of it. It seemed normal that the three of us would take family portraits together, my mom and I wearing the aromatic wildflower corsages he'd pinned on us earlier that morning. It wasn't odd to me that my mother wore a wedding set and somehow worked the fact that she'd "break up with him if he ever left his wife" into consistent conversation. It just was what it was. He'd come home with treats and presents in his grip and bags of "big city shopping" my mom had asked him to get. She would get dressed up, have her hair done at the beauty shop, and put on a full face of makeup when she knew he'd be pulling into town. Happy family time filled the moments he was in Lordsburg, and then the time would come for him to go back to the other place. *His* home, though I never heard them call it that.

Not knowing the details, one might look at the three of us together or at those expensive family photos (done twice each year) and see nothing but a typical happy family. If I'd ever spoken a word about "surprise kisses" when Daddy left on work trips, most people probably chuckled to themselves and remarked about how cute it was.

Our family time involved average things. There were nights at the movies, camping trips, and fishing expeditions. His parents adored us and visited us regularly. I grew up knowing them as Granny and Gramps and loved them very much. When he was with us, there was no shortage of affection, holidays, KFC picnics, evening walks, inside jokes, board games, and all the things that I was pretty sure other families did.

The goodbyes when he was readying to leave seemed to last forever. I was required to be there. If I were riding my bike (which he taught me to do), over playing at Melanie's, or even spending time with my grandmother, it was mandatory I be home as the goodbye ceremony began. He would give me a big hug and a kiss and tell me to "be good to my mom." (Not *for* my mom, but rather *to* her.) Then my mom would cry, he would hug her, and they'd make out a little. I was around four or five when I became aware of how this ritual played out every single time, so I didn't really know what *making out* was.

One day, as children often do, I fired off roughly twenty questions about their kisses and why they were different from mine. I saw an unjustness in it.

They dubbed them *surprise kisses*, and it was funny for a while. Then one day I moved past joking about it, and I said I wanted a surprise kiss too. I was tired of being left out of something special. In the explanations they'd given, neither of them used words like *romantic, couples*, or *grown-ups*. I think the definition I'd gotten must have been something like, "When you love someone, you have a fun surprise kiss." When my mom's boyfriend broke down what a surprise kiss was (normal people know this as French kissing), I was grossed out and decided I did not want any part of that! They both assured me it was nice. He told my mom to give me a surprise kiss first, just to see what I thought.

I didn't like it.

They laughed; it was all fun family stuff.

Then, as he said his last goodbye to me, he gave me a surprise kiss too.

I *really* did not like it.

"Surprise kisses" became an occasional thing, even though I didn't like them. I would bully myself in the back of my mind about it being normal and brief, that I needed to stop being such a baby. I responded this way a lot, deep in the back closet of my brain.

There is another memory, fainter but equally uncomfortable, of a similar situation; only it didn't involve the goodbye routine.

The three of us were on the couch watching a movie, and the two of them started making out. It was fairly aggressive, and at one point he gave my mother a hickey. Even as a little girl, I knew that I wanted to be anywhere but there beside them while they were groaning and panting.

Movie nights, like goodbyes, weren't optional. In fact, looking back—unless there was some sort of home project happening—when he was with us, my presence was expected.

Unsure of what to do, and afraid to bring any attention to myself by leaving the couch, I became fixated on the hand-crafted yellow coffee table directly in front of me. I loved the story of how my mother's great-uncle, fingers permanently bent from arthritis, had whittled and assembled it by hand. It was beautiful, but for me this table was the focal point where I would disassociate from the hard-to-handle things that would come. This became another fun and playful thing for them. He had my mom give me a small hickey to show me that it was OK, then he gave me a deeper one.

And not just that one time.

This memory is much less vivid—I would question if it had happened at all, except for a school photo (another semi-annual photography torture) where my sweet little six-year-old neck has a hickey, deep purple for the entire world to see. The photographer alerted Child Protective Services, and they paid my mom a visit. (If you know anything about how things were done—especially small-town things in the 1980s—the fact she did this was very progressive.) The social worker caught Nora on a day her boyfriend's train was heading in, so she was channeling her inner 1950s housewife—done up beautifully, our house pristine. She was in the middle of baking an apple pie and had chocolate chip cookies cooling on the counter. Surrounded by framed family photos (twice a year, every year), the social worker left appeased. In her report, she penned we were a happy family and it had been a simple misunderstanding. My mom took a perverse sense of glee over having "fooled that woman," citing that nothing happening was "any of her damn business." In the home tour, my mom had been able to hide the sex pillow she'd made for her boyfriend, which always sat front and center on their bed. The woman had no idea about the very open sex life between the two of them, which took place all around our home and that I had no choice but to witness.

The woman had no idea what was happening to me behind closed doors. No one outside of those walls knew—*I* didn't even know.

1982 family photos

age 6

Misty dressed as Casper for
Halloween

Occasions

{To the small, aching girl who longed to be celebrated: "You Are Enough" by Sleeping At Last}

During summer breaks, I would often go to Phoenix to stay with my aunt. I lived for those summers. My aunt, uncle, and older cousins would play with me, color with me, and take me to the movies and other favorite places. There was this amazing Mexican restaurant called Poncho's, where you raised little flags and your waiters would bring you anything you wanted as often as you asked.

Flag up, "Three tacos, please!"

Flag up, "An enchilada and some rice, please!"

There were one or two locations, one with a giant fountain full of pennies and wishes. It was the sort of magic I lived for! Toward the end of our flag raising, it would finally be time for the giant, warm, pillowy sopapillas. My eyes would grow so big that my face hurt as I bit off a corner, letting the honey flow like amber magic. (To this day, sopapillas are one of my favorite things to eat. The way restaurants now try to offer diners fried tortillas slathered in Hershey's Syrup and whipped cream should be against the law!)

Poncho's is no more, so if you're planning a trip to Arizona because my beautiful memory has made you hungry, I apologize. Even so, I'll always encourage trips to the Southwest, for myriad reasons. If you've never had a real sopapilla, then I strongly recommend you arrange your travel plans immediately. (You're welcome!)

During those visits, we would shop, play in the pool, watch cable TV, and make runs to Taco Bell and Baskin Robbins—two other magical places that my small town did not have. Since my aunt and uncle worked during the day, a family from their church would watch me. I would eat chocolate pudding, ride bikes, and play Star Wars action figure–inspired games with their son Bradley during the long summer days. When the end of summer neared and it was time to go home, I was devastated. Sure, I missed Melanie and her family and couldn't wait to tell her all the things, but mostly I just knew I didn't want to go home, though I never understood why.

Nora hated that I loved going to Arizona, or that I spent time with my Aunt Gloria at all. Whenever Gloria's family would come to Lordsburg for a holiday or a long weekend, they made it a priority to spend time with me, and my mother developed a taste for making the visits as complicated as possible. There were so many manipulations, stipulations, and any other "-ation" she could conjure up, with no reason other than to hurt someone. That someone was usually me. When it came to my Arizona trips, though, it was complicated. She did not want me around, and she also did not want me to be happy. Not having to deal with me won out most of the time. I was lucky that way.

As I neared middle school, some sort of shift occurred. I could feel changes and things that were building but could neither articulate nor understand them. I would miss parts of days or evenings I simply couldn't account for. In some strange way, I felt this was very bad, yet also as it should be. There were many times I lived more by watching my life unfold than contributing or doing much about it. As time passed, the one thing that was always clear was that my mother's contempt for me grew.

In the spring, my mother had promised me she would do something amazing for my eleventh birthday. I still managed to find excitement where my birthday was concerned, even though every single year my mother notoriously went above and beyond to ruin it. Secretly, I doubted she would follow through with her promises regarding my eleventh, but the anticipation overtook any doubt.

On the morning of my birthday, with every hour that passed, crushing defeat began to take over. A few minutes before we were heading to my grandmother's for lunch (as we did every Saturday when her boyfriend wasn't around), I asked her if she even knew it was my birthday.

"Of course, I know. I was there, wasn't I?" She began to lecture me about how I was selfish and didn't deserve a birthday. I was a lazy, bad kid and a complete idiot if I thought she would waste a penny on my day.

Over lunch, no one said anything. When Mommy brought out the Saturday lunch dessert, it was cottage cheese and fresh canned peaches—my least favorite. (Cottage cheese and fruit do NOT a dessert make.) After my mom left and I retired to my Saturday afternoon routine of playing out in the shed while listening to Casey Kasem's countdown, I allowed myself the sadness. I was eleven now, and for the first time I could recall, I let myself sink deep into a dark space. The anger toward Nora's meanness evaporated, and I surrendered myself to the things she seemed to believe about me.

After a few hours, my grandmother told me we were going for a ride and had to stop by my mom's house on the way. She pulled a ten-by-thirteen-inch covered cake pan out of the trunk, but I was so lost in my sad abyss that there was no room for curiosity. I begged her not to make me go in, but she reassured me it would just be a few minutes. I spent Saturday nights with my grandmother, and my biggest fear was that I would get into that house and my mom would do something awful, guaranteeing that I wouldn't be allowed to leave.

Nora cried what seemed to be genuine tears as my friends all yelled, "Surprise!" She was so proud that I had never suspected a thing. For years I would hear about the huge surprise party she threw. It was clear that it had ranked up there in her mind as a crowning achievement. There had been five friends, no decorations, no party favors, and no food other than the cake my grandmother made. The plan was to watch *Howard the Duck*, eat cake, open gifts, and be done.

I loved every second of it, and it didn't occur to me that her crowning achievement had required no real planning or effort at all until I was well into my thirties. I had always seen it as this rare, magical moment that occurred within the walls of our usually dark home. My mother lorded it over me whenever she needed to remind me of the un-grateful piece of garbage I was.

Many years later as a mom, I understood. There were often times when I would completely pour myself into something amazing in the name of love-filled motherhood, and the receiving child would not care. There is no deny-ing it—that feeling sucks. I do feel bad if it was how I made my mom feel that day. But also, to advocate for the eleven-year-old me, the whole thing was unhealthy.

Christmas the same year, we followed our early Christmas routine of dinner and opening gifts with my mom's boyfriend. He always spent the actual holidays in his real home with his real family, so this became how we did things.

There were three gifts beneath the tree for me. My mom went on (and on) about how money was tight and I needed to be grateful that I even had *three presents*. They watched as I opened the first one, and then the second. Together, the two boxes had revealed an ankle length, straight black skirt and a cameo collar, long sleeve white blouse. I was eleven years old and in the sixth grade.

Before I said a word or even had time to react beyond my confusion, my mother exploded. "See? I told you she wouldn't be grateful! I kept the price tags on there so she could see the kind of hard-earned money I spent on her, but she doesn't care! She is so spoiled!"

My entire memory of this fake Christmas Eve seems filled with multicolored squiggly marks of confusion. I had no idea what was happening.

He asked her to calm down.

Shaking, she lit a cigarette. "READ THEM, you little selfish brat! Read the tags!" She was screaming, spitting on me as her voice raged. I fumbled, searching for the tags. My own voice shaking now, I read $68 on one and $87.78 on the other. I was eleven. I had no concept of what either one of those prices meant. Hot tears made their way down my cheeks, and her boyfriend escorted her back to their bedroom.

I was devastated and angry all at once.

I was sad that this had been my Christmas—the terrible clothes, the way I seemed to disappoint my mother simply by existing, and also the fact that I hated the terrible clothes.

The tags showed more money than I understood, yet I didn't know how to be thankful.

Eventually, the two of them emerged from their bedroom. He gave me a reassuring, apologetic smile, and though my mother's hate-filled eyes still aimed their darts at me, we moved on. In our family, the tradition was always that the youngest opens gifts first, and so, since there was the unopened third gift, it was still my turn.

My mom made some quiet remark about the only thing I'd asked for (which I knew had been a Tiffany cassette tape), and I allowed myself a tiny breath of hope. He winked at me, and with a rush, the negative feelings were gone, and I ripped open that box.

I could see that inside were three cassette tapes, and my heart soared. Music was everything to me, and I'd wear whatever clothes Nora wanted me to as long as I could retreat to the blaring headphones of my Walkman. Everything leading up to that moment disappeared. Christmas was saved and I could not wait to retreat to my bedroom and lose myself in my new music.

Except Tiffany wasn't among the three cassettes.

There was an ABBA tape, a Queen tape, and a Sesame Street disco tape. I had no idea who the first two were and was deeply offended by the third. Scared to reignite my mother, I looked up at her with a weak smile and saw nothing but smug satisfaction glistening in her eyes.

It was her boyfriend's turn to get mad. "What the hell are those?"

She had not been expecting that.

"Nora, this isn't what you said you were going to do. What did you do?"

She sounded nervous, though it was apparent she tried to hide it. "I wanted a few tapes from Columbia House, and none of the music she liked was on the list of free tapes, so I just picked three."

"But I gave you money to buy her the tape on her list. You said you'd bought the damn Tiffany tape!" He was controlled, but definitely angry. This wasn't a version of him I had seen before.

"No, I told you I ordered tapes for her. I did use the money you gave me to pay for the cassettes I ordered. I had already spent so much of what you gave me on the new clothes."

"Yes," he snarled, "something else we will talk about later. I do not understand why you do things sometimes."

She was full of charm and word-twisting magic where he was concerned. Eventually, he gave up attempting to reason with her logic. Even to me, it was clear that the two of them were not having the same conversation. In the end, she blamed him for always taking my side and told me I'd ruined her Christmas.

Because we had to fit our Christmas in where his schedule allowed, I hadn't been able to spend that Saturday night with my grandmother. She picked me up for church the following morning and brought me home after lunch. My mom was napping, and he was getting everything together for his departure. (The grand goodbye ceremonies had dissipated by this time. She would still go through the motions of an agonizing departure, like a woman sending her soldier to war, but my presence was no longer welcome.)

We exchanged casual greetings as I made my way back to my room. It was more normal when he was there, as though some sort of canopy shielded me from my mother. It was the first thing I saw as I walked through my bedroom door—propped on the handle of my stereo was the Tiffany tape. Stuck to it was a Post-it with a smiley face and his messily scrawled, "p.s. don't tell your mom."

I never spoke about it to either of them. I was over the moon! Ours was not a home where any noise from my room was allowed beyond my walls, and the best part about it was that my mother had no interest, so she never even noticed.

On *actual* Christmas morning, a strange scratching and animal noise awakened me long before the sun came up. Once I worked through the fear I had about the beast that was presumably there to kill me, I felt something nibble my toes. There, in the dark of my tiny trailer bedroom, I fell head over heels in love with a playful puppy I could not see.

The Christmas before, I had begged for a puppy. When I'd been given a stuffed brown and white Pound Puppy named Spot instead, I had loved him as though he were real. In the hours that I'd lie awake, waiting for sleep, I would stroke his velvety soft fur while confiding the deepest parts of my heart.

There in the dark, I introduced this magically alive puppy to Spot. It was the three of us against the world! My heart felt so happy that I could burst. When I heard my mother up and around, I went out to tell her about the German shepherd puppy that had appeared on Christmas night. She thrust a letter at me—a letter from Santa.

I was past the point of believing in jolly Saint Nick, but there was something truly magical about it all. A puppy was my heart's deepest desire (superseding even the Tiffany tape), but I wasn't about to ask for a puppy. The letter from Santa (and not in my mom's or her boyfriend's handwriting) said her name was Betsy, and she had chosen to love me and to be my best friend.

The gift of Betsy (whose name I detested) was the best thing I remember happening to me. I am eons older than that Christmas morning of my eleventh year, and I can still feel the swell of joy, love, and gratitude over beautiful Betsy. The most amazing part of her to me was that she seemed to mirror those same feelings—ABOUT ME! *ME!*

I loved everything about her—her smelly breath, over-sized clumsy feet, and the way her soft, wiry hair felt so warm when I hugged her. My world instantly revolved around Betsy, and I wanted to do everything with her. When the reality of this set in, it was pretty much the beginning of the end. My mother started demanding Betsy stay outside, all the time. We lived in a single-wide trailer with a small side yard. Betsy was just a baby, and the desert can get so cold. We had no doghouse or shelter for her, and she was lonely at night. Betsy would curl up, pressed against the aluminum siding beneath my bedroom window. When she would whine, I tried to reassure her through the window. With Spot in my arms, I imagined how sad Betsy must have been, how lonely ... *Did she worry that I loved Spot more?*

Spot's shiny brown nose was scraped with chew marks from the night they met. There in the dark I would caress those teeth marks while attempting to soothe Betsy through the window. I needed to be loud enough that she could hear me, while quiet enough that my mom could not.

I needed to reassure her that I loved her more than anything in the world.

As a sixth grader, I woke up every morning, made my own breakfast, and got ready for the day. I would then walk to school, go through an entire school day, and walk home. As I'd turn the corner, I could see Betsy at the fence, dutifully waiting. She would get more and more excited with each step I traveled. She had so much energy, and as she was growing, it was clear this tiny yard was not meant for her. She didn't care, all she wanted was me.

Once home, I would change clothes and start my homework at the kitchen table. This was usually two hours of schoolwork plus going wherever my mom deemed we needed to go (such as meeting a friend for Cokes at the truck stop), and it cut my available time significantly. My mom still had me going to bed at eight o'clock, despite that I never fell asleep until well after midnight.

Even at my age, I knew Betsy was not living her best life. She was lonely, and I developed not only a consuming desire to spend every waking second with her, but a cancerous guilt that I hardly got to spend time with her at all. I knew she was sad, and I hated myself for doing that to her.

Nora hated Betsy. She ensured the relationship between my dog and me would be a failure. She ignored Betsy, kept my out-of-school time so full, and then berated me about how much Betsy loved me and just wanted to be with me, but I was so selfish that I ignored her ... over and over again. My mother would force me to beg for her permission to go outside, and even then, would search for silly, microscopic reasons why her answer was no. Betsy dangled like the proverbial carrot, just out of reach, always whining beneath my window or begging me to play from the other side of that screen door.

For the two months Betsy was mine, she was my one ray of light. She also became the ideal weapon to hurt me. I came home from school one late-February day, and Betsy was not at the fence waiting for me.

My mom had given her away. She said Betsy deserved better than me. For many nights after Betsy left, I fell asleep sobbing into Spot's fur. I was consumed with worry that Betsy thought I hadn't loved her. I begged Spot to somehow let Betsy know she was the very best girl.

To this day, feelings so complicated rise to the surface when I see a neglected dog outside. Guilt, shame, immeasurable sadness, and so much grief—how can something so long ago still stir such an ache from deep inside?

I turned twelve in the pediatric unit of a Silver City, New Mexico, hospital. My mother, nearly one hour south, neither called nor came to visit. My grandmother made the drive up and brought me flowers. They were fake and shades of blue, arranged in a cobalt wire basket with a felt bunny stuck inside. She was worried about me, and she didn't try to hide it.

I had been diagnosed weeks before with mono. Everyone talked over me, no one explaining what mono was or how I'd come to have it. At the time, I was pen pals with a girl named Christie from Missouri, who had multiple sclerosis, and my child-mind decided these big m-words were the same. (I was never good with large, overwhelming words.) I'd been told the day we became pen pals that Christie was going to die.

Therefore, I believed I was dying.

Gone was the future I imagined, the hopes I allowed myself to conjure during endless games of MASH (Mansion, Apartment, Shack, House) and daydreamed escapes.

I did the most natural thing that an eleven-year-old girl in my shoes would do: I wrote a goodbye letter to Joseph. I poured out my heart to him and told him I was dying. I did this in history class because what did school matter anyway?

My mother found it while going through my room and decided it was a suicide note. Immediately, she scheduled a top secret visit to a psychiatrist, with my grandmother along for moral support. She barged into the appointment, angry and firm on the resolution that she wanted me committed. Ever the naive child, I had no idea what a psychiatrist was, why we were meeting with one, or that Nora had even found my letter. As the realization of the latter began to hit me, I was mortified! I did not want my mom reading those words written to the only boy I had ever loved!

No matter how much I argued that the letter was not a suicide note (and what even *was* suicide anyway?), she would not be pacified. She embarked on this mission with a purpose, and she would not be swayed. Eventually, the elder women were escorted to the waiting room, while the psychiatrist attempted to get to the bottom of whatever circus we'd brought to his office. When I refused to speak to him or even look in his direction, he called over a pediatric specialist colleague, and she suggested I be hospitalized for monitoring and evaluation.

It felt like an excruciatingly long period of time in that office alone with him. The air was heavy, thick, and void of light. He had plants and every piece of furniture or decor contained some element of brown. He wore a tweed jacket, had a gray beard, and smelled of bark. While he attempted to engage in conversation with me, I sat trapped inside myself, unable to move or say a word. When his colleague came, she brought with her some sunlight. I saw then how the plants could grow, and when I attempted to wiggle my fingers and toes, I felt them move. Not only did she smile, but she *was* a smile, and as long as she stayed, I could tell her anything she wanted to know.

My grandmother sat in my hospital room on my twelfth birthday, still believing I had wanted to take my own life. Twelve years earlier in that same city, she had been the first to hold me close. She had given me my name.

The weekend after my mother took me home, she threw me a slumber party for the birthday I'd celebrated two weeks before. It was a lackluster affair. She served dinner, had a small, plain cake and a huge, boxed gift. She made a dramatic display over how my gift was *so perfect* and she could hardly wait to give it to me.

"You've asked for this more than anything in the world!" she squealed. More than anything in the entire world I wanted Betsy, and I wanted to be back at the hospital. I did not want to be home, I did not want to be with her, and I certainly did not want to be having a sleepover with anyone. I was numb those days. The hospital and the details around it—my health, lack of energy, what I can only imagine now was the start of depression—left me feeling incapable of much. Still, when it came time, I began to open the gift. She did not try to mask her frustration with my lack of excitement, but I had grown so used to living in the shadow her disappointment that I didn't care. Between this and the fact that gifts from my mother seldom brought joy, I merely went through the motions without enthusiasm.

Inside the very large box was a pastel rainbow blanket that her boyfriend had crocheted.

I had never wanted it. In fact, I had made it clear, over the months he'd been crocheting it, that I hated the blanket. I thought it was ugly, old-fashioned, and resembled a baby blanket stretched out to adult size.

I looked to her. Underneath the tears welling in her eyes, I saw it there—that familiar smugness masked as something else for our guests.

"Thanks, Mom," came my monotonous response.

"You're welcome, baby. Happy birthday!"

Gray Scale

{For him: "Praying" by Kesha}

A couple summers ago, when I stumbled upon the old letters between my mom and her boyfriend, I decided to reach out to him. I'd acquired a handful of things from my mom I felt belonged to him, that I wanted him to have. For obvious reasons, we had not stayed in touch, and when I found him on Facebook, I sent him a message. It was honest and from deep within a space I wasn't even aware existed.

After I reached out to him, I penned a short personal essay to him and posted it on my blog. He doesn't have cause to cyberstalk my online spaces, so I never imagined he would see it. While it was *to* him, it was really *for* me. A form of closure and cerebral processing that I could give to myself. (To this day, I am proud of that post. It may not be the most eloquent or profound piece, but it is personal.)

In the direct message, I asked him if we could talk. I would have been willing to say everything that I was wanting to say in a message conversation, or even over the phone. I have heard a lot of inspirational speakers talk about *big endgame goals.* You know, where you establish what feels like a larger-than-life goal and then create smaller steps toward it. While I would have been willing to say the things I needed to say in those ways, my *big endgame goal* looked like my husband, Chris, and I flying to Texas and having dinner with him. Chris, bless him, is no threat to this man. The two of them always got along and (to the best of my knowledge) had a mutual respect between them. For a long time, I resented my husband for this. I didn't understand how he could be jovial and relational with this man when Chris knew what he'd done. Ever that lost little girl deep inside, I was still waiting for someone (anyone) to find me worth fighting for.

By the time his and Chris's civility wasn't an issue for me, my mom's boyfriend was no longer a fixture in my life. I don't know how it happened, but I am grateful this is their truth.

I did not say in the message that I wanted to fly down and talk to him. What I said was I had some things I felt belonged to him that my mother had no business keeping. I reassured him there was nothing in me that wanted to visit negative experiences from our past. I made it clear that, though what happened was not OK, I had made my peace with him. I wanted to talk with him about so much more than the abuse because our lives were so much more complicated than that.

Since I reached out, I have shared with a handful of people my desire to see and talk with him. For the most part, people seem unable to understand. I get it. A few of these people genuinely care about me and cannot imagine why I would put myself through that. When I first began talking about this hope I had, I wasn't looking for approval or advice.

A few months ago, Chris and I were sorting through some things we'd put into our attic, and I came across the package I had set aside for *him*. The boyfriend. Curiosity got the better of me, and I logged on to Facebook to see if he'd ever read my message from years before.

It is safe to presume he did because it seemed he had since blocked me. A few minutes of further digging confirmed his two adult sons did the same. My immediate reaction was shock. I felt a range of rejection, hurt, and a hundred other complicated emotions which evolved rapidly, until suddenly the ironic hilarity of the whole situation settled in. It was not lost on me that my child molester—the man many held responsible for the loss of my family—felt threatened by *me*, and on social media no less.

It also oversimplifies a truth far more complex than that.

The first Christmas I was a mother, I mailed him a Christmas card. This decision was more impulse than planned. My mom was busy with work and caring for my grandmother, so I told her that I'd be happy to handle her Christmas cards. She was stressed over it, and though it may seem old-fashioned, this is a task I actually enjoy.

As we were on the phone, her going through her address book while I observed my daughter playing with dolls on the floor, she came to his name and made a joke about sending him and his wife a card. (He and my mom broke up the year before, and Nora has always been well cast as the bitter ex.) I said, "Sure, I'll send him a card." So she gave me the address.

My mother has always been the sort to accept a dare thoughtlessly—the more rebellious, the better. As she grew older, I suspect hindsight left her with some regrets. She phoned back just a few minutes after we hung up and asked me to not include her if I decided to send him a card. She made it clear she wanted me to jab him in this way, but that she wanted it to appear she'd had no part in it.

I never imagined their relationship would end. When it did, I wanted to be really proud of my mom. I told her that

I was proud of her and allowed myself to be the rock she leaned on, but I knew that she'd had little to do with the decision to call it quits. Whatever the reasons were on his end, I was grateful.

I was by her side through the deep depression and suicidal chapter following their breakup. I was there as she made many self-destructive choices, and finally began to make some healthy ones. For that I was incredibly proud of her. Through those highs and lows, I made sure she knew I loved her unconditionally and wasn't going anywhere. I provided for her the love which I had always hoped she'd someday give to me.

I did send him a card. From a very raw place, I wrote about how, while the sexual abuse inflicted on me had been a very wrong and cruel thing he'd done to my childhood, I was grateful that I was able to understand my little girl in ways no one had understood me. I mentioned her early childhood had also seen trauma before she came to our family. I wrote about how God can bring about good from even the evilest of actions, and I wrote that I forgave him.

And I did forgive him.

I meant all of this, and I don't regret having the courage to say any of those things. It had been fifteen years since the abuse ended. However, saying it in a Christmas card, knowing that his wife and family would probably see it, is not something I am proud of. However deserved it may seem, it was immature and petty.

I can't blame him for being skittish. It is irrelevant whether that holiday card caused problems for him—I shouldn't have sent it. I was a new mom, and my advocate-supermom senses were all tingly and heightened. These are poor excuses for doing such a mean thing. The truth was that I *had* forgiven him. I believed the things I wrote, but the second I delivered the message in such a careless way, it didn't matter.

And we come to the part of the story we've been headed toward for a while now. I will tell you I talk about events directly, and, depending on your standards, it may seem graphic. If you worry you may be triggered, please skip ahead. You don't need that, and though it is an important part of my story, the actual details aren't the heart of this book.

My mom's boyfriend sexually abused me.

The abuse went on for roughly a decade. At various points from ages two until twelve, I have brief recollections of incidents. While I don't know specific details (I was a child), I know enough to be certain thirty years after the final incident that it was real. My mother, whether consciously or not, offered up her innocent little girl in exchange for a life where she could buy and do whatever she wanted, when and however she chose. No longer chained to the life of a waitress, her freedom cost me my childhood.

We live in a world where the only options are victim or survivor, but neither seems to fit quite right for me. A man may lose the use of his legs in a tragic accident, surviving the trauma but remaining a victim of his paralysis. He would not be a survivor of paralysis until he was no longer paralyzed. This is where the minimization of abuse takes place. We are, from that moment on, both victim *and* survivor. There is nothing wrong with this. No matter how we try to mold, twist, and manipulate perceptions of the words themselves to bring the validation we seek, we are both.

There is this idea that healing from abuse of any kind is a mountain we must bravely climb. The notion that those of us affected will ever reach a point when we've beat the trauma is naive. While most abuses can occur within minutes, the effects of them worm their way deep into the fibers of our being. Though this ugliness may lie dormant for years, it will reappear.

One day, within the first six weeks of my twelfth year on this earth, my mom's boyfriend put his hand between my legs while we were watching a movie on a Friday night. I sat on one end of the couch, he in the middle, with my mother knitting on the other end. My memory has him reaching his arm around my shoulder to fondle my nipple for an eternity before moving down to begin touching my vaginal area, but my rational mind questions the plausibility of this exact placement. I am guessing the first part happened before a resituating occurred to move into the second. It doesn't matter *how* it happened because it did happen.

And it changed my entire life.

My twelve-year-old body, that Friday evening in May of 1988, had an orgasm. Times were different then—I had no idea what a climax was, or even much about sex at all beyond the things I'd heard or seen from the two of them. I remember the very quiver that exploded inside of me—how incredibly terrifying and sickening it felt, while also somehow wrongly feeling good—and this would cement itself into my memory forever.

It would be nearly two years before I would feel it again with a boyfriend and be able to identify what had happened.

Ten weeks prior to this "family movie night," I had been hospitalized for contemplating suicide. On paper and to my family, this was the reason. In truth, however, the team of doctors working with me knew something bigger was wrong. These doctors knew of the presence of abuse even before I did.

Every day for the thirty-eight days that I resided in this hospital, tucked under the vast desert skies of Silver City,

New Mexico, the smiling female doctor would subtly educate me on the boundaries of my body and then question if anyone had ever violated those boundaries.

Every single time, I told her the truth as I knew it.

"No." *No, of course that never happened to me!* Panic mounting inside me, I felt the temperature in my hospital room rise significantly as our daily talks took place. I was less reassuring and more emphatic that this had never happened. No one in my life would do that to me. I thought about uncles, Melanie's dad, cousins, and various male friends my mother had. None of them would ever do such things. The mind, though, is an amazing organ whose capabilities we simply cannot grasp. In those thirty-eight days, the one person who never crossed my mind was my mom's boyfriend, this man who taught me to ride a bike and spent hours playing board games with me. The man who took me on daddy-daughter dates and knew the songs I loved most on the radio. This man who did not come to mind once, as if memory of him had been switched off: my *daddy*.

That's what I called him, almost from the beginning. *Daddy*.

And wasn't he?

While my father was a stranger, this man stepped up. He provided the T-bone steak and baked potato dinners we always had when he came to town. He was also the one whose money bought the Hamburger Helper and bologna sandwiches I learned to make myself when he was at his real home and my mom was lost in a depressive fog. He made my mother light up like a sunrise when that train whistle blew. Long before cell phones and social media updates, she had his schedule down to a science. No longer working, due to the comfortable life he provided, she lived for that man's cowboy boots and Stetson to walk through the frame of our small, single-wide front door. It was an

actual blooming/wilting occurrence which I grew up believing was normal.

This is what love looked like, wasn't it?

Even so, when the doctor had asked her question, this
man, who was a prominent fixture in my daily life, never
found his way into my thoughts.

In the hospital, I was so far removed from my life's version of normal. I adapted, almost instantly, to a new normal. I was such a master at compartmentalizing, that even
in the quiet moments, I never thought of my actual life,
my *real* life. Even if I had tried to analyze if the everyday
occurrences at home were normal, what other *normal* did I
have to compare them with?

*Didn't daddies have wives and children in other towns some-
times?*

*Weren't parents pornographically active, all over the house, re-
gardless of whether the daughter was in the same room?*

*Didn't mothers crumble into a verbally abusive and en-
raged-sad state, leaving your home shrouded in drawn curtains,
cruelty, and clouds of heavy cigarette smoke until Daddy reap-
peared?*

What defines childhood *normal*? This was mine. I didn't
know any different.

Up until the hospital, he gave me baths whenever he was
in town. I had spent portions of my early childhood in
the New Mexico Children's Hospital for a hip disorder. My
mother had been taught how to do therapeutic massage to
help with pain management, but she never wanted to do
it. From as early as I can remember, it was not uncommon
for him to get me naked and lay me on my stomach so that
he could slather my body in Icy Hot for one of his special
massages. Pornography was a major fixture in our home,
both in print and video forms. The gigantic things—which
were, in reality, the very opposite of normal—were so mun-

dane that I didn't think much about them at all. During those thirty-eight days, safe in that hospital, none of these things came to mind. None of the strange violations, which the doctors urged me to remember, were accessible to my brain.

There was nothing abnormal to report.

Until that first Friday night, anyway, discharged from the hospital and back home.

That night, as *it* happened, I could feel a familiar fog begin to descend upon me. It was warm and heavy and somewhere I knew I had been many times before. Just as I was about to surrender to this safe space, an alarm sounded, bringing a sense of clarity. All at once, I thought about the smiling doctor's words and questions. This *was happening,* this *was real,* and *this was what she had warned me about.*

Though chilled, I did not panic. As the clarity continued, I experienced a flood of memories from countless other times this abuse had taken place. At twelve years old, I was able to understand that somehow, I had blocked every single instance, gaze zeroing in on the coffee table while retreating to somewhere deep inside. As my body rebelled against the dark reality of what he was doing and climaxed, the words on repeat within my mind were only, *Dear God, please don't let me forget. Help me remember.*

At some point the movie ended, ice cream bowls were rinsed, and I was in bed. One to lay awake for hours watching the clock, I must have fallen asleep quickly that night. I woke with a sense of urgency that following morning, asking before I was fully coherent, *Do I remember?*

I did.

I thanked Jesus then and there. Wrapped in my soft-worn Holly Hobby sheets, I sobbed unfamiliar, grown-adult, guttural, quaking tears of relief. I didn't know what to do or why my memory mattered, and still I found myself overwhelmed with gratitude that my memory had not failed me.

Later that day, across our fence, I spoke the words aloud for the first time, to Melanie.

To him,

I wanted to sit across a table from you, breaking bread, and taking in the years which lie evident upon our faces. Lifetimes have happened since those days when I called you *Daddy*. Bad things happened then under that label, but good things did too.

So many good things.

Life is never black and white. While there were storms of mental illness inconsistencies raging within my childhood home, you offered a balancing sense of certainty. You are the only other living person who knew those parts of her like I did. There are so many things that only you could share with me, about her.

Monopoly is still my favorite game; you were the only person patient enough to play it with me. You instilled in me a love of board games, and I'm thankful. You taught me, while never getting angry or acting impatient, to ride a bike. You stood on that street, from blazing afternoon sun through dusk, taking pictures and cheering me on. When my own mother couldn't bring herself to leave the walls she found solace in, you ventured outside for camping, shopping trips, fishing, walks for ice cream, bike lessons, and actual conversations with me.

It has been hard to reconcile, at times, the faithful and stable parent you were beside the monstrous things you did. Empathetically, a part of me wonders why, and possibly what darkness befell you, leading you to take such actions. In truth, though, I don't think I really want to know. I am grateful for the dad things you did, and that you stepped up at all to be that presence in my life. You were her boyfriend;

you had other interests in me. You could have chosen to use me and not also invest in me, but you brought the gray scale middle, too, and it is within that vastness which some of the better parts of my childhood took form.

Hurt people *hurt people*—this is enough for me.

I don't think I would have said most of these things to you, though, had we met to share a meal. I would have asked you about her, and maybe *why her*. What about her made you decide to love her? What about us made you stick around for decades? I do know in my heart that you did not prey on her to tarnish me. I know that you genuinely loved her, loved us ...

Even so, I know what you did. We both do.

I know that the *only* reason she came to my wedding was because you made her.

I know that the *only* reason she came to help me after my cancer scare was because you forced her hand.

I know, too, there are many other scenarios just like those, unknown by me.

I am grateful. Even then, even when there were chasms between us, hardened boundaries of both security and pain, you looked out for me. As odd as it may seem, you always had. I see this now.

When I was young and still in that house, she sought to wound me, and you swooped in to provide something better and balance me out. This was separate from your darkness, and I may not understand it or what motivated you, but within my space of growth and healing I am finally able to see what it meant for me.

It meant I had someone who would validate me and have an interest in attending school programs. It meant I had someone willing to read me stories, color with me, and listen to what the mean kid at school did when I was having a hard day.

Maybe it seems twisted and incomprehensible, but this doesn't make it any less true.

I remember that the rare times you were able to attend a school concert or play were the best.

I think I'll always love you, but only in recent years have I allowed myself to accept this.

I forgive you, which is ideal letter talk, but probably would not have been verbalized across our shared table space. I abhor what you did, but I also understand that, had you not been there, my childhood would have been *all* darkness under that roof. There would have been no one to see me, and no one to care.

I do wish we'd gone to dinner.

I wish you'd responded to my note.

I genuinely wish I knew how you were, could tell you how she is, and *who* she is now. I wish, strangely—unexpectedly—that I knew you outside of the tornado of good and bad that rested just beneath the surface of all those strange family photos.

It is hard to reconcile compartmentalized pieces of a girl from the gray, but I am trying.

~M

Voice

{To both of them: "My Tears Ricochet" by Taylor Swift}

It is so easy to hear about child abuse horror stories and get angry at the adults present when it looks from the outside as though they did nothing to help the victim. In the years that followed my abuse, there were a lot of those people who had things they wanted to talk with me about. Like Amy. These things always revealed that there were suspicions—red flags—but they dismissed them, and because of that, they felt they owed me somehow.

We live in a world filled with "I wish I would have ..." hindsight, but the uncomfortable truth is that things are seldom so simple. History is filled with stories of early corporations who created a tattle culture to motivate employees to work harder. Initially this seemed like a productive idea, but time and time again, it would slowly backfire. Horrible work environments were created, and, while we can't blame all inequality on this practice, that manipulated divisiveness did not win humanity (specifically those oppressed) any favors. Whether we admit it or not, we long for community connection. A person's subconscious can look forward, projecting a likely outcome should they report a suspicion and it turn out to be false. The threat of a lost relationship, or whatever their investment is, may trigger the self-protection instinct.

Being wrong would be embarrassing.

Someone could get hurt.

Someone could retaliate, and I may get hurt.

I may never see that child again.

Most of the time, people had not consciously processed the things they saw until they stood at the end (knowing about the abuse) and traced backward, revisiting those red flags and feelings. We want to blame because we feel powerless, and blame feels like doing something, but it really isn't.

There are two people in my story who own the responsibility of what happened to me, and they are my mother, Nora, and her boyfriend. Period.

The other people around did exactly what little-girl me needed them to do: They LOVED me.

But when I needed to be saved, I saved myself.

It goes back to that Phoenix afternoon, dancing beside my aunt's pool. It can trace back to so many moments when I took charge shamelessly to advocate for me. Maybe it even trails all the way back to the afternoon of the anthill. Yes, Amy may have lifted me up by my chubby arms, but only because I sat there pleading my case.

I was a twelve-year-old girl, unprepared for the choice and consequence I suddenly found myself dealing with. I sifted through that overwhelm and mulled it over. I moved slowly, making small maneuvers based on prayer and intuition. Then, with a wisdom from somewhere beyond myself, I took a stand for *me*.

First it had been confiding in Melanie, whom I had sworn to secrecy, because I was still trying to process and figure it all out. While it did not seem real to me, and I definitely did not welcome the feeling that my life had been turned inside out, I also knew my trust had to be given sparingly.

Next, I wrote to my Aunt Gloria. I told her everything and asked her to take me to Phoenix to live with them. Rationally, this seemed like the best plan of escape. I never doubted their love for me and knew I needed to get as far away from my home as possible.

Four days after the last incident, I had a postdischarge follow-up with the smiling doctor. (She was a pediatrician. She was friends with the male psychiatrist who had suspected sexual abuse when I froze in place of interacting with him. He was technically the doctor in charge of my care, but she was the face because he had no idea how to reach me.)

Nora, her boyfriend, and me, our happy little family, had gone up to Silver City for the appointment. We had lunch at Wendy's, and even though Nora objected, her boyfriend treated me to a Frosty. He decided to wait in the car during the appointment while she sat in the waiting room looking at magazines. The doctor pulled me back alone because, while times were different then, she'd also had zero interaction with my mother during the thirty-eight days that I had been under her care.

The second the doctor's gaze met mine, I believe she knew what was coming. She never said it, but I am convinced she believed I was suffering from memory repression, that it was just a matter of time. When I blurted out what had happened, her response to me was one of immense relief and concern.

In all our time working together, I had never shared anything out of the ordinary with this doctor. She had no idea how my mother could be. She earnestly believed that my mom loved me and would do all the right things for me. She made me believe my mom needed to be told, despite my hesitation. When I look back, I am sure she thought my reluctance stemmed from the shame of what I'd been through. In my twelve-year-old mind, her boyfriend was my abuser. I was so fresh and young that I could not comprehend my mother's complicity.

Nora responded with grief and tears, and—for the first time ever—I relaxed and allowed myself to believe she really did love me. She told me she was *so sorry* this had happened and cursed that *son of a bitch.*

The doctor handed my mom some pamphlets with resources and numbers to call, should we need them.

"Come on, baby." Tears still on her face, she wrapped my hand in hers, and together we headed for the car.

She pulled the seat forward, trembling, so I could climb in the back.

"Well, how'd it go?" The tone of his voice was so normal, goosebumps pricked my skin.

As she slammed the heavy Pontiac door, however, the real Nora emerged, leaving me both terrified of what would happen and in awe of my mother's performance. The entire forty-five-minute ride back to Lordsburg was filled with her rage and insults while I sat wound into the tightest ball I could manage. There, in the most distant corner of a suddenly claustrophobic car, I chewed every single one of my fingernails down until they bled.

The next day, everyone in my middle school learned about the abuse. It started with a hushed confession to my few close friends, me begging them not to say anything. They'd been concerned by my absence and how I didn't seem myself. By lunch, word spread. I don't blame them—this was hot gossip—and we were all just small-town kids.

For the whole of my life, I had ached to fit in and belong in a town where that seemed impossible. Suddenly, with a horrific story to share, all the cool kids knew my name. Big eighth graders vowed their protection, and with each promise of support, I grew more confident in the road ahead. As the afternoon bell rang, I found myself braver than I'd been before.

I still, over thirty years later, remember the way it felt to speak my truth, a little louder each time, confirming to one person and then another. Every time my mouth formed the words, I gained more of what I needed to fight for myself.

To advocate for little-girl me, and also for twelve-year-old me.

Beyond my school campus, I opened my mouth and spoke the truth to every person I encountered. Grocery store clerks, postal workers, church members. It didn't matter if I was beside my mother or alone.

"Misty, you look cute today! How are you?"

"Well, did you know that my mom's boyfriend has been molesting me?" I'd ask, my voice level.

It didn't matter the questions—*How's school? What are your plans for the summer? How are you feeling?*

For the first time in my entire life, I no longer noticed my mother's reactions to me. I simply knew that as long as I kept sharing my story, shame could not take up space in me. Somehow, I would be OK.

July 1911 Last photo of Nora & Misty together until her wedding 6 years later

Summer

Home

{For this scared girl of twelve, navigating so much uncertainty: "Oblivion" by Bastille}

I have always taken solace in the water. In my littlest years it was the kiddie pool in Melanie's front yard, and as I'd gotten older it was within the water of a bath. I could feel the hard parts of me melt into the liquid as it ebbed and pooled around me, filling my crevices. When a swirl of hard-to-breathe-through thoughts threatened to rise to my surface, I would take my hand to gently paddle in the water beside me and count my breaths.

In, out, in, out. Water, air ...

In the summers we camped on the lake, and on the best afternoons I'd get to go out into the fishing boat too. There, on the quiet of the lake, I would secretly dip my hand into the cool water, imagining it a wooden paddle.

In, out, in, out. Water, air ...

During the last months, after I'd told my entire world what Nora's boyfriend had done to me, I would spend hours pouring water slowly from one cup to another. Over and over, losing time in the sound of the water.

As a teenager, I took every opportunity afforded me to head to the river. My favorite Saturdays were spent in floating tubes, hands gently paddling through the water's surface, the sensation of peace flooding my soul.

There were conversations happening in the space all around me. For the summer, my mom and her boyfriend did the best they could to cohabitate with me. For the most part, they pretended like I didn't exist, and I was more than happy to be left alone.

The power had shifted between the two women in our home. If I opened my mouth and asked for something, I usually got it, no questions asked. This had never been the way of things before. Nora no longer derived a sick sense of pleasure from denying my requests. My benefits came by way of drinks from Sonic, swimming at my friend's house, and watching HBO. I spent the summer sleeping over at Melanie's house whenever I wanted, except for a month spent in Texas with my cousin, which included a road trip to Oklahoma. The Martinez family was putting an addition onto their house, and this created an extra level of excitement. I fell in love with Def Leppard in those days as the music blared over the sound of saws and hammers. Looking back, it sounds like it belongs in some coming-of-age Judy Blume book. *Twelve-year-old girl is swept up in hard life things and a growing sense of magic and empowerment the summer before seventh grade.* In truth, I was still insecure, overthinking, awkward me. While, in a moment of necessity, my survival instincts had kicked in, I was still just that messed up, broken girl wanting someone to find her worth fighting for.

One August evening I wasn't allowed to go to Melanie's because my mom and her boyfriend were taking me to dinner and a movie. He was still pretending I didn't exist, which made me feel like even more of a third wheel all evening. On the way home, I was in the backseat while the two of them carried on a conversation in code.

"She'd never suspect."

"How do you want to do it?"

In my mind, it was clear they were plotting to murder me, and I had no idea how to protect myself. This might seem like an overdramatic conclusion, but even though I'd been living my best summer, I still felt as though I was on the cusp of a huge shift. My death would solve all their problems, so that was where my mind went.

The next day, he left for the train while I lay in my room, planning my escape. My mom called me into the kitchen and motioned for me to sit across from her at the table. The afternoon sun was hot through the window beside the kitchen table. She had been almost nice to me that morning, so I took my seat heavily guarded.

"Do you remember the Children's Ranch in Idaho that came and spoke at the church?"

I did, faintly. It was months ago. I also knew my mother refused to set foot in church, which piqued my curiosity.

"You are going to go live there for a year." She began crying as she spoke. Those ten words were a struggle for her to voice, the last three seeming to almost break her.

I was momentarily stunned before the emotion hit me like a gut punch. Deep tears flowed well before my brain had processed what she'd said. For months I'd known foster care was a real possibility. I also had no clue what foster care was. But I had seen a glossy ad in the Sears catalog that showed two girls sharing a bunk bed, and my mind had daydreamed that my foster home room would look *just like that*. In my daydream, this bunk was shared with another twelve-year-old girl who would be my very best friend and the sister I never had.

Never, in all the afternoons I'd spent fantasizing about this possibility, did I think I would be punished by being forced to leave my home and family.

"I promise you," she said, determination creeping back into her voice as she took a drag of her cigarette, "you can come home after a year, unless you want to stay."

"I won't." The words felt like rocks as they made their way through my throat. The sunlight swirled through the air with smoke. If I tried hard enough, I could blur her face completely.

"You might! It sounds like a lot of fun there!"

I focused my gaze on her face, and she shifted just slightly. "No, I meant I won't come home again because you'll never let me."

I was angry, but in my core, I knew this was true. I guessed *he* was making her choose, and so she had. I hated him for forcing her, I hated her for choosing him, and I hated me for not being loveable enough that everyone would just choose differently.

She was speechless; she looked as though I'd slapped her. I don't remember having any further conversations with her about it. She was excited as she packed my things, acting as though she was getting me ready for summer camp.

That summer had been my third year attending church camp. I liked going because it meant I got to leave home. The year before, I was sent home early because I was vomiting blood and had a high fever. My mom had been off traveling with a friend, so my grandmother picked me up. I spent the following weeks watching TV movies, taking antibiotics, and peeing in saucepans because I just couldn't manage the cup. The back pain was the worst part of the entire ordeal, and our local doctor had been so confused as to why it took me so long to get better. This memory became one of many that, once the adults had clarity about the abuse, suddenly made sense. That urinary tract infection turned into a raging kidney infection. It seemed from there I transitioned from one illness to another, until my diagnosis of mono just seven months later.

When Nora packed me for summer camp, she would pack the worst things. She did not allow shorts or swimwear. She offered up logical (to her) excuses why I must spend the camp session in stiff blue jeans, dress slacks, and long sleeve, button-down shirts. None of her excuses stood out as odd to me, though, because in most situations she went to great lengths to complicate things for me. The lack of friends I made was unsurprising because I looked ridiculous and smelled of secondhand cigarette smoke. It wasn't all bad though—in her own ways, Nora demonstrated love to me. My mother loved me by smoothing a flat sheet into my sleeping bag. Down on her hands and knees, in the heavy, old sleeping bag that had once been Papa's, she wrestled to get that sheet as smooth as she could before she rolled the bag tight. As she did that, I'd feel delight in knowing that when I came home from camp, I would spend my first night back in clean, ironed sheets. As uncomfortable as I felt in those hot, sticky clothes, crawling into that cool sheet come bedtime were the times I felt most wrapped in my mother's love.

She also kept jars of the combined grape jelly and peanut butter in the cupboard because she knew I loved them, even though they were more expensive.

Nora spent so much time deliberately lashing out, wounding me, and yet, these silent gestures of love shone through. It was almost as though, amid the cruelty, she couldn't quite help herself.

It seemed unfair to be forced to sit and watch my mother pack my things for a second time that summer. This time, while most of my clothes were being packed, she refused to include anything I really loved. My framed photos of my grandfather and the gold square frame of my grandparents when they were young and elegant were things she said the home would not allow. Also in the elimination pile were my book box, my Walkman, all cassette tapes, and all notebooks and journals. The only "personal" item she allowed me to take was Spot. He had been my biggest source of comfort after Betsy went away, and again in the nights leading up to my departure. Had she not allowed him, I would have hidden him in my clothes.

As she packed, overenthusiastically animated, I thought about those clean sheets and jars of sandwich spread. In the same way that one of my favorite children's books illustrated moments of the baby telling her things goodnight, I sat there painfully aware that I was bidding mine goodbye.

Goodbye clean sheets, a symbol of mom's love.

I had told Melanie and her family about being sent away. Their reaction had been delivered with so much love, humor, and honest disappointment. They did admit, with sadness, that maybe it was for the best. Their home was where I felt the most seen. Though they were unable to stop the situation, they gave me life in my last New Mexico days, and I was so thankful. Lorrie made me tacos with soft and warm homemade tortillas. Melanie and I danced and sang to music and watched *Dirty Dancing* on repeat (thanks to cable television), and they tried desperately to teach me some Spanish to take with me, though in that regard I was hopeless.

Less than one week after my mom told me the news, the car was loaded. My grandmother, aunt, and I set off for Idaho.

I was mad at my aunt, though I didn't understand why. Internally, I am sure my broken blame shifted from person to person, based on the moment. I was wounded and masked that with anger. I could not bring myself to acknowledge my mother's role, so anger became my fallback. My aunt never mentioned my letter or why I couldn't live with her. This spelled out REJECTION, in glowing neon letters.

I was mad at my grandmother too. *Why had she told my mom about the stupid children's home? Why didn't she love me anymore? Why didn't she want me to live with her instead of sending me so far away?*

No one had talked with me about what my mom's boyfriend had done. No one in my family reassured me, offered comfort, or said anything. It was simply life as usual, with an added element of awkward tension that ended with a road trip to Boise.

In the hours along the interstate, my grandma tried so hard to connect with me. Eventually, she roped me into playing a game of cloud guessing, where you point out turtle and dragon shapes in the sky. Despite the heaviness around the reasons for our drive, those cloud games still live in my heart as one of my most meaningful memories with her. Every time I see cottony clouds, my eyes search for the shape of magic. Once my gaze latches on to something, I send an *I love you* out into the universe, meant for her.

I had looked up *Idaho* in the encyclopedia prior to the trip and was so happy to read that it was home to many trees. As much as I loved the New Mexico and Arizona desert landscapes, I was looking forward to a life with trees. When I could bring myself to pray, I would beg God for a great tree to lose entire afternoons reading long books beneath. As we pulled into Meridian, Idaho, however, I was disappointed. We had stopped at a local old-school drive-in called The Hungry Onion because we thought it would be nice to get some lunch before we arrived. (We were close—you could feel the sharp shift in the air.) I don't remember what I ordered, but I do remember the butterfly-laden sense of doom consuming me. My anger resurfaced, and I found myself feeling more and more trapped. I didn't understand how they could be so calm and upbeat about everything, as though we were on some fun adventure. In addition to the mounting panic over what was actually happening, I was devastated by the lack of trees. I had been promised the "City of Trees" by that dusty old book. What I saw instead was so much dry yellow. There were scattered trees here and there as we drove the final leg of our journey, but mostly Idaho seemed to be desert, too, without the red rock and breathtaking beauty.

I begged to go home.

The answer was no.

Idaho

{To this season of childhood, the people, and the time: "Broken" by lovelytheband}

My first road trip consisting of more than a half-day's drive happened when I was ten. My mom was searching for any excuse she could find to make me unable to go to Phoenix that summer. She couldn't bear to have me home with her either. There had been an endless array of talking to anyone who would listen that her nerves could not handle it.

Her boyfriend had helped her invest in fifty percent of a convenience store called the Quick Stop. Over the course of the first decade of their relationship, he had invested in many ventures for my mother. There was a bookkeeping class she took, a hotel she managed (with the hopes of buying), a knitting shop she turned the front half of our trailer into, and a chocolate-making venture. Many of these lasted years, some overlapping with others. With each new adventure, Nora would blossom with a surge of confidence, and I more than anyone else loved her like that. In the end, she wouldn't keep up with whatever she needed to, or she'd have a major falling out with a business partner or customer, and the business would simply be no more.

The Quick Stop had been my favorite! I loved going to the store with my mom. I loved restocking the candy and snack shelves, organizing displays, and helping keep inventory in the back. On the long days when I was left to entertain myself, I'd spend hours in the windowless back room with floor-to-ceiling inventory shelves, my imagination running wild. I seldom interrupted her because her usual retort was snarky laughter and telling me to go play on the highway. As much as I tried to spend my hours at the shop being helpful while staying out of her way, by the time summer came, she'd tired of having me around.

Being a typical kid in America, I always wanted to go to Disneyland. My mom had been several times before I came along and loved to show me the photos and tell me all about how magical it was. As much as I maybe should have grown up resenting those pictures, between you and me, I loved them. I loved all her old photos so much; she eventually forbade me from ever looking at them. She displayed them on a bookshelf in our kitchen that was OFF LIMITS to me. While other kids would sneak alcohol or watch dirty movies, when I was home alone, the most rebellious thing that I could think to do was to pore over those aging albums that smelled of old glue, dust, and mystery.

It was not abnormal for Nora to talk about how she was planning a trip to Disneyland while making it clear that this was an experience I would have to earn by being *good enough*. Good enough involved giving daily foot massages, washing dishes, keeping my room clean, no back-talking, not asking to do anything, not asking her for anything (like dinner, for example), and being happy to play in my room, alone, without making any sound, ever. A child can do those things for a while, but the second an eight-year-old says they are hungry after a day of no food, the response delivered would be a well-rehearsed monologue about how I "must not want to go to Disneyland after all." She'd remind me she knew I couldn't do it, while also repeating how spoiled I was.

Eventually, whenever the dangling promise of Disneyland came up, I filtered it along with everything else she said. I knew it would never happen. So, in my tenth summer, when she began talking about the *California trip*, I couldn't believe it. She informed people I wouldn't be going to Arizona because I was going to California. She always said *California*, which, to me, meant the beaches and Disneyland. I knew nothing else about the state, nor did I see any other possible reason to go.

One afternoon, a random array of clothing was thrown into a backpack, and I was told that the time had finally come for the *California trip*. The packing for this was nothing like camp packing. My mom seemed excited in this frantic, yet not-entirely-positive way, but I didn't care. CALIFORNIA! BEACHES! DISNEYLAND! I told her that I loved her and may have even squealed a bit. I told her that I couldn't wait to fill our own photo album with pictures of us together at Disneyland.

"Oh, I'm not going with you." She continued filling the bag with random things that made no sense, though I no longer noticed.

"What? Why? Who is taking me to Disneyland?"

"You are going to California. It's time to go; we don't have time to talk anymore." She put my bag in the backseat, and I climbed in the front, scared and confused.

Everyone always talks about how big Disneyland is, but to me, from the cab of an eighteen-wheeler cruising down the interstate, it looked like a half-inch oasis. If John hadn't told me what it was, I never would have known. This is the same story regarding my first glimpse of coastline.

"There it is, over there! That's the Pacific Ocean!" he said. Honestly, it looked like every other flat horizon.

I had gone to California with my mom's friend John, who was a trucker, and his son. His son was a year younger than me and didn't want me there. (That made two of us.) The trip was just under five full days. Short of showering in truck stops with complete strangers, every second was spent in the cab of the truck. The days were long, but I enjoyed the road. The way the world whizzed past us was invigorating.

My second major road trip was the one to Idaho. It felt a lot shorter, but also like an eternity. My first impression of the Gem State was very small farming communities, the old-school hamburger drive-in, and its giant yellow onion-shaped water tower. As we left our lunch spot, the small town gave way to farmhouses and fields of crops. The date was August 20, 1988. Farmers on tractors were plenty, but trees were not.

The original presentation we had seen was on Mission Sunday at our church. With slideshow photos and glossy pamphlets, our congregation was shown this beautiful and smiling life of animals, children, and idyllic country living. If I were to speculate what my aunt's and grandmother's first impressions of the Christian Children's Ranch were, I'd guess they found it safe and inviting. Physically it would prove to be safer than my childhood home had been, but beyond that, the "safety" aspect becomes complicated. In pretty much every way, the real-life community was nothing like the images we'd seen months before.

Four ranch-style cedar homes flanked a short dirt road that led to a mechanic shop and barn at the end. The first building on the left held two administration apartments and the office. The second building on the left and the two on the right side of the street were homes. Each home was designed to house ten children and a set of houseparents. In most cases, the houseparents had children of their own, and then the remaining number were *Ranch kids*. The houses had a mix of boys and girls, ranging in age from newborn to seventeen.

On that first day, the short dirt road between the rows of houses was not filled with happy, playful kids as the slideshow had led me to expect. The children of all ages were not eager to feed the chickens so they could take a horse ride before dinner. Even with my limited life experience, I couldn't help but notice that the element of brokenness felt heavy in the air all around. If the two women in my family noticed, they didn't say a word. I was twelve and naive, yet the heaviness of it caught in my chest. My grandmother confessed similar observations to me many, MANY years later. I imagine she was internally reassuring herself that she was doing the right thing, the best thing, for me. Honestly, she really was. It was the best thing in a situation with few to no good options. Sometimes all the choices before us are terrible, and we just have to pick one. This was *that* one. There was no decision she, or anyone, could have made to protect me from life.

The drive to that little community nestled near the bank of the Boise River had taken days. The days had dragged on. Once we were on the property, everything unfolded so fast. There was a meeting with a lot of strange faces where I met my new *mom* and *dad*. There was a rush of busy as everyone readied for an annual summer open house event happening that evening, and of course my aunt and grandmother were welcome to stay. There were a few dozen pairs of eyes that watched my every move. There were giddy children asking things that were none of their business, promises to keep my secrets, and instant ugly nicknames. I had never imagined being a foreigner in a place far away from home, yet there I was. Once the festivities faded to night and my family drove away, I was terrified and alone. The only comfort I had those first nights was Spot's plush comfort and caressing my finger over the deep teeth marks in his nose. Had Betsy felt scared and alone after my mom had sent her away too?

The Ranch considered most feelings dramatic. For a kid, it is nearly impossible to comprehend that a place with no familiarity is a safer and better alternative to the ones you know. As an adult, it may make sense. As a child, crying yourself to sleep in a room that is not your own—with strangers, foreign sounds, smells, and atmosphere feelings—is traumatic. No one should ever be punished or shamed for this.

Mom and *Dad* Thompson, in the beginning, were the worst. *Dad* told weird jokes that I'd never heard. He had an odd laugh I didn't know, and a temper I did not trust. I knew angry, scathing women, but angry men I did not. *Mom* Thompson had this way of saying kind things, but with less kind things layered just beneath the surface. When you were in trouble and Dad Thompson would break out the paddle, mom would sit there and watch with a smirk on her face. These two people became the new outlet for my blame. I wanted to hate them so badly, and I tried. On the outside, I followed the rules and played the game, but inside I directed as much responsibility for my situation toward them as possible. They, along with the administration staff, were the Bad Guys of my unfolding story.

Resentments grew when the staff went through the very small number of things my mother packed and threw most of it out. I was angry when they made comments about the heavy cigarette smell lingering on my clothes. I wanted to scream when Mom Thompson made comments about how inappropriate my clothing was, when I had ironically come from a mother who had intentionally bought me the most old-fashioned and ugly clothing she could find, just to make my life more uncomfortable. Everyone loved to talk about how white my skin was while I sounded like a Mexican. Most of those early days had me wondering if I had simply traded one set of complications for another.

On my second day, I got in trouble and had to write sentences because I had not rinsed all the shampoo from my head. In truth, my hygiene habits had looked like quick, cold showers in the dead heat of summer, my mom washing my hair over the kitchen sink one to two times a week, and her boyfriend giving me baths before bedtime when he was home. I had no idea how to rinse suds from my own hair.

I was mad when they wouldn't let me call my family. I felt irrelevant when they told me my mother was an untrustworthy liar, and then followed that with *we know you claim you were sexually abused, but your mom said you lied, and no one believes you and you aren't allowed to talk about it as long as you live here.* I hated them for forcing me to call them *Mom* and *Dad.* They weren't my mom and dad.

I fell in love with music from a young age, and that music helped me survive the worst things. It was so confusing when the new adults in my life told me all the music I loved was satanic and I couldn't listen to it anymore. There was no respect, no understanding, no attempt to get to know me or to learn how I was feeling. There was no getting down to my level to explain to me why I couldn't have the only things left that were familiar. I was simply told they were *bad*, and the telling implied that I must be stupid (and very sinful) because I should have known better.

You don't want to make Jesus sad, do you?

God is a vengeful God; we have to fill ourselves with holy things.

This new place became a strange home with foreign rules that I did not understand—nothing made sense to me. I also didn't understand why I was instantly treated as so untrustworthy. I had been hurt, and because of that, I'd not only lost my entire family, my home, and my friends, but it was made clear that I was even more of a "bad kid" than my mom had ever made me feel. The Ranch life became an imprisonment of sorts. I lived this fishbowl existence—on one hand, I would always be the freak for others to observe. On the other hand, I would always be on the outside, looking in at the entire world which I ached desperately to be a part of. Hardest of all, I stood outside a 2000-mile window, distantly observing as my family went on with their lives, sans Misty. I would spend the next several years watching as close Children's Ranch friends went home to be with their families. Eventually, I came to see that while the Ranch was labeled "a place for troubled youth," more than ninety percent of us were really from broken and troubled parents who'd made us casualties of their own journeys. The problem with labeling hurt kids "troubled" and presenting them that way to the world is that they will be treated as such.

Even worse, the kids themselves begin to believe it's true.

If you've never experienced this sort of life before, then let me tell you the one part that was pure magic and, honestly, unlike anything else in the world. In the closed-off and sheltered state of our group home, there was a camaraderie that developed among the kids. It was us against the grown-ups, even though I doubt any of us ever really expected to wage a war. I imagine we wanted those adults (or any real, grown-up people) to find us worthy of value. Sometimes it seemed like they did, but usually that approval was merely a result of conditional love.

On August 20, 1988, I became a resident and remained in care there until August 20, 1993. Those five years felt like fifty, and some seasons within them are still hard for me to reconcile as having been only weeks or months. Anyone who has lived in anything similar can tell you that time is different in such a snow-globe way of life. In one week's time, it truly is possible to form your most intimate friendship or to "go out with" and wrap up all of your trust and security into one boy. These are levels of relationship that many don't achieve after decades of connection out in the real world. It's a weird phenomenon. Psychologically, living through shared traumatic experiences can bring very different people into such a connected and intimate bond. No matter what any of us had been through, we still had an innocence of childhood, which made these bonds more intense.

Forging such connections within your abandonment and rejection is a rare, beautiful gift. The very defeating downside is when those friends go home and new ones come. This cycle is unending and never gets less soul-crushing.

Idaho, for me, became about loss.

The Van and the Fishbowl

{Song: "Girls Just Want to Have Fun" by Greg Laswell}

The adjustment period of my new life seemed to last an eternity. I was learning brand-new things—and failing at them—constantly. Looking back, it's fair to say that I had adapted pretty well, quickly. (Considering I was suddenly living in a house filled with other "troubled" kids, two full-time parental figures, constant noise, and a fair amount of drama which were the complete opposite of what I'd known.) I wish someone would have noticed that then.

This new life looked like lots and lots of chores. Laundry was done with a wringer washer, on the porch, and then dried on the line. As a girl deathly allergic to bees, my laundry day was a constant source of anxiety because those Idaho yellow jackets loved to hang out on clothes pins in the beating afternoon sun. There was a never-ending list of hand mopping, woodwork polishing, and porch sweeping that needed to be done. The seemingly unnecessary chores were my least loved parts, but the bigger chores were something I found gratifying. I loved bucking hay, weeding the garden, and tending the animals. I not only learned to ride horses, but also overcame my fear of them and grew to love those rides.

Life for Ranch kids existed on a level scale. Once your first thirty days had passed, you'd automatically move to level one. Level one held the basic amenities: $6 a month in allowance, one fifteen-minute family phone call per week, an early bedtime, and no extra privileges. Permission and privileges had to be earned. Level two took one up to $8 a month, a twenty-minute weekly family call, a possibly later bedtime, and the possibility of a monthly day visit with family. Level three saw $10 a month, two fifteen-minute family calls each week, more privileges and permissions, and the option for overnight visits with family. Level four was reserved for ages fifteen and up. Level four was *the* level to be on. Though the $12 a month wasn't much to brag about, within the system built to control behavior, it felt like the closest thing to freedom we'd get. Level four meant a kid could be trusted and was of value. Level four was a rare achievement and came with a sense of pride.

Should a kid, at any level, get in major trouble, they would revert to their thirty days and start again. Evaluations happened once a month and were filled out by houseparents. They'd have a meeting with administration, and if everyone agreed a kid had earned a new level, the kid would then be brought into the meeting and told of their promotion (or demotion in some cases). These monthly meetings happened for everyone. This wasn't a time to check in and see how a kid was doing, at least not in my experience. Instead, it became a laundry list of mistakes my month had held or of times I'd shown exemplary behavior.

Once my initial thirty days had passed, I was allowed to receive letters and weekly phone calls. My mom, grandmother, and aunt would have to decide between them who would be calling me on Saturday mornings. To be clear, no one assigned them Saturday mornings, but the women in my family have always been morning phone people. The members of this new family of mine (adults and children alike) were not morning people of any sort, and so these eight o'clock Saturday morning calls weren't gaining me any popularity. Calls, for group-home kids, consisted of sitting in a room next to the houseparent so they could listen to whatever was being said. Such surveillance wasn't exclusive to the phone. Letters were read by a houseparent before they were given to the child or mailed out to the child's approved contacts. Things like this have an awful way of adding to the dirty and unworthy feelings kids may already have about themselves. Pre-Children's Ranch, I often questioned if I was garbage, but usually I felt my mother was wrong and that I wasn't. In the Children's Ranch setting, I was just garbage. All of us were. We had opportunities to "get better," but the truth was that playing the game and compartmentalizing was the only attainable option. When I was focused performatively on playing the part to move up the levels and be seen as a "good" kid, I was one version of Misty. Whereas when I was with my friends and staff wasn't in earshot, I was another version. Both were variations of truth condensed to what I deemed those in that situation would like the most. That was, in every instance, the end game—to be liked, maybe even loved. No one, including myself, had untethered access to the truest parts of me. When I'd catch a glimpse, I would shut it down and bury it. I was convinced that this was the horrible, unlovable, and easy-to-leave part of me ... I knew I couldn't afford to let her out. Over the years, the more people I met or situations I was in would result in more boxes for me. I became an expert in transitioning from one to the next as needed. This coping strategy served me well, for a time, but long-term it was an impossible solution.

The school we attended in those early days was a very small, private Christian school. We would pile into two vans (a girls' van and a boys' van) and make the forty-five-minute drive out to our little country school. Not once, but twice, in that first school year, I slammed my hand in the huge metal sliding door of the girls' ugly, mint green van. It was 1988 and these vans were decades older. The girls' van, in addition to being mint green on the outside with larger-than-life stickers on the sides announcing to the world that we were part of the Christian Children's Ranch, had bizarre yellow and brown plaid upholstery inside. Piling out of that monstrosity on the Ranch property or at the school was fine, but climbing out if it anywhere else was a huge embarrassment. The only thing that could have made the experience marginally worse would have been if a marching band had escorted us into the parking space while an emcee shouted, "The Freaks are here, the Freaks are here!" The adults couldn't relate to how hard these parts of our everyday life could be because people's perspectives of them were far kinder. *What saints! Giving their lives to help these terrible delinquents!* With us, people watched and stared. People pulled their kids closer, and often made it very clear that they were well aware of what *bad kids* we were.

The other consistent place these vans took us was to church. I had grown up attending church, and unlike some of the other kids, this should have been a comfortable experience for me. It wasn't. While church folk loved the houseparents so much and raved about what good people they were, the kids were treated like criminals. Other kids made fun of Ranch kids often and seldom included us in activities or invitations. As in all situations, there were a few exceptions. I feel such an overwhelming gratitude for the exceptions I knew. The empathetic and gracious souls who were willing to thwart the system in place and accept us. I learned so much from these kind people and had the closest to normal moments of my teen years because of them. Being thrust into this sort of fishbowl life had left me craving *normal* more than ever.

That dumb van is like its own person in my memory. It was the faithful transport for so many fun road trips where we held lively conversations and played group games. It was also where secret lovers held hands and where I first "made out" with a boy. This ugly fifteen-passenger van was a vehicle that seemed to announce with its appearance that the circus had arrived. The van that, until the day it died, likely still had pieces of my flesh and blood ground into its doorframe.

Twice.

Dad, with his syrupy southern drawl, would habitually warn us to watch our fingers whenever we slammed the door. As a preteen I was obviously above having to heed his warning. It was snowy outside, so I must have been at the Ranch for at least four months. I should have known better. I'm sure I was screaming and wailing like a toddler because, truthfully, I had never felt such pain! Dad rushed into action, placing my fingers in the snow. Despite how I'd ignored his very relevant warning, and even though I'd taken his attention away from the dozen other kids he was responsible for, he never got angry or made me feel dumb for what I'd done.

My bruised fingers were not broken, but they had distorted into abnormal shapes and were turning all shades of black, purple, and red. I had them wrapped until my black, brittle nails fell off. It was spring the second time it happened, just a few months after the first. It was just as bloody and terrible as before, except without the immediate aid of snow. It was only the second time I had been able to close that guillotine of a door after months of inability because my hand had been so damaged.

I was, and may always be, a slow learner.

This time around, though Dad didn't get angry, it did become something he would tease me about from that day on. It was joking in love, and it made me feel special, as though I belonged and was a part of something. This was when I began to accept that this bald and flawed man was somehow *my* dad. I started to see these two parents for who they were, without the filters of my resentment, sadness, and homesickness.

And it turns out my house mom Julie wasn't smirking when we were in trouble—she simply had a slight case of resting joy face.

Thirteen should be an exciting birthday by any kid's standards. I had made it through the strangest Christmas I'd ever known fairly unscathed. While Christmas in many American households can be a materialistic disaster zone, in my birth family it wasn't like that. Christmas at my grandmother's was all about family. On the other hand, Christmas with my mom was, as any holiday with someone who has an untreated mental illness, unpredictable and unhinged.

The first Christmas I spent away from my family involved a manger in place of a tree—because a kid in our house had an allergy—with all the presents piled in and around it. What else can be said besides that it was weird? It felt wrong and creative all rolled in to one. Christmas itself was a gluttonous binge on all things gift wrap and charity. (*So many people* buy gifts for foster and group-home kids.) I had never in my life seen anything like the volume of presents. While I know that I unwrapped more gifts that Christmas than I'd gotten total in holidays past, I can't recall what any of them were, other than a solitary gift that came in a package from my mom. In it was a blue plastic container of body powder that bore a fifty-cent price tag. Its lid was held onto the base with two pieces of Scotch tape. Inside, the "springtime" scented powder smelled exactly like Comet cleanser. The only other thing in that box, which had cost four dollars to ship, was a note that said, "I couldn't do much because money is tight. The Children's Ranch is costing me all of my money, and times are hard."

Because my houseparents read the mail, they said it was their duty to tell me that no one in my family was paying for me to be there.

In March, when I turned thirteen, there was no gift or card from my mom. She had managed to send my house mom Julie the recipe for my favorite dinner after I begged her for months. Our standard Ranch groceries came from food donations, the food bank (which we were required to volunteer hours for), and government-provided staples. Sometimes we'd have to whip up the most creative meals because we only had weird items in the food stockroom. Other times, we'd spend eighteen months eating weekly pineapple Bundt cakes because we had cases and cases of mix brought in. This didn't stop Julie! She went to the supermarket to buy the ingredients for my birthday meal, then made that dinner for our family of twelve plus my two friends who were sleeping over. Those cheesy, bean-covered taco burgers were the best thing I had ever put in my mouth! I now understand what a sacrifice that was since their ministry position paid hardly anything, and groceries for such a large group couldn't have been cheap.

My two good friends, Tammy and Dee, spent the night, and it was honestly the best birthday I could imagine. We listened to (approved) music, talked, and told stories. It felt like everything that a thirteenth birthday in a Judy Blume novel would be, so I knew I was lucky. It's only now, reflecting back in my forties, that I imagine the absence of my mother's cruel manipulations hanging over that day is likely what made it all lighter, though her disinterest must have hurt.

That summer brought with it an all-new experience as a Ranch kid. It seemed as though every week had work groups camping out on our property and spending time with us while doing missions projects for the Ranch. When the groups were there, we would have late-night bonfires, game nights, hikes, and whitewater rafting trips. Those days were the best! During the other parts of the summer, we would climb into our trusty friend, the mint green van, and drive around the country representing the Ranch. If you have never had the honor of watching a Christian Children's Home give a presentation for you then you really missed out. We made up a wide range of sizes and ages of awkward kids dressed in weird clothes singing songs and performing cheesy skits so people would give us money. It's a little exploitive, but most of the people from far away churches didn't treat us the way our local ones did. They'd take us to restaurants and out for ice cream. They would ask us about ourselves and really try to make our time special. We were usually divided among parishioners' homes, and in that setting, it was easy to revel in the momentary environment of *normal.*

Getting to travel was invigorating! Summers spent this way instilled in me a love of road trips. The engine would overheat, stranding us for hours. We ate gross tuna fish or ham and cheese sandwiches that had reached temperatures no food should reach and held our bladders far longer than we liked. We also belted out the songs we loved, told stories, and played hours of I Spy, and no adult ever told us to be quiet. On occasion, there was money in the budget for a movie, or someone would donate tickets to a water or amusement park. I fell more and more in love with road trips and the satisfaction of adventure.

It wasn't an easy situation for anyone. As Ranch kids, we were blinded by our own broken hearts and youthful inability to comprehend anything else. There was significant trauma happening in most of our lives—both in the back-home lives and in the daily abandonment-laced ones we lived within a fundamentally sheltered environment. This wasn't exclusive to us; the adults were affected too. These people had given up their lives—often at the sacrifice of their own family's and children's best interests—for these seemingly self-centered and angry kids. At the best of times, it was an amicable cohabitation with minimal drama, but on average, someone in our family of twelve was likely dealing with a personal hell of apocalyptic proportions. The legalism, constant scrutiny, and absolute lack of trust (on all fronts) was exhausting for everyone and just not a healthy situation. This cycle existed because the kids weren't able to trust the adults, and the adults weren't able to trust the kids. It was a spin cycle of skepticism and fear. Being a group-home kid gave me the opportunity to do a lot of things I never would have done otherwise. When you're stranded in the middle of nowhere with a broken-down van and eleven other miserable people, it is hard to take comfort in melted cheese sticks and dried-out peanut butter and jelly sandwiches. When you're on your first roller coaster or you and your friends have the run of an entire luxury health and fitness center where the owners also plan to cater in dinner for you *and* give you gift certificates to go shopping, life is pretty great. The children's home life felt a lot like the whiplash of those two extremes, every single day.

The owners of a posh local health club would shut their doors and invite the entire Ranch in twice every year. All day long, we would roam around and swim, play basketball, attempt racquetball, and just hang out and act like normal kids. We had as much soda and as many snacks as we wanted. The televisions in every corner of that building played music videos, and we drank it all in. We ate delicious food that none of us had to cook or clean up after, and then we were given the chance to go shopping for brand-new things later! The adults relaxed and let us be kids, and that was the most magical part of all. Every August, just before school started, and every December, just before the new year, we had our days.

It was easy to live for those days.

In between those two amazing days each year, there was a church who would also come in and rent out Chuck E. Cheese for us. For four hours, we had free rein over every arcade game in that building. We hung out with our friends like were we normal kids. We ate pizza, drank our fill of suicide sodas from the fountain machine, and then cashed in our tickets for pure-bliss nonsensical junk.

My very favorite Ranch kid perk, though, was that I had an automatic scholarship for church camp. One Sunday after church every summer, I climbed on a bus and headed to camp. On that bus, I was no longer a *dirty Ranch kid*. I was just a teen girl. Sometimes I reconnected with friends from the previous summer, and sometimes I made new ones. I packed my own bags with things like shorts, T-shirts, and flip flops, built my own reputation, and lived the normal life of a middle school/high school kid for an entire week.

That first summer when I was thirteen, our house family went hiking up in the Boise foothills. My house mom Julie was so *different*. While other kids were coming in after school and eating donated chocolate muffins or homemade cookies, we were allowed to split an apple with another person and spread a tablespoon of government-issued peanut butter down the middle. We washed plastic bags to reuse, did our laundry on a wringer washer, and hung everything on the line to dry. This wasn't a Children's Ranch thing; this was a Julie thing.

Prior to being a Ranch kid, the idea of peanut butter on an apple would have seemed disgusting. The first few times I was subjected to such culinary torture, I made myself gag. The same was true for the occasional bagel with cream cheese—shared of course—and cups of yogurt. None of these things had been a part of my diet before, but decades later these are among my favorite snacks to eat.

So, there we were, hiking and having a great time, when Julie decided that we should start picking up trash from all around the foothills. My house mom was crunchy, gluten-free, environmentally responsible, and health conscious long before such things became trends. While scouring for trash down at the bottom of a small ravine, I saw what looked to be an awesome small trashcan! This is important because, for the first time in my life, I was decorating my space the way *I* liked. I wanted it to be so stylish and cool, but I also knew (because my mom Julie had told me about ten thousand times that it had to be *free*) I'd have to get creative. A super cool trashcan seemed like the solution to my interior design dilemmas. It was like being at HomeGoods and seeing this absolutely amazing thing and knowing it's the one thing home has been missing! That ravine was my HomeGoods, and that bin was my thing!

My houseparents told me not to go down the hill for the trashcan. They claimed to be looking at the same exact bin I was but somehow did not see its magic. I went anyway. I was thirteen and obviously the expert in this situation.

The two things gained from that adventure were the scar that still sits on the right side of my nose (though it is smaller now) and the absolute divine miracle that I did not lose my eye. This was also one of the ways we confirmed I have wonky vision with almost nonexistent depth perception.

What wasn't gained? My dignity as I tumbled down the hill and the terrible five-gallon bucket missing half of its bottom.

To recap:
- Late summer/early fall: became Ranch kid.

- Winter: slammed fingers in van door.

- Spring: slammed fingers in van door, verifying I am a slow learner.

- Summer: tumble down steep hill, nearly taking my eye out on rebar sticking out of ground.

Mom & Dad and their daughters
1989

Misty & Aunt Gloria
First family visit. 1989

T, D & M

BFFs

friendship♥

Dad

{To the man who chose to be my dad and showed me a father's love: "Storyteller" by Morgan Harper Nichols}

Aside from the dad jokes, the significant details of my house dad that stand out from that time were pretty silly: the sound of his boots coming in the house, screen door smacking the frame behind him; the large refillable cup almost always in his hand; his gap-toothed smile that lifted his entire face with an almost childish crinkling around his eyes—I think I loved that about him from day one, though I didn't know how to acknowledge it. Any devotion to the new parents seemed a betrayal to my mom. While it is natural for this mentality to set in, Nora went to great effort whenever she'd call to remind me that they were trying to steal me from her. She made it a competition and spun reality to make it seem as though these two people were the reason that I wasn't at home with her, where I should be.

That was the most confusing part about visiting my family—on the phone, my mother *missed me so much* and hated our separation, but every visit found her absolutely disinterested in anything concerning me. Every time I boarded the plane to go home, I was hopeful that I had finally earned her love and would get to be a normal girl with her normal family. Tucked inside my desert-bound plane, I would daydream about embracing her while she tearfully told me she'd send for my things because I was staying home. Five to seven days later, I would return to my actual home, devastated all over again.

This house dad of mine, the only real dad I ever had, confused me often. The way his brain worked, the things that triggered smiles and laughter or spurred anger, never quite made sense to me. He relentlessly teased me about the stupid things I did (like the van door and the bucket) in this way that never made me feel foolish at all, but instead made me feel seen and loved. There would be days when I'd tag along on some errand or another while he listened to Paul Harvey on AM radio. I enjoyed the time I had with him, even when I felt like I shouldn't.

Without knowing it, I was learning a lot about fatherhood, daughterhood, marriage, and manhood from my dad. While it gets a little confusing to talk about "my mom," because there was my house mom Julie Thompson and my birth mom, Nora, I can just refer to him as my dad. He was always the only one.

What I was most aware of in those days was my education in Satanism.

Conversations about evil things like rock music, synthesizers, and Saturday morning cartoons, the fundamentalist blame for everything was on Satanism. Self-proclaimed former Satanist turned Christian, Mike Warnke, became a prominent source of information to the staff, which in turn trickled down to us. We saw him live, read his books, and listened to tapes of his experiences and warnings. In the late 1980s, there was a mounting panic which somehow managed to weave its way into a majority of news stories and scandalous topics on daytime talk shows. Authors, both Christian and non, were hot on the trend, weaving it into their works. This would later be known as the Satanic Panic, but in those days, this was just life.

So many things were dubbed *satanic*, and how were we supposed to know? Once upon a time, I had loved the Smurfs and never suspected the underbelly of evil that it was subtly implanting into my psyche. In this impressionable time, there were two major elements that deeply impacted me and laid the stones for paths my life would one day take. One involved developing a sold-out belief that I was solely responsible for the lives and salvation of people I loved, and the other was the miracle of allowing myself to trust my house dad.

Anything which warned of Satanism was required reading, even without having been vetted by the adults first. This was how, at thirteen, I was allowed to read a memoir about a woman who claimed she'd been significantly abused by an underground satanic ring. They'd forced her to do porn while raping her. With each pregnancy she had, they sacrificed her babies to the devil in snuff films. The things depicted in those pages still haunt me. As a girl who was an abuse survivor, it was almost re-abusive to read those pages. I read that book at least a dozen times. (The book referenced here is *Satan's Underground* by Lauren Stratford. I do not recommend reading it, and I do remember later learning she'd lied.)

I had grown up knowing Jesus and, to the best of my knowledge, loving Jesus. I knew the Bible stories I'd been taught, the verses I'd been rewarded for memorizing in Sunday school at the little yellow church, and the childhood songs I sang for my entire life. Then, one regular family movie night—something religiously done in group-home families, complete with my house mom's stovetop popcorn, served in a five-gallon bucket and devoured as though we may die tomorrow—the VHS movie *The Toymaker's Dream* was chosen.

Upon realizing this was a recording of a stage performance, disappointment set in.

I missed watching current movies. Movies had been such a big part of my pre-Ranch life. I wasn't always the biggest fan of classic Disney films or old musicals, so my attitude about such things wasn't always mature. That night as they gathered us around to watch some weird video tape of a play, I felt annoyed.

When the movie ended and the home video–quality credits began to roll, my cheeks were still wet from the tears over what I'd seen, aching to my core. I had no idea why I felt so overwhelmed. I watched *The Toymaker's Dream* four more times over the weekend. The parental figures seemed excited that I was so enthralled by this masterpiece. To be honest, I was doing research. I was on a mission to solve the mystery of how this movie affected me the way it did. Nothing had ever reached that deep place before and I wanted to understand.

In 2006, I was at my mother's house, going through boxes of photos and letters with her. She had dozens of letters from when I was at the Ranch, about half of which she had never even opened. I wasn't quite sure how to feel about that, remembering the painstaking effort I poured into the pages I had written her. Casually, I questioned her about it.

"I knew everything about you and everything that was going on, so why read a letter?"

She had known nothing about me at all. Our five-minute phone calls once a month hardly told her anything.

One of the letters I found, which she had at least opened, was an emotional plea for her to watch *The Toymaker's Dream*. "It will all make sense," I had written. "It will change your life, I promise." I went on to tell her how worried I was about her, how I loved her so much, and how I prayed for her every day.

Every single word I had written was code for the most gripping fear I had ever known—my mother was going to burn in hell, and it fell on me to save her.

These thoughts which consumed me as a teen girl were the product of an environment so heavily saturated with talk of Satan, fears of hell, and the evil people outside in the real world. At one point I became convinced that all sexual abuse connected back to Satanism, and I became terrified about the gaps I had in my memory. The fears were crippling. I was still forbidden to talk to anyone about what I'd been through, so this was a fear I walked in alone.

It was my fear, my very unhealthy coping mechanisms, and this completely overwhelming need to be everything to and for my mother that suddenly the responsibility to give her eternal life was heaped on my mountainous task list, topping:

- make my mother love me,

- solve why I'm such a pathetic and unlovable person and then fix it,

- lose weight/be pretty,

- change everything about me so that the people I love won't be obligated to stick around anymore, but instead they would just want to be there!

I wish I could curl up on my sofa and watch *The Toymaker's Dream* whenever I wanted. I wish I could share with the whole world the feeling that performance left me with. In all the ways that every single thing connected to God had become wrapped up in shame and fear, that production had the opposite effect. *The Toymaker's Dream* is a play about a toymaker who deeply loves the toys he creates, but they turn against him because they were deceived. The whole play is a brilliant analogy for the story of God, Jesus, and how it all unfolds. For me, it tapped into these things I had never doubted and made them visually engaging, without all the darkness I'd grown accustomed to.

When I was thirteen, I wrote that letter to my mother (hopefully just the one) insinuating she was going to go to hell. I had the best, most loving intentions. I deeply felt that it was my job to save her, as soon as humanly possible.

Sometimes the people who love us hurt us when they speak their truths. Sometimes the ones causing the pain are us, even with the best of intentions.

In school one day, we were shown an episode of a daytime talk show where Anton LeVey and his daughter were guests. He was the head of the Church of Satan. It was chilling, and there was absolutely nothing educational about it. Having us watch the show was simply to validate that the Satanism we were being taught was true—to prove that all the horror and evil in the "outside" was real. There was the living proof, dressed in black and green.

The product of this obsession divided our small community of group-home children. On one side, we had a blossoming obsession with Satanism, the devil, devil worship, and a hatred for God. On the other side was an obsession with Satanism, crippling fear, and the crushing burden to save the world.

Neither side was healthy. Beneath the surface of the strict regime that ruled in our lives was an undercurrent of a youth-driven one. There was a developing hierarchy of consequence, sense of justice, and all-around disinterest in anything involving the adults "above" us. We were what we had. *We* were who we could count on.

The one exception for me was my dad.

His jokes, his laugh, his crinkly-eyed smile. His ugly, plaid recliner no one else was allowed to sit in, his shiny bald head, that slow southern drawl, and his insistence of listening to AM talk radio. In those early days living as a kid in his house, and especially later in life, I learned so much about manhood from him. He wasn't afraid to show his emotions, and when he loved someone it was with an unwavering support.

I knew he was reliable, and what he said was what would happen. I knew he didn't want to control me with fear. I knew, when I looked at him in the moments he thought no one would notice, he, too, was heavy with the weight of having to save the world. Instead of a mother who was a mistress and an abuser, though, his burden was a world of kids who knew nothing about fatherhood, daughterhood, marriage, or what it meant to be a man, outside of him.

I never saw it coming, and I'm not quite sure when it happened, but one day I felt safest when my Ranch dad was around, and I allowed myself to rest in that feeling.

For this girl, my dad was light like the sun.

Womanhood

{To the kids we were, trapped in all the in-betweens: "Cosmic Love" by Florence + the Machine}

I was thirteen when the pivotal moments of a girl's life happened: my first period, my first kiss, my first tampon.

I was eleven and still living with my birth mother in New Mexico the day my school held the presentation about menstruation. No one had paid attention, so naturally I left the entire thing with far more questions than answers. I talked incessantly about it with my mom that afternoon, but she was no help. A few weeks later, I lied and said I'd started my period. I wasn't sure why, but it was premeditated. I didn't tell friends, just my mother. My mom proceeded to share the news with her boyfriend, her friends, and our family. Whenever one of them would ask me about it, I would just divert the topic away from my great feminine deception.

I began to wear pads, here and there, when I could remember that I was supposed to be having periods. Because I hadn't paid attention that afternoon in class, I had no idea how long they should last or that anything like cramps were involved. I was banking on my mom not caring enough to pay attention to these details, and I was right.

For some reason I had known, in the deepest part of me, I should lie about it and remind the members of my household, on occasion, that *I was a woman now*. On the day this "blessed event" happened, my mom went to a friend who had "resources." I have no idea who this person was, or *why* they had a massive stockpile of pads from the 1950s, but my mother stashed a box of feminine hygiene products beneath our bathroom sink, which only confused me more. The pads, which seemed like extra long, twin-size Barbie mattresses, had silver rings on each end. When I had no idea what I was supposed to do with those, my mother showed me to wear it smoothed, front to back. One end of the lining stuck out the front of my pants, and one end out the back. It was uncomfortable, super awkward, and whenever I wore it, I was convinced the whole world knew. As if I wasn't already struggling with not fitting in. I probably managed one fake-cycle day here and there.

There are many odd little lies kids conjure up, and for a long time I thought this was one of those dumb things. With all my current over-forty wisdom, I believe this particular lie wasn't. Aside from lying to Mr. Hernandez about the two hundred dollars I'd stolen, I remember lying only a handful of times. In one such lie, I was around eight or nine and grounded to my room for a weekend. I had a black and white thirteen-inch TV in my room, so it wasn't the worst thing. I played Barbies, watched cartoons, and, honestly, had a great time, save for one thing: I was hungry. I kept telling my mom, but she didn't care.

Those were actually her words, "I don't care! You're grounded. Close your door."

When I braved crossing into the hall because I needed to go to the bathroom, Nora exploded.

"Go to your room, young lady! I don't want to see you, hear you, or be made aware that you are anywhere near me. Got it?"

And so, I peed on the ugly, mint green carpet in the corner of my room when I couldn't hold it any longer. This might be the first time, I'm not sure. I have faded memories of waking in the middle of the night and relieving myself in that same spot because I was too afraid to go to the bathroom. Those nights always played out the same—I'd wake and lie in bed uncomfortably for a long time. After I tried to find the courage to climb from my bed and go to our trailer's only bathroom (which adjoined with my mother's bedroom), I would finally give in and take to the corner.

Ours was a fourteen-wide trailer, my bedroom as small as an afterthought. I had a twin-size bed, a small dresser, and a bookshelf which Papa had built shortly before he died so my books would have a home. There was hardly any floor space beyond that. I can't imagine no one knew—urine leaves a horrible smell. While I know it wasn't an everyday thing and may not even have been a very frequent one, it couldn't have been a well-hidden secret, yet no one said a thing.

That afternoon, not long after I found relief in the corner of my tiny bedroom, a neighbor came over, and my mom went out on the porch to talk to him. I tiptoed into the kitchen and grabbed the closest cup I could find and the only packaged food in the cupboard—a bag of Nestlé Toll House chocolate chips. I sipped water for the rest of the day and made those chips last as long as I could.

I hid the evidence in my bookshelf, but months later, my mother found it. I denied having taken the chocolate chips. I would forever be subjected to the retelling of how I was such a liar, and whenever my honesty was in question, this was the ONE incident Nora would revisit.

One night when I was eleven, I had this terribly vivid dream. I was walking in a dark, damp brick alley. I can still remember that the air smelled faintly of garbage, rainwater, and soot. As I made my way down the alley, a figure in a tan trench coat began following me. I knew in my gut that this person intended to hurt me in the worst of ways. My heart began to race as I realized it was up to me to save myself. As the alley stretched on forever ahead, I woke up. Not three seconds later, my bedroom door opened slowly. In total darkness I saw the faint shape of his figure.

"I'm awake." I spoke the words firmly and matter-of-fact-ly. He retreated, saying nothing, and closed the door behind him.

This was before I went into the hospital. This was before I unearthed repressed memories of what was happening. It's such an important moment because I instinctually knew that I could trust my intuition, even if it didn't make sense.

As crazy as it may sound, I also believe it was from this place that I crafted the lie about my period. I don't know if he'd had a vasectomy or not, but I believe the idea I'd begun menstruating spared me worse abuses.

At thirteen, when I actually became a woman, it was a quiet event. I told a foster sister, who in turn gave me the details about cramps, PMS, and all the things I'd been clueless about. The Ranch did not allow the use of tampons due to the risk of toxic shock syndrome, which I was OK with. Even though my older, and therefore wiser, foster sister said how much better and easier tampons were, the whole thing sounded terrible. *No thank you!*

One actual menstrual cycle later and I wanted to return the whole idea of becoming a woman.

When I was twelve, I fell in love again. My very first love was Joseph, but since I was now living my new Idaho life, there was no future there. (There had been no future there anyway, let's be honest. I was just an annoying little kid. Even so, this was how I had given my heart permission to move on.) In the very early spring of 1989, I fell in love with the new kid—resident bad boy and all-around Seattle grunge-head, well before Seattle grunge was a thing. We were exactly the same age, and his name was Ricky. In a sea of conservative white people, Ricky was familiar to me. An instant connection happened, not because we were soul mates, but because our spirits recognized similar hurts and early-life longings. Also, he was Mexican, and I found that familiarity comforting.

Ricky was my first real boyfriend.

For fourteen days, after agreeing to "go out," we kept our relationship a total secret because the Ranch rules forbade romantic relationships. Also, we were twelve, so we must have been in on the secret, too, because we avoided each other like the plague.

I cried for days when we broke up.

Ricky was always meant to be my first real kiss. That Idaho afternoon a year before, when I allowed myself to love him, I had known it.

By thirteen, we were no longer traveling to the rural country school for our small education. The Ranch was now renting the gym of a church where we'd set up a makeshift school. For middle and high school physical education we had begun going to the Boise YMCA. From a group-home kid standpoint, this was a pretty big deal. For that one afternoon each week, we were free to roam the entire facility and did as we pleased. We could swim, we could work out, we could play ball.

We could meet boys in empty closets and kiss ...

In all honesty, the closet/kiss thing only happened once for me. It was my first *real* kiss, and it was with Ricky. I still had heart eyes for him. Even though it had been a year since we broke up, I asked him to kiss me. I asked *him* to be my first kiss. Ricky was a little heartbreaker, charming in the best ways, with his dimply grin and dreamy eyes. All the girls loved him, in that way young teen girls love hard but shallow, though it felt so gut wrenchingly deep. I knew I would never "go out" with him again. I knew this unrequited love could consume me. I also knew, as miserable as loving him lonely was (and any woman reading this can identify with that thirteen-year-old feeling), it was a healthy and a normal thing to go through.

The truth was that, shamefully, I was scarred inside by the kisses I'd known before, and I could not let those live on as first kisses any longer.

Those were never *my* kisses at all. I wanted a beautiful story to share when someone asked me about my first kiss, so I took it upon myself to get that story. I walked up to my crush, who did not love me back, and asked him to be my first kiss. Being the lover of girls that he was, and especially a lover of girls loving him, he agreed.

By movie and romance novel first kiss standards, mine was lacking. It was in a dark closet, barely qualified as a French kiss, and lasted a handful of seconds. His hands were on my hips. I was nervous; I'm not even sure if I really participated at all. It began, my insides exploded, and then it was over, and I stood alone in a closet.

Some months after that kiss, which I replayed as I fell asleep every single night, school was out for summer, and I was headed on a backpacking trip. This was my first *Ranch kid* summer. This backpacking trip wasn't about the missions work crews that visited over the summer, or about getting solicited donations from churches. This trip was about us and our friends, staff, and adventure. I felt both lazy, wishing I could stay home, and restlessly ready for adventure. If memory serves, this was a long drive to a remote trail on which we hiked about ten miles into a rugged area where we camped for a few days and then hiked back out and drove home. My pack weighed far more than I deemed acceptable, and I was even less excited to have to wear a giant black garbage bag when it rained. We all looked ridiculous, like wet and whiny California Raisins. The actual trip felt like miserable and grueling work. I hated backpacking, I had decided. I had never been camping outside of the summers my mom, her boyfriend, and sometimes his parents had spent at Quomodo Lake with his travel trailer. Those summer adventures were serenely magical and, while I had loved camping then, it turned out that wasn't real camping at all.

It was my dad who was heading up this insane excursion. When I look back, it only solidifies his hero status in my eyes. We were angsty teens, and this couldn't have been the dream backpacking adventure he imagined.

Thankfully, we all survived, though not all of us unscathed ...

While there were other frustrating elements of the adventure, I remained present and grateful to be there because Ricky and my best friend Tammy were too. The three of us palled around, allowing our vulnerability to emerge with the actual hiking, heavy packs, and extreme beauty surrounding us. We had some deep conversations on that trip. The one thing I had never seen coming was Ricky and I becoming close friends. I was grateful that my first kiss belonged to someone I could trust with pieces of me, even if it was a foreign concept.

It was also sweet that he was actively worried about me when I almost died.

I was still new to the whole menstruation thing. I had not come prepared. Tammy and I were the only girls brave and dumb enough to sign up for the trip, so we were staying in a tent together. When I confided in her that my period had shown up (in the early days, a girl is seldom regular), she went and got the only adult woman along for the journey. Mrs. Newbern, thankfully, was prepared.

Sweet, beautiful Mrs. Newbern handed me a tampon. Due to the nature of the trip, an exception was being made, and this was the only option I had.

Of course, I knew how to use one, I lied.

No, I did not.

It started as a discomfort. After about twenty minutes I could barely walk, I certainly could not sit, and to be honest, I was sure I was dying inside. Something was terribly wrong.

Tammy tried so hard to help. She was a fourteen-year-old girl; I am not sure what either of us expected her to do. I lay in our hot tent sobbing, writhing in pain, each second getting worse, when she finally ran to get Mrs. Newbern.

Mrs. Newbern was this sweet, beautiful woman with the creamiest olive skin and the gentlest voice I'd ever heard. Before this day, we had exchanged fewer than ten words with each other, as the nature of her job at the Ranch and my position as a kid assured our paths did not cross. This sweet stranger of a woman kneeled in front of me as I lay screaming and writhing in pain and dug that forbidden cotton monstrosity from deep within my nether regions. While I was on my period, isolated in the mountains of Idaho, this saintly woman not only inspected my unshowered vagina, but she saved me. She then taught me how to use a tampon. I was mortified, humiliated, and indebted to her.

And I was alive.

Most importantly, Ricky sat as close to the tent as rules would allow, worried.

This was the first time in my life I recall anyone going above and beyond to help me and someone else I cared about being worried about me. Bonus points to me because I did not die from the humiliation of this boy I adored knowing I was an idiot who couldn't use a tampon and had to have it dug out.

When I emerged from the tent, Ricky told me he was glad I was OK. I could see in the way that his eyes shone, while his features relaxed, that he meant it. The majestic Idaho wilderness was just as beautiful, and our adventure went on as intended.

When school resumed in the fall of 1989, I marched into that building with a confidence I had never begun a school year with. Sure, I was wearing donated clothes from our clothing room, but so was everyone else. I was away from my family, hurting, messed up, and angry. Every other girl in the van that morning and in our rented classroom that day was just like me. I was a saddle-sized-pad-packing girl, just like the others. I'd had my first kiss and had a real best friend.

That week marked the anniversary of my first year as a Ranch kid. I held out so much hope that I'd go home like my mom had promised, but I knew deep down that would never happen. This permanence was the one detail that set me apart from the others.

That first day of my eighth-grade year, I knew I fit in, I was loved, and I was accepted.

I was normal.

It turns out normal hasn't ever been something that suited me well.

My cycle was irregular. I could go three months with no sign of a period, and then a pain would rip through my abdomen and the flood gates would instantly open. That first day of school, I bled through my favorite jeans, and everyone in class saw the blood on the seat of my chair. I died a little. By the halfway point of the school year, everyone knew that if I was on my period, there would be evidence everywhere. Embarrassing, but also oddly accepted.

This included my seat in that poor mint green van. Prior to that day, it was simply the spot where I usually sat. After that day, it was mine. With pieces of me left in the door frame and now the upholstery, I was organically staking claim to this new life of mine.

Devotion

{To early teen me and her sad friend Ricky:
"Alone" by Trampled by Turtles}

When I was fourteen, I made a suicide pact while playing The Game of Life with Ricky. I was staying in the house he lived in (where Tammy also lived) because my houseparents left their job and moved on so Dad could pastor a small-town Kansas church. I didn't know myself well enough to be conflicted over their leaving. Shortly after their departure, maybe a week or two later, Dad came back to tie up some loose ends. Upon seeing him, my heart leaped with something that felt a bit like belonging, but also deep loss. It seemed foreign and very much like a feeling that I didn't have rights to, so I stuffed it deep down.

While the new houseparents settled in and adapted, those of us who lived in the house were divided up among the other houses. Our small group-home community was a cluster of three houses, two management staff apartments, an office, a car shop, and a barn. We weren't in school, so it must have been spring break or early summer vacation. The days were long over at Ricky and Tammy's house. Lazy days filled with the two of us rotating between playing board games at the long kitchen table, built to feed eighteen, and sometimes sneaking into the laundry room to kiss.

We weren't dating.

I was still hooked on him, but I cared more about our friendship than any attraction. Our little trysts were less sexually charged and more about grasping for some sort of human connection.

Tammy and I were drifting apart. She was transforming into a more legalistic, good Christian girl, and I struggled to relate. I knew I was a disgusting and damaged girl, so I related more to the Rickys of the world. Tammy was one of the only girls in their house, with houseparents who had no children of their own. I had never in my entire life spent so much time with so many boys, and I loved it. Before temporarily moving across the street, I hadn't really known many of the older high school boys. They intimidated me during school because my self-esteem was so far in the gutter, and because *high school boy* was a language with which I had no grasp. Ricky was comfortable for me because we'd been a part of each other's lives in many ways for a long time, at least by group-home standards.

The average Ranch kid lived there for three to six months. The setting, the circumstances, the situation, and the environmental structure made those months (however short or long) fairly intense. Intense trauma connects people. All any Ranch kid ever longed for was to *go home*. It did not matter how unhealthy their "real home" was—I was the classic example of this—we simply ached to be there again. When kids left, always with sobs and tears and tightly gripped hugs, they promised to write or call. They meant it when they made such promises—we were deeply and intimately connected. Our lives had been forever changed, and we could not imagine a future where we weren't in one another's lives. Then they would return to normal lives and eventually not want to remember Ranch life. I understood. I was jealous, but also sometimes it broke me.

The suicide pact between Ricky and I was not serious. We gravitated to the game of Sorry, with darker secrets and whispered rules. It was all harmless; we were bored and young and stupid. I've heard ER doctors, nurses, police officers, and paramedics can have really dark senses of humor because of the things they witness. This isn't entirely different from kids in our circumstance. We had seen abuse, many variations of trauma and neglect, and needed to maintain some form of rebellion against the very structured system that rubbed our sense of comfort the wrong way.

Had Ricky called me out on the promise I had made to end my life, would I have done it? Honestly, yes. Not because I was suicidal, although I didn't see much of a life worth living. I would have done it because I loved Ricky, and when I took a hard look at my life, he was probably the one person in the world I was closest to at that time. I would have done anything he asked me to do because that was how I was learning to love—to sacrifice myself so that the person I cared about knew they were of value. Desperately, I ached for someone to love me like that.

The new houseparents were different. Their sense of humor was different than *Mom's* and *Dad's* had been. They argued a lot and arguing often led to pouting and weird adult behavior I couldn't understand. Were they good people with genuine hearts for kids like us? Yes. Were they a good fit for the job of parenting us? Probably not.

They were the type of people who would have done great as part of the summer groups that came in, spending fun time with us while performing short-term mission projects. They went into the job expecting to save us. They wanted to make such a difference and reap the reward for their amazing acts. I don't judge them for that; I have been there. I have loved so deeply because I needed to feel like I made a difference. Differences got made, but not the ways we hoped.

Jobs like theirs have a high burnout rate, and they seemed to spiral toward that quickly. They then spent the rest of their time as houseparents operating more by oppression, shaming, and ridicule than anything honest or empathetic. I wish I could go back in time and whisper such truths in their ears, as much for our benefit as for theirs. They were good people with really good hearts.

Sometimes good people can hurt people too.

Life transitioned to a new normal and I adapted. I was becoming skilled at getting up the morning following a guttural loss. With all the changes, my mother's lack of care remained a constant. The new houseparents found it acceptable to talk about this with me, whenever or wherever they chose. There was no consideration for my heart, however undeserved my sense of devotion to her was. I did, in the interest of survival, finally surrender to allowing a controlled closeness with them to evolve. I genuinely admired certain things about them and, of course, wanted them to love me. While I never felt like they were my parents, I desperately wanted to keep the peace while somehow managing to earn their love. I was learning how to be a compartmentalized version of myself so others would find me good enough. With them it worked, for the most part. They remained my houseparents until the August afternoon I left for college.

As this new normal began to develop, some kids left while new ones came, and once again it was time for the school year to begin. The start of my freshman year marked the anniversary of two complete years at the Children's Ranch. A visit home that second year had me asking my mother when I was going to come home to stay. The simple words seemed like an ungraspable concept to her. She had turned my room into her sewing room, replacing the carpet (though never saying a word about the damage I must have caused to the corner of that small space). She had given my furniture and bedding away, except for the rickety book-shelf Papa had built me. She was giddy as she gave me a tour of her new car, new (massive) stereo, new television, huge collection of VHS movies, and all the other new things she had acquired. It was not lost on me that my mother's contribution to my birthday and second Christmas had, once again, been nonexistent. Her apology had come, once again, with the excuses that she could not afford it. On every phone call, she complained about how my hospital bill was draining her and that she'd been advised to file a malpractice lawsuit against the pediatrician who'd admitted me.

That fall, as I was spending my days learning government and algebra, she wrote to me about how she and her boyfriend were taking a big vacation to Las Vegas. I wasn't the best at geography, but I did know that Nevada was closer to Idaho and begged her to come visit.

"PLEASE drive a little further and see me," I'd begged. I knew this was possible, and my heart flipped rapidly as I allowed myself to entertain the thought. My grandmother, my aunt, and my grandmother's brother, Dale, had managed to drive up and visit both springs. I realized, for the first time, it was painful for me to live somewhere that my own mother had never been. As a mother *should be*, she was the most important person in the world to me. That I lived a life with people she didn't know and slept in a bed that was housed in a decorated room she had never set foot in seemed the saddest part of my life.

She promised she would try but "didn't think *he* would allow it. It's *his* money," she reminded me. It was up to him.

It was always up to him. Just before I had to hang up (these new houseparents weren't fond of her early morning calls either), she subtly jabbed me with how things could have been different if I had made different choices.

"So, you're never going to come see me then?" I did not hide the crushed sound of my voice.

"I am sure I will! Someday I will just show up and surprise you!"

I wish she'd never said those words to me ...

They say the majority of a brain's coping mechanisms are formed by age two. It's something like seventy percent, leaving another twenty percent to be formed by age seven, and the last ten percent to marinate and develop during the remainder of adolescence. Perhaps this is how it is under normal, healthy upbringings, but I am living proof that this is not always the case.

My mom and her boyfriend did not come to Idaho to visit. As the weeks passed and I kept looking for them to appear on our winding, riverside road, a little part of me withered. Once I had seen and given voice to this need, there was no going back. I was both angry with my mother and desperate for her come. I joined in on the bad-mouthing my houseparents did of Nora, forming some ill-comforting alliance. It felt good to be understood and validated for a second, but I also allowed shame to grow because she was my mother and I loved her.

During those still warm months, a work group came—friends of my houseparents. These were the early, preburnout days when they were still trying to connect with us. Their friends had brought a video camera and one day suggested I should make a video for my mom.

I poured my soul into that video. I walked around introducing her to every single kid I could find. I told her about school and what I was learning, with the camera directly on me. I was radiant with happiness because I was able to finally share this world with my mom. One of the things I was most excited about was that Tammy and I had planned an epic slumber party. The summer groups had helped the Ranch build a small school, and we had jumped through all the hoops required so we would be allowed to have the party in the brand-new building. My house mom and her friend were chaperoning, which was perfect because these were the early days, so we could get away with more. We watched *Steel Magnolias* and *Weekend at Bernie's*, ate so much junk food, and did a fashion show, which turned into a moon-the-judges/strip show.

This last part I had forgotten about until 2006.

When I'd found the (many unopened) letters I'd sent my mom, it was just after my grandmother's funeral in August of 2006, and grief was thick. I was still a protector of unending love and grace where my mother was concerned. As I sorted through that box of letters from me to her, I reminisced. My heart broke with each unopened envelope, and toward the bottom, I came across an unopened manila bubble mailer. It was decorated with stickers and had a six-page letter inside about how I could not wait to share my life with her. I talked about how I felt split down the middle and just needed my life to be whole, that I might not survive if I did not learn how to be complete. I was far more splayed open on those pages than I had any memory of being. All at once, I was surprised the houseparents had read it and allowed it to be sent, but then realized maybe they hadn't wasted their time because they knew she didn't care.

With that open-heart letter was my video tape.

She had never seen that silly girl, glowing and so eager to share herself and her world with her mother.

It hadn't ever mattered to her.

After that video was made, I began daydreaming that one day I would come home from school and my mom would be sitting in my bedroom waiting to surprise me. I would walk home as fast as I could, nearly every day, and bust into my room, so happy to see the dream come true.

Of course, she was never there. Deep down I knew she wouldn't be.

I sometimes imagined I was her. I would pretend I was there in that space to surprise my daughter. I would run my fingers upon the varying textures of clothing hanging in the closet and pause to admire how well the shoes were organized. I would linger on the spines of books, feeling impressed that my daughter was so well-read. All around me, I would absorb the sense of detail with which she had decorated her space. I would be sad, as a mother, that she was living in a world I knew nothing about. Pinned notes and photos of friends would inspire a smile to spread on my face, and I would admit to myself how much I missed her and how deeply loveable she was.

This never happened. It was only ever me there, pretending.

I played this little game most afternoons. Every great once in a while, I still do.

Ranch Life

1989-1992

Brother

{To my brothers R and J: "Tether" by Chvrches}

The spring of my eighth-grade year found most of the kids in the Ranch obsessing over love. I had no idea what silly girlhood crushes were supposed to be like. My only experiences were with Joseph and Ricky, each very different in nature.

Once, at a weekly YMCA physical education day, gossip made its way to me that a high school boy named Ryan wanted to go out with me. I knew him the way that one knows someone when you live on the same parcel of land. I'd spent some time with him during the days at Ricky's, and this idea that he would like me seemed preposterous. I became self-conscious around him, but also, I began to notice him in ways I hadn't before. I found myself embarrassed and jittery in his presence. I analyzed everything he said or did around me. *Did this prove he liked me? Did that?*

He was playful and teased me often. Because he sat near me in school, Ryan began opening up to me about his family and his pre-Ranch life. Even though I never imagined he would ask me to be his girlfriend, one afternoon I was blindsided when he told me that a boy in his house named

Mike liked me, and I should go out with *him*. Mike was this shaggy blond-haired, hazel-eyed, wide-smiling stupid middle school boy I had never given a thought to. Mike felt like the sort of kid I would reluctantly have to babysit, even though we were close in age. Mike was the sort of boy to flatulate, laugh about it, then not comprehend why the girls in the room didn't think it was funny.

The only boyfriend I'd had was Ricky. While I hoped I would one day look back on a life filled with many boyfriends, I knew Mike was not going to be one of them. It seemed to mean a lot to Ryan, however, and so when Mike asked me, I said yes. Eleven days later when Mike touched my arm and tried to kiss me, I broke it off. I just couldn't. I had tried. Instead, I sucked in my gut and lay across my bed in an attempt to zip up my tightest jeans. Then, as dusk was approaching, I walked past Ryan's house as he was washing dishes. *Wasn't this how girls got a boy's attention?* Did I want Ryan to want me? I did. Also, I wanted him to love me. Although I did not understand what that meant exactly, as his gaze lifted and followed me from his place at the kitchen window, I suspected those tight, acid-washed jeans were the way to get it.

The next day, he passed a note to me, telling me I was hot and he liked my jeans.

My grandmother had reluctantly bought those jeans for me when she visited the month before. We were at a thrift store, and I knew I had to have them. They were amazing! They were skinny jeans—before skinny jeans were even a thing. They were so tight that I could not sit down in them. I could barely walk. Once they were buttoned and zipped, while I was horizontal, I'd have to have a roommate grab my hand and help me stand up without bending my body. The feedback from many of my nonadult people were that the jeans looked hot. I liked the way it felt when someone thought I was attractive—I wanted *more* of that. If the skintight, clearly too small jeans were what people liked, then I needed to work on being smaller, too. Ryan's note had been the validation I'd been waiting for. So that day at lunch, I made myself throw up for the first time.

In my legalism-filled adolescence, there were no helpful after-school specials bringing awareness to things like eating disorders, teen pregnancy, or rape. We came home, did chores, and watched reruns of *Little House on the Prairie.* My favorites were the two-part episodes about "Sylvia." She was beautiful and sweet, and a rape victim. She had a father who didn't believe her and punished her for having a teen pregnancy. She had Albert, with his beautiful, kissable lips, who loved her and was willing to move heaven and earth for her. I loved the darkness of it, but also, I surrendered myself to needing an Albert of my own. This was how a boy would really love a girl. I wanted to be loved like that.

I continued making myself throw up, sneaking laxatives from the medicine shelf behind my houseparents' bedroom door, or faking stomach aches in order to skip meals all together. Eventually, the jeans were comfortable enough for me to sit down, and that was the day Ryan asked me to be his girlfriend.

I had a boyfriend who was a high schooler! It didn't matter that we were being educated in a two-room school, with middle and high schoolers in one room, working independently, and elementary kids in the other. It didn't matter that he sat next to me in class and the idea of middle and high school division was nonexistent. He held my hand once, on the way to the YMCA for PE. We were in the ugly mint green van, and, with my hand tight in his, I sat there pouring more of myself into that van's DNA. Blood, skin, and, this time, hope. I soaked up everything about that moment. He was much taller than me, and this made me feel safe. His hand was so warm and much larger than mine, and I wanted to disappear into him and stay there forever.

Before Ryan became my boyfriend, I felt like I could almost be myself with him. Even when he teased me, he felt protective. I knew if I'd needed a confidant, I could probably trust him. After I agreed to be his girlfriend, I seemed to retreat somewhere inside of myself and avoided him.

On two separate YMCA days, news spread to me that Ryan wanted to meet me in an empty room so we could make out. I liked him a lot, but he was a high school boy and I was scared. I wasn't sure what I was afraid of, but I knew I could not bring myself to go to that room, so instead I placed myself in situations where I couldn't. The idea of what could happen in that room made my insides churn. My roommate had been sneaking out to have sex with Ricky at night, so for ease of escape, she had hammered some large nails under our bedroom window. She said the boys could switch, and Ryan could just sneak over into our room one night. While I liked Ryan, I lived in a state of panic every single night that his six-foot frame was going to climb up those nails and come through my window.

One day, a few weeks into our relationship, I was delivered an ultimatum by a third party. I would either meet Ryan in the ball closet of our school's gymnasium or he would break up with me. I knew I didn't want to lose him.

I went to the closet.

I imagined this large boy overpowering me. I felt manipulated. I wanted him to love me, but also, I needed him not to. I felt sick.

"Do you not like me?" Ryan asked.

"I do, I really do," I reassured him.

"OK." He reached for my hand and held it loosely. The light was faint, bleeding in around the door. I could see him, and also not. "Is it OK if I hug you?"

It was. His arms wrapped around me, and I sank into his large embrace. My entire body exhaled with the exchange of his warmth enveloping me. Hugs were against the rules too.

"This is really nice." He was right; it was. We were breaking all the rules, yet nothing truly bad was happening. The safety I loved about him consumed me.

"I think we should break up." I wasn't surprised by the words he'd spoken into my hair.

"I'm sorry." And I was. I wanted to live inside his hand, his arms, everything he had unexpectedly come to represent for me. But I couldn't give him the things girls were giving boys, and I did not know why. I felt broken, deeply sad, and ugly. I also felt like I let him down.

"This," he spoke, still wrapped warm around me, "makes me realize I can't kiss you. If I'd snuck inside your room one night, I think I would have let you sleep with your head on my chest. It feels like kissing you would just be wrong. Does that sound terrible?"

"No." It didn't. Reluctantly, I pulled back from him, straining to see his face. "I know exactly what you mean."

It was the best breakup in the history of breakups. I had entered into something I wasn't ready for, only to realize that I already had a deep connection with this boy who would be the closest thing to a real brother to me. A prayer prayed for years had been answered by this boy. For many months, we had been talking and building something that we thought was headed in one direction, while really it was bigger than either of us understood. It wasn't just us, either. Somewhere along the way, the administration took lenience where Ryan and I were concerned. While a six-inches-apart rule was strictly enforced between boys and girls, no one batted an eye when Ryan would give me a hug. On car rides he would sometimes reach for my hand, and this became such a second nature reality, I wouldn't realize it happened until a new kid would point it out and ask if we were boyfriend and girlfriend. We would laugh and talk about how repulsive that idea was. I would like to think it was this unexplainable tether between us which set the wheels in motion for Ryan to be moved over to my house, but I'm not sure we had any real power in that decision. His houseparents were moving on, so a game of musical houses brought my heart-brother home to me. There we were, allowed to interact as normally as possible. While it was technically against the rules, I was allowed to stand in his doorway and he in mine. Often, on those dreaded Saturday mornings when my mom called, he would crawl out of his own bed to sit beside me through the conversation. We never talked about the extra hard things, instead we simply slipped into orbit together, anticipating needs and filling some unknown void.

Long before any of that happened, though, in the space between our breakup and the sharing of a Ranch house, I walked in darkness. I battled with bulimia and cutting. Beneath my clothes were razor blade scars in the shape of initials of the people whose love I was desperate for. I was branded, belonging to my mother, belonging to Ricky, belonging to fleeting crushes and desperate dreams. Upon my wrist, ankle, and inner thigh were deep scarring scabs from eraser burns. I hurt. Pain was bubbling forth from somewhere so deep within me. I did not know how to react or how to handle it, so I would simply expel some agony from myself a bit more.

That summer, just before my freshman year, we were traveling, doing our Vacation Bible School (VBS) and church touring. I was feeling particularly awful about myself, so I wore my favorite skinny acid-washed jeans. It was hot, and jeans seemed like the wrong choice. They were loose-fitting by this point, which seemed like something I should have felt happy about. All the girls were doing it—playing the game of fingers down throats and popping stolen ex-lax when we could. Partly, I think I did these things because it was what I thought I was supposed to do. Maybe this is why we were all doing it—simply because we were all doing it. We did not know it was stupid or dangerous; we saw a means to an end. Whatever end I was hoping for, however, wasn't going to be found in a toilet bowl.

The last time I took a laxative as a part of this weird game I was playing with my life was that VBS day in the jeans. I had taken two because, as I said, I was feeling dark and down. I craved the feeling of control that I believed would settle in eventually.

The joke was on me, however, as I took to the stage to sing with my fellow Ranch kids and my jeans were ruined by dark liquid pouring out from me. I couldn't feel or smell a thing, though everyone else could. A trip to the emergency room, two IV bags, and a legally required physician's counsel had me discharged that evening as "fine." I don't remember how honest I was with the hospital staff. I do remember leaving there feeling terrified and knowing deep down—one hundred percent—I was anything but fine.

School started, the slumber party and video to my mom happened, and life went on. One afternoon, I had terrible cramps and was sent home from school. Because my houseparents weren't home, I was sent to Mrs. Newbern's house. The irony wasn't lost on either of us—the reason I found myself in her care again involved my period. She had me rest on her daughter's bed; eventually, she came in with a cup of tea and sat down to talk. While she, like every other staff member, knew it was my accusations that I'd been molested which led me to the Ranch, she was the first one to state she knew it was true. She'd gone on to say that it was obvious I had been violated and that it made her angry because I had not deserved it. She explained to me how shame worked. It was through that beautiful, vulnerable heart I came to realize any shame I had ever felt relating to the sexual abuse had been born long after the abuse stopped. It grew from the abandonment and rejection from my mother. It was watered and grown out of the staff not believing me and forbidding me to talk about it, even though I'd never mentioned it to them. It matured every time the rules, realities, and decisions of the Ranch made me feel like a bad, dirty, worthless girl.

That Saturday, my youth group was having a party at a church family's home. We were eating pizza and watching *Gleaming the Cube* (thus beginning my lifelong adoration of Christian Slater) when one of our adult leaders mentioned something about sexual abuse. It was just after the movie had ended, and kids were gathering to play a game. He knew I had been abused, and he was curious how it had been handled. He was a police officer and somehow connected to the Ranch board, but beyond that, I didn't know how he'd known. It felt significant that, while I hadn't spoken in years about what my mom's boyfriend had done, the conversation came up twice within one week.

I didn't know this man asking questions, not really. I knew I liked him and felt like I could trust him. He was a good dad, super funny, and most important, he never treated me the way most other people treated Ranch kids. This was not the normal confidence I felt around men, and I trusted my instinct. I answered all his questions honestly.

Before I realized it was happening, a new investigation was underway. Police came to the Ranch around school hours to talk to me. I was assured that something would happen this time, and the various adults around me were chastised for not having treated me better. It was a surreal experience. It was 1990, and no one could understand how I had never been examined or interviewed by police when the truth was told the first time around. It seemed the entire, inconclusive investigation happened over my head and around me—done without me at all.

My mother was angry and had made a big, dramatic show of disowning me over the phone. That evening, feeling overwhelmed from awful things that I didn't know how to process, I ran across the street. I saw one of the boys sitting on their side porch and asked him to go inside and get Ryan. It was dusk; the sky transitioned through hues of purple and pink. We weren't allowed outside after dark. We weren't allowed less than six inches apart. We weren't allowed without adults present to supervise. Somehow, none of that mattered.

The two of us sat on the concrete step, Ryan's arms wrapped tightly around me. I told him, for the first time ever, my truth. Since leaving New Mexico, I hadn't spoken a word about any of what had happened, outside of answering investigation questions. While those answers were pieces of the truth, they did not form *my truth*. Like I could no longer keep myself sealed tight, it poured out of me, and he scooped it all up, making it his story too.

Nothing came of the investigation. Any faith the staff had regarding goodness in my mother was gone by the end. They decided I was not allowed to stay in her home on visits. She never argued with this because she hadn't wanted me in her home in the first place. The ache for my mom's love didn't exactly go away, but there were people now who validated me, people who were willing to fight for me. These things allowed me to see that my mother was equally—if not more so—to blame for what had happened at the hand of her boyfriend.

I slipped into the start of my third Ranch year far more damaged than the two before, or maybe just more aware of my brokenness. I was babysitting for people from church here and there, making minimal money, but enjoying the normalcy of it. I was a good kid; the adults trusted me. I knew beneath the surface, I was garbage, but I did my best to not let anyone else in on the secret. The one and only person who saw the whole truth and loved me despite it was Ryan. My ex-boyfriend-turned-brother was the only thing keeping me present. Even though I felt I was my most real with him, and it seemed he could see right through me, I don't think he had any idea how I was playing with my life.

To Whats UP

Well I don't know what to say But that you are a very special person Who has touched peoples lives and help people out with problems, and don't let anyone tell you your not special.

I love you lots

through for me is Ryan. He is my brother, blood or no blood, he is my family when no one else was there. I can pull it all out to him and even though he is no longer in arms length, she still he cares. then

Milly,
How are you doing? I'm doing fine but working 10 to 12 hours every day. I miss you at home especially during Christmas. Mom and I decided not to put a Christmas tree because there was only going to be the two of us here. Is there snow up there yet? So you can have a white Christmas. We don't want any snow down here.

I still think of you as my daughter

PS money is to get you something.

Journal entry   after Ryan left...

Her boyfriend

My 'brother' Jared

Jared & Ryan

Ryan

Mint

{To Nora: "Gravity" by Sara Bareilles}

I hated the color mint green. My mother had insisted on carpeting my childhood bedroom with that terrible color. I hated that carpet. I hated the ugly mint green van. It was embarrassing and represented all the things about my freak show life I detested. As a March baby, I hated that my birthstone was close to the color mint green. Whenever mint green clothing in my size would come in through our donated clothing room, staff would set it aside for me. Something about mint green seemed to make others think about me, even though I found the color cringeworthy.

My second Christmas in Idaho was vastly different from the first. I was thirteen years old and had been invited to spend Christmas with a local family I'd never met before. Just like in the movie *Annie*, where Little Orphan Annie gets to go to Daddy Warbucks's home, and everything is special and wonderful, and then someone realizes just how special Annie truly is. This is how I see that Christmas—through the filter of a nostalgic childhood movie with a happy ending.

I don't remember their names or many details about the adventure. It seems I was skilled, by this point, at slipping into a hidden space of self-protection and allowing some part of me with no memory retention to seamlessly navigate on autopilot. Even though I had been so nervous, they were kind and funny. For Christmas, they gave me several gifts, but the only two I can recall were a mint green sweatshirt with matching mint green socks.

I loved that shirt and those socks—they became my favorite possessions.

My Christmas family took me to their niece's Christmas Eve wedding. The ceremony was at an old church, in a dimly lit chapel with walls built of smooth stones. The wedding was beautiful, and by this point, I realized that this was a good family, and I was safe with them. The bride walked down the aisle to Firehouse's "Love of a Lifetime." I had never heard that song, nor had I heard of someone walking down an elegant, candle-lit aisle to a recorded rock song. It seemed immature, inappropriate, and all at once amazing and wonderful. As though I were starving for music beyond easy listening Christian, lyrically, I fell further and further into the notes. As the chorus made its second appearance, I saw tears sparkle as they caught the light on the bride's cheek. I knew then, in that chapel and with those lyrics drilling themselves into my core, that I wanted to be a part of these people. They were a family, exactly like the kind I dreamed of. I had been alone and thrown away, and there, in that room on the Christmas Eve of 1989, I felt like I had finally found something too.

After Christmas, they took me to a youth retreat in McCall. There, anonymous among teens I had never met, I got to play the role of a normal teenage girl, my favorite part to play. I lived a worry-free existence of gossip, giggles, and sugary soft drinks. It was heaven, and my appearance there required no explanation.

The first evening I was back in their home, we went to see *Batman* with Michael Keaton. I pledged then, in this new life I desperately craved, that my heart would forever love both Michael Keaton and *Batman*. I allowed myself to accept that this could be my life, and as our days came to an end, they asked me if I would like to come and live with them. My answer was an emphatic *YES!* It had been a long time since I'd been able to wish for good things to find me, and that Christmas, I let go of my walls and need for control, and allowed some hope to seep in.

I believed I would be going to live with them; however, I never saw them again. I knew that Christmas had felt like the start of something for me. It was ushering in something life-changing, and in my thirteen-year-old naivete, I assumed it was this new family with their ideal, normal life. I didn't know yet that reality isn't like the movies, and families don't happen the way Annie's did. I didn't know that after our few days together, they tried desperately—these nameless people from a tiny blip in my life—to get my mom to relinquish her rights. They had done it by trying to give her money, by hiring an attorney, by any means necessary, and they had failed. My mother gloated to them that she didn't want me, but she wouldn't let them have me, either. I didn't know any of this, because once again, the big things happened over my head and around me, leaving me out entirely.

Time passed and I began to accept that I wouldn't be living with them after all. I wasn't allowed to call them, though no one had ever told me why—so they disappeared from my life. Without any of the bigger details, I just assumed they'd come to their senses and didn't want me after all.

That Christmas was the prologue to my eating disorder, to my skin carving and burning, to the darkest places I would ever dare to go.

Early in the fall of 1990, I began to notice a certain blond-haired, hazel-eyed boy differently. Now inches taller than me and less middle school annoying, I realized I might actually like Mike. Tammy had gone home to her family, and my roommate and Ricky had been kicked out for sneaking out at night. The romantic interests and friend pool primarily consisted of the few of us still lingering plus a lot of new faces.

I confided in Ryan that I thought I might have feelings for Mike. While, several months before, he had been the guiding force in the pity relationship I'd had with him, this time Ryan was vehemently not supportive. He told me I deserved better.

It had been a lifetime since spring. So much had happened, even more so when filtered through the intense trauma-bonding of group-home adolescence. I had changed; we all had. When Mike's best friend William asked me if I liked Mike, I said I did, and soon I was his girlfriend once again—only for real this time.

I loved Mike. I never saw that coming. My heart has known real love in many forms, so I can look back at the boys of my youth and be able to sift out the girlhood crushes and silly infatuations from the loves which held some pieces of truth and substance. Our relationship was real. People who say teenagers can't feel love clearly haven't dealt with teens in active states of personal trauma. Emotions play by no rules.

This love was life-defining.

It was unhealthy.

While I had kissed Ricky a handful of times, the first time I ever *made out* with someone was with Mike, in the doorway of the ugly green van. It was emotional, it was lust-filled, and it was intense. The very first time Mike kissed me, we were in the kitchen of his house. As we stood there, awkward and young, this boy's eyes glazed over, and he moved in to kiss me. It was nothing like kissing Ricky had ever been. From that day on, I kissed my boyfriend every chance I got. On the front step in broad daylight? *Sure! Why not?* In the van during the middle of the day? *You bet!* At the basketball court? *Yes sir!* We gave in to the moment whenever it struck. Bases were taken, though we never went all the way home. I don't, for one second, doubt we would have if an opportunity had presented itself.

Sometimes we would get in trouble and have to stay apart for a while. Usually, this was because we were fourteen and not "legally allowed" to have a relationship by Ranch standards. This never stopped us. While I would miss kissing him, he would spend school days penning me long, handwritten letters, and then turn around and spend the nights recording me mixtapes. Sometimes those tapes had songs from the radio, and many times they were him talking to me—really, truly talking to me—about the often-unspoken things. The boy knew the way directly to my heart.

I called him Michael. It sounded grown-up, it felt intimate, and we were both drowning in the intensity of a very heavy, adult relationship. I smile a little now when I think back to my childhood obsession with *Grease 2*, dancing around my aunt's pool to those songs I knew by heart. In that movie, the female lead character, Stephanie, falls in love with her Michael, and when I was fourteen, I'd fallen unexpectedly hard for mine.

As the months passed and autumn became winter, I noticed there was an odd leniency developing where our relationship was concerned. While the adults had no idea we
were making out in creative corners of our tiny little world
or that his hands knew things about my body that even I
didn't know, it seemed as though our love had transcended
the rules of the Ranch and had won over the world. By
this time, their houseparents had left, and Ryan was in my
home. (Mike had not been brought into our house for obvious reasons.) Around Thanksgiving time, Ryan had been
allowed to ask Mike over for a movie, and he and I had been
allowed to watch shoulder to shoulder while sharing a bowl
of popcorn. The unspoken reality was that Mike was not a
friend of Ryan's, and there was no real closeness between
them. This was all a sneaky attempt on our part to pretend
we were a *normal* couple doing *normal* things. Even so, my
houseparents made it clear they were willing to turn a blind
eye, within reason. A dinner here or there at one another's
house became a regular occurrence. It was as though we
were allowed to have a relationship, though no one was
willing to verbally grant their permission.

In early December, cloaked in an unfamiliar courage, I
asked my house mom to take me Christmas shopping so I
could buy Mike a gift. He did the same with his houseparents. One evening, we had a Christmas party at the school,
hosted by volunteer staff so our own staff could attend an
employee celebration. We stole away to the tiny home ec
kitchen, where he kissed me gently and said he had a gift
for me. He produced a square box from his back pocket,
opening it to reveal a silver bracelet.

"We are young and dumb, but that isn't forever. You make
me so happy, and I swear I will never leave you," he said,
as he clasped the bracelet on my right wrist. "Even when
we can't be together, you are mine. I will marry you some-

day. I love you." He kissed me again, and hand in hand, we emerged back to the party. When friends asked what was going on, I told them we were engaged. Because I was fourteen and in love and completely clueless.

The evening we decorated our Christmas tree, my house-parents invited Mike over. It was strange and wonderful. My gut told me something was off, but I reminded myself that I could be insecure and paranoid—always waiting for the big, bad thing to happen—and it didn't matter because I loved him and he loved me, and we were allowed to be together.

We all drank hot chocolate and laughed. At one point, Ryan and I exchanged a glance which may have been a unified questioning of which version of *The Twilight Zone* we had stumbled in to. Before Mike headed home for the night, my houseparents had us pose together in front of the Christmas tree for a photo. He kissed my bracelet, a twinkle in those hazel eyes, before he crossed the shared yard and disappeared into his house.

The afternoon I came home from school to find the developed picture of Mike and me waiting for me on my bed was the same day he told me his mom wanted him to come home.

"For Christmas?" I'd asked. I hadn't gone home for Christmas, but I wanted to.

"To stay."

I was happy for him. This is one of the ways in which I know my love was real. While I was devastated for me, I wanted that for him. His mom lived in Colorado, but they were moving to Phoenix. This felt like a miracle to me, and further confirmation that we had something special. If I could work hard and be a better kid, maybe I could convince my family to let me come home. Maybe I could live with my aunt in Phoenix after all. I knew it didn't have to be the end for Mike and me.

The days before he left were hard. He began lashing out at his best friend William and me, saying William would take his place after he left, which was laughable. William was younger and annoyed me more than any person ever had. I knew that, as happy as Mike was to be leaving, he was struggling too. I, on the other hand, was doing OK. I felt like this was the most difficult thing I had ever faced and also that it shouldn't have been. It seemed out of place to me that, after everything and everyone I had lost, this boyfriend of four months would hurt the most.

On the day he left, they allowed him to come into the school to say goodbye. He pulled Ryan and me out onto the landing where he kissed me as we both cried. All at once the pain was flooding hard and fast. As he left the classroom that day, he passed my desk and saw our Christmas tree photo. He asked me if he could have it.

"I can't," I barely managed through the tears.

"Please?" He did the same, through his own. In a romantic gesture, perfect for the year it was, my boyfriend took off his favorite denim jacket and placed it in my arms. "Please?" Softer the second time, he gestured toward the only photographic proof I had that we had ever happened at all.

I couldn't say no to him. And then he and my photograph were gone.

Christmas morning had me in bed with a very sharp knife and plans to dramatically stab myself to death. It seemed poetic, I guess, to target Jesus's birthday as my big day. I wasn't thinking about my pact with Ricky from nine months earlier. No, I was consumed with my broken heart. It hadn't been just the loss of my boyfriend; it had been the years of so much loss, and Mike had been my unexpected breaking point. At fourteen, as illogical as it was, I needed to have it out with God. I had remained faithful to him and never blamed him for anything that had gone wrong for me. For as long as I could remember, my life had been a continual raging sea of loss, and I had reached a point when I allowed myself the possibility of questioning God's goodness. Why had he never let me matter to someone who would stick around?

What about me was so impossible to love? So unworthy?

Instead, the sweet youngest son of my houseparents came into my room and asked if he could snuggle with me while I told him a story. I said yes and slipped the knife between my mattress and box spring.

I don't know that I would have succeeded in taking my life that morning, but I know I could have made everything so much worse than it felt.

Unlike many who left with promises to stay in touch, Mike kept his word at first. He'd call or send the occasional note in the mail. Nothing other than "I love you" seemed deep or heartfelt. I was looking for evidence his life had stopped mattering like mine had when he left, even though I knew that wasn't true. He had a new home in Arizona, and a new school. I needed him to prove that I mattered, and he couldn't do that. He knew they listened in; he knew they read his letters. But also, he was just a fourteen-year-old kid. It was hard to see that truth about us—our relationship had been so much bigger and more intense than either of us were capable of understanding. There was nothing he could ever have done to take away the pain I blamed on his absence.

One night in February, I was having a rare heart-to-heart talk with my house mom. She said that I was stronger than I thought, and the way she spoke made me believe, for a moment, that there might be some truth in her words. For the first time in months, I felt something emerging that was more than hopelessness.

Then, in the same reassuring tone she'd spoken the other words, she said, "The love between you and Michael is very real. We didn't realize that. If we had expected that, we wouldn't have let it happen. We'd known he was leaving since the school year started, so it seemed like overlooking your relationship was OK."

I froze. Calmly, I asked questions. While they had good intentions, allowing us some form of normal relationship because Mike would be leaving the Ranch, they failed to take any responsibility for how that oversight allowed something deeper to develop. I felt like a science project; like a specimen ... like a pawn. I cried myself to sleep, my arms wrapped tight around his jacket, as I had every night since he'd left.

By morning I had found a numb sense of clarity.

My first real love was with a boy named Michael, the one thing about my life that my little-girl self would have adored. We had a fairy-tale romance constructed of beautiful, handwritten love letters, mixtapes, warm kisses, and all the things that boyfriends in the nineties were supposed to do. There was a lot of kissing, seizing every opportunity we could. Where Mike and I were concerned, the group-home element didn't deter us too much, but also, maybe the rules kept us safe enough. We had a lot of opportunities to spend time together, and the feelings we developed were real.

I could still smell him there, on the collar of his jacket. I tucked it into the back of my closet with the hidden box of notes and tapes.

Our relationship had been the most beautiful thing I had known, but it was time for it to be done.

I washed my face, got dressed, and hugged Ryan before we walked side by side to school in silence. Within a week, I ended things with Mike. This was the one and only time that I was allowed to make a long-distance call to him. It wasn't fair for him to drag around the dead weight of a relationship neither of us was ready for. Two weeks later, a bit numb to everything, I agreed to date a boy at church. He was nice to me, funny, and altogether different from Mike or Ricky or Ryan. I needed different. While internally I felt ambivalent toward the people around me (Ryan being the only exception), I just wanted to make it through each day unscathed.

yours a a WAY to Shelter...
... All I WANT is a
family, And to live a
normal life like a
normal kid. Without "levels.
And I WANT to live with
parents who don't Scare
the crap out of you
when they are mad. I
WANT parents who don't
have spur-of-the-
moment-mood adjustment.
I WANT to live with Paren
I can talk to, Who under-
stand me. I have so much
tension, And I have
been so emotional
lately. Oh well. I better
go. I will...

journal entry 1992. age fifteen

Brittany

{Song: "Grey Street" by Dave Matthews Band}

At fifteen, I was allowed to have an *approved* boyfriend. When the obnoxious, redheaded boy named Jim, from youth group, asked me to be his girlfriend, I said yes. Though he wasn't someone I was seriously interested in, he came from a very approved church family, and I was already good friends with his sister Kara. Except for the occasional fifteen-minute monitored phone call and sitting next to each other at church, ours was a nearly nonexistent relationship. While I, for obvious reasons, could no longer spend the night with Kara, I did get to hang out with their family on occasion, and those moments always made me feel normal. Their mom was so kind and when I look back, it may have been her I loved most during those get-togethers. She stood nearly a head taller than me and had the kindest eyes.

It was one afternoon during my second month volunteering as a candy striper, and the middle of my third week as Jim's "girlfriend," when my houseparents couldn't pick me up from the hospital after a shift. They coordinated with Jim and Kara's mom to pick me up and keep me at their house until someone could make it into town to get me later that evening. Naturally I was thrilled! Any opportunity to play normal was welcome. Kara and I settled onto the couch playing a video game or something while their mom moved around the kitchen prepping dinner. Jim was sick and upstairs in his room, or maybe he had a broken leg ... I can't remember. I didn't even see him. Kara thought it was gross that I was going out with her brother, so when her mom realized she had to run to the store for some tomatoes, there was no mention of me sneaking up to see him.

The reason I can't recall what Kara and I were doing, or what ailment kept Jim out of sight, is because they didn't matter. I was going through the motions on the outside, while in complete shock internally because the normalcy of it all was far beyond my comfort zone.

For Kara this was a normal school day. I was going to eat a normal, weekday dinner with their family. There was a TV on. It was a lot to process *before* their mom left for the store. As the reality of her walking out the garage door sank in, something internally exploded.

Normal kids were left home alone, *unsupervised*.

She hadn't given any foreboding warnings because a Ranch kid was in her house; she'd just smiled and assured us she'd be right back.

I do remember I sat frozen on the couch until I heard the garage door announce her home. We must have been watching TV because I was so far inside of the freak-out happening in my head, there was no way I could have maintained a conversation or video game.

Later that evening I was walking the long Ranch drive with my closest girlfriend Brittany. I wanted so badly to share with someone the magic that the afternoon had held. Being left alone for what must have been only fifteen minutes felt like the most amazing thing to ever happen to me. Naively, I began to tell Brittany about it.

Brittany didn't understand—she couldn't. Her dad was the administrator of the Children's Ranch. With excitement dripping from my luscious secret, Brittany began probing for more, "And so, did you sneak in and see Jim?"

"No."

"You can tell me! I'm so excited, what happened?" she squealed just enough, her own anticipation building, that I allowed her excitement to validate my own, even though we were clearly on completely different pages.

"Nothing." I giggled back.

"Did he kiss you?" She paused her step and looked at me so longingly, as though she was trying to excavate the dirty details from deep within me. I felt so stupid then, getting excited over nothing. Clearly my magical moment would only be magical if I'd done something like kiss my boyfriend, and also sad that I hadn't thought of it then.

"Yes," I lied.

Brittany was so excited that I allowed myself to feel good for a moment. *What would it matter anyway? Who would it hurt?*

"Oh my gosh! How long was their mom gone? Did you guys, like, *make out?*" Her accentuation on the allegation carried with it an electricity unlike any of our very safe conversations had held before.

It was not lost on me that we were supposed to be best friends, but I was very reserved with what I could share with her. Her family had moved there just after Mike had gone home, so it wasn't that I had many juicy secrets to share, but I hadn't been very forthcoming regarding my feelings about things either. As much as I may have wanted to tell her everything, as I imagined best girlfriends did, the fact that her parents were staff created a huge chasm between us.

"I'm not sure. It went really fast. Maybe fifteen minutes."

"FIFTEEN MINUTES?! Oh my gosh, Misty! Did you have *sex* with him?"

What?! I stopped midstep, in complete shock. "NO!" The whole situation felt out of control as I once again began slipping into that place of overwhelm inside.

"I knew it! You did! I see it on your face. How did it feel?"

And there I was—a dirty Ranch kid. I couldn't possibly have been without adult supervision for more than a minute or two without climbing the stairs and having sex with a boy I wasn't even sure I actually liked. A dirty Ranch kid who wouldn't be happy with a stolen kiss, but instead had to go straight to sex.

I knew that, as such, she wouldn't believe me. She'd decided my guilt, and I already told a little lie, so why not turn it into a big one? "It felt weird."

We walked and talked a bit longer. I'd retreated so far inside my own sense of shame that I managed only one-syllable responses. We parted ways with the usual hug, me grateful the moment was over.

It turned out our walk would be the most pleasant part of the nightmare. It wasn't even an hour before her father was over and meeting with my houseparents behind closed doors. When I was finally pulled into the meeting, I knew what it was about and had prepared to come clean.

"I'm sorry I lied to Brittany. I didn't even see Jim when I was over there."

"Why would you lie about something like that?"

"Honestly, I don't know. I feel so stupid."

"Hmmm. This isn't making a lot of sense. Could it be that you told Brittany the truth, and now you're trying to get out of trouble by claiming it had been a lie?" Though Brittany's dad was talking to me as though I were five, I understood how this theory made sense too. I was calm and sad, direct and telling them the truth as brokenly and honestly as I could, but it wasn't good enough.

I was finally sent to bed where I cried myself to sleep.

The next morning, I was not allowed to come out of my room until the other house kids had left for school. I was ordered to put on an ugly dress and help them pack up my belongings for storage. Just before the kids were home for lunch, my house mom brought me a dry tuna sandwich and a copy of the book *This Present Darkness* by Frank Peretti. "You really need to read this book," she'd said.

Sequestered away from everyone in the house, I spent the afternoon reading. After dinner, Brittany's dad was back and the four of us were once again behind the closed door of my houseparents' bedroom. This new routine went on for many, many evenings. During the days, I sat alone reading that book and its sequel, *Piercing the Darkness*, over and over again. After dinnertime, I was manipulated and interrogated.

"Just tell us the truth."

"All we want is the truth."

"Aren't you tired? Don't you miss seeing other kids?"

I was, but with every tactic used to manipulate the answers they wanted, I felt stronger in my conviction to tell the truth. *Wasn't this what being tested looked like?*

On the fourth night they told me Jim had confessed. His sister had confirmed we'd had sex while their mom was at the store. I was in shock. I felt myself retreat so far inward as I tossed around the possibility of their words. *Why would they say that? Why would Jim confess?*

Even so, I left the room that evening standing by the truth that I'd lied about the whole thing.

It was the night that Brittany's dad pulled out the old brass frame that held a faded photo of my grandfather which I remember most. With his patronizing smile, he referenced the photo and challenged me to consider what this man would think. "He loved you. I know you've always said you really loved him. What would he think of this situation? How disappointed he must be in the girl you have become."

His words stung, but over that they rang true. Would Papa want me to lie just so I could get the interrogations to stop? I didn't think so. But of course, he would be disappointed in the girl I had grown into.

Everyone was.

On the final night, as I waited to enter the room and go through the same routine, Ryan pulled me aside. "Please, whatever is happening, just do what they want. I hate watching you go through this. I miss you, and honestly, I can't keep being in charge of a house full of kids night after night."

"I am telling them the truth, and they won't listen." As the words came out, I felt the literal exhaustion carrying them. For nearly two weeks, I hadn't shared an interaction with anyone who genuinely cared about me.

"Then say what they want to hear. It sucks. This will just go on and on if you don't."

I knew he was right, and I knew I couldn't go on like this much longer.

Just like all the other nights, I was taken into my houseparents' bedroom, the dark wooden door closing behind me. I looked at the lines etching the faces of my houseparents. I took in the still condescending look of Brittany's father. I wanted to scream *ENOUGH*, but I surrendered to the realization that it wouldn't change anything.

In the end, to them, *I* didn't matter. I'd been so busy resuming the role of my advocate that I failed to see the parties to which I protested only saw me as a bad kid, and beyond that I didn't exist. They'd made up their minds, and in that moment, so did I.

Enough, Misty. "You want me to tell you that it's true. That I had sex with Jim. So I will. I went into his room while their mom went to the store and had sex with him."

Ten minutes later, I'd been sent to bed for the night, and my houseparents resumed a normal household evening without me.

The next morning, my house mom brought me a pregnancy test. I was informed I'd be taking them daily until I got my period. As I sat, embarrassed, peeing on the little white stick as she stood on the other side of the door, I began to panic—*what if I'm pregnant?* That was the power the daily psychological abuse held over me ... Even though I knew I'd never had sex before, and even though I knew I wasn't pregnant, I still panicked.

Three test-filled mornings were accompanied by three further isolated days reading and rereading the Peretti books, and then finally my period came. It was the first time I'd been grateful for it. It felt like a miracle because my cycle had proven itself to be the least reliable part of my life, and that was saying a lot.

For thirty more days, I rotated between two ugly skirts and tops I'd been given to wear. I dug a ditch just outside of the school windows, twelve feet long and five feet deep. I then filled the ditch in. I scraped paint off fence posts near the barn and then painted the posts the same color. Toward the end of my thirty days, when I was once again allowed social interaction with other kids, I had to sit on our front step after school and cut thick, black inner tubes into "rubber bands." Though my daytime hours were still isolated, and once again had me reading the books, I suspected the purpose of my rubber band late afternoons was to embarrass me. I didn't care. By the end, those sessions usually had me in tears because my right hand ached so badly from the cutting. Once they were done, and my Thirty Hours of Physical Labor was marked complete, the "rubber bands" were thrown away. My right thumb developed an aching burn and stiffness that winter and was finally diagnosed with arthritis roughly four years later.

Once the thirty-days punishment was over, I was allowed to unpack my things and resume my everyday life. As I pulled Papa's photo from the box, I sobbed. "I'm so sorry, Papa. I'm so sorry I'm not better. I don't know how to be better."

For a long time after that, he lived in the back of my closet, upside down. I couldn't bring myself to see his face, and to this day, whenever I see a photo of this man I still love so deeply, I am taken back to that evening.

It was several months later when I happened to run into Jim's mom in the church kitchen. I had gone to great lengths to avoid their family whenever we were at church. Her outrage at me was understandable. She stood with a pitcher in her hand, screaming at me. She told me I should be ashamed of myself, that I was pathetic and a slut ... that I had no idea the damage I'd caused.

I absorbed everything she said, my eyes glued to the linoleum floor, painfully aware of the dozens of eyes and ears nearby, frozen and taking it all in.

No one came to my rescue, and no one intervened as this woman in her forties verbally assaulted a fifteen-year-old girl. No one stepped in because they all knew I was just a dirty Ranch kid, and whatever her reason, she was justified.

A few weeks later I heard her husband had died. They'd learned he had cancer around the time my own life had blown up, and they'd had many months of intense grief and stress. My takeaway was not that her anger toward me was a reflection of a grieving wife and mother, but that I had traumatized their family during an already horrible time and would have to bear the burden of that reality for the rest of my life.

I perceived it this way because this was the message with which the news had been delivered.

Our Ranch family left that church then and moved on to church-hopping within the approved network of local churches. It was made clear my actions had brought shame upon our houseparents, and this was best for the family.

When I was forty-four, Jim popped up in my "people you may know" on Facebook, and on a whim, I messaged him. For nearly thirty years I had carried this heavy regret. To the point that, when I would allow myself to think about it, waves of crippling nausea would debilitate me.

I poured my heart out in apology over Messenger. I knew nothing I could say would help repair the damage of what I had caused in his family.

He had no idea what I was talking about. He remembered we'd "dated," but not much beyond that. We chatted about his family, his life in the decades since. It was a nice conversation and he assured me I had nothing to feel guilty about, that whatever had happened hadn't really impacted them enough for him or his sister to remember it.

Sisters

{To my sister: "Renegades" by X Ambassadors}

As a girl, I lost hours praying for a brother or sister. I was willing to accept either until my cousin Kyle stayed with us one summer. He was older and slept on the top bunk in my bedroom in our little narrow trailer. The short life-chapter with Kyle was the best one I lived inside of that trailer. My partner in crime, ever patient to play Barbies in exchange for adventures hunting frogs, I hoped Kyle would never leave. Once he did and life resumed to the former normal, my prayers leaned a lot heavier toward begging for an older brother.

Logistically, this prayer made no sense, but I was a dumb little girl with no real grasp on how families worked and became.

Growing up, I was told that my biological father had a son and daughter, and sometimes when I would daydream about having a real dad, I'd imagine how awesome life would be with them too. Having nothing to base these imaginary people on, I would reference various characters from TV. It was never very fun imagining them, though, so eventually I stopped. While I didn't have a real dad, I did have a dad (of sorts), so that part was easier to imagine. The sibling ache was so raw that I could not bring myself to accept that there could be an actual brother and sister out there somewhere. *Did they know about me? Did they ache for me too?*

On the flip side, the dad I did have, my mom's boyfriend, had two sons at his real home. A handful of times when I was young, I asked my mom about my "brothers" and when I would get to meet them. This conversation never went well, and eventually I began to accept that these stranger-boys were never going to be the older brothers I prayed for.

Thankfully, those sibling prayers were answered on a timeline that was not my own. I have never been sad that I walked through the abuses of my early childhood alone. I know that there were other homes which harbored other evil secrets, but I have always felt relieved that the little gold and white trailer knew only mine.

June of my fifteenth year paved the way for some defining moments. While I felt like I was on decade ten of group-home life, it was only my third summer there. It was the first summer I didn't fly home to New Mexico for a visit. My grandmother was dealing with breast cancer, though no one had told me. She sent me a letter in September explaining the months of my family's silence. I understood why they felt the need to be quiet about it, but also, I knew that, once again, being excluded had contributed to my damage.

One average summer Sunday in early June, our house got a new girl. This sort of thing happened all the time, and though it carried an exciting energy of change, it also brought the dreaded annoyance of changes and intrusion. My roommate, prior to this twelve-year-old invading our space, had been the sweetest little blonde five-year-old girl named Maegy. We were two girls in a house full of boys, except for our house mom and our houseparents' birth daughter. The details were different in every house because the parents set the tone for that house's lifestyle. There was a house that loved board games, Renaissance-styled things, and role-playing games. They were a theatrical group, very artistic, dramatic, and nurturing. Within their house, emotions were high, but there were attachments formed between the houseparents and the kids. They marched to their own rhythm, which most of the other staff did not approve of, so in addition to being labeled the *fun house*, they were also the outcasts.

This was not the house I lived in.

Reconnecting with former Ranch kids always reaffirms what I imagined they thought our house was like. From the outside looking in, our house appeared to be run in a stricter and more oppressive way. There were unrealistically high expectations on us kids, while we were also held at a distance, with little to no nurturing or emotional connection. Though it wasn't always like that, this perception isn't far from the truth. When Maegy needed comfort from a scraped knee or a bad dream, she knew to seek me out. When she was consistently punished in borderline child abuse by today's standards, it was me she turned to for love and guidance. I would comfort her, sure, but I would also talk with her about her sassy attitude and how to change certain behaviors. Within our house, we had our own undercurrent of how things were done. The boys looked to Ryan, and sweet little Maegy looked to me. It worked, and I was happy. Throwing this new twelve-year-old girl into the mix was not ideal. I was resentful of the kink her presence had created.

Also, she annoyed me.

My ability to empathize with Sherri, the terrified and confused twelve-year-old girl sleeping on my top bunk, was nonexistent. I had no grace for what she was going through because I had never been able to relate to overdramatic and needy people. She wanted to be coddled, reassured, and comforted 24/7, and I was very much the wrong person to do that. I did not waste an ounce of thought on how wrong it was that she had been placed in a group home on her twelfth birthday. She was jealous of my bond with Maegy, and no matter how often I explained to her that Maegy was five and we'd been together longer, she couldn't understand.

When Sherri witnessed me handling many of Maegy's disciplines, she grew even more jealous. She began doing blatantly rude things, assuming I'd take her into the bathroom and spank her or put her into time out.

I did not do this. She did get in trouble by our houseparents, and her consequences were as awful as Maegy's often were. Sweet, feisty Maegy was not sad for her. Maegy was relieved that maybe she would no longer be so scrutinized. I was not sad for Sherri either because she was annoying and I just wanted her to go home. I was happy to torment her subtly and reject her demands for coddling.

I was so annoyed by Sherri, and most people around at that time would be in complete agreement with me. She was *a lot*. But also, a bitter sort of apathy settled into me. While I was falling asleep wishing to wake up in a world where Sherri would be going back to her real home, there were other elements at play. No matter how unkind I was to her, this girl would not give up on her obsession to have me love her.

Not long after her arrival, Sherri got her period. That day, I eased up on her a little bit. I also told pretty much every single person I saw. I told my boyfriend Ben, who she was obsessed with. Her reactions were always so dramatic that it was fun to tease her, and sadly I was not alone in this. Later that evening, Nora called me, and I told her too. She asked to talk to Sherri, and though I'm surprised the houseparents allowed it, Sherri got to talk to her for a moment. I don't know what my mom said to her, but Sherri developed an obsession for my mother, too, which, admittedly, I liked a little. She began talking about how great my mom was and how I was so lucky. It was ignorance, but the fact she believed it seemed to validate that secret little-girl hope inside of me. I wanted my mother to be a great mom, the mom I deep down believed she was capable of being. Sherri was the first person ever to believe Nora was this mom, and I plugged into that. It didn't matter that she had no honest-to-goodness clue about Nora at all.

The significant thing the summer brought, in addition to the arrival of Sherri, was my relationship with Ben. This was entirely different from my other relationships because this one was "legal and permitted" by Ranch rules. I was fifteen and had worked hard, so I was on a high enough level (within the behavior-based level system) to have a relationship. Being slightly younger than me, Ben was technically not old enough, but because he was a staff kid, it was OK. I was becoming good friends with Ben's sister, Missy, and liked their family and loved that their lives were far more normal than mine. It was summer and life was good. There were sunny days, bike rides, swim nights, horseback rides, river rafting adventures, and camping trips to the mountains. The only bad thing, really, was the annoying twelve-year-old taking up space in my room.

In those same first few weeks of summer, I received a letter from my father.

My mom had reached out to him and given him my address, should he want to contact me. I chose to ignore that I was fifteen years old, and she had apparently known how to get in touch with him all along. When I spoke to her about it, she said that she believed he should finally step up and be my dad. She had zero faith that he would act on it.

But he did.

With those handwritten pages there were a few photos—pictures of my older brother, a photo of my older sister with her husband, one of my father taken at Disney World, and a photo booth frame of my father and his two younger daughters. In his letter he called these faces my brother and sisters.

It felt like the moment I had ached and prayed for.

Growing up, whenever I had daydreamed about my father, 1980s actor Joe Penny was the face and voice I knew. Every time he appeared on my TV, I felt the pang of my familiar childhood father-ache. Having an actual human being on the other end of a letter or phone call was incomprehensible. While my life had held many instances where I needed the presence of a counselor to help me process what was happening, the addition of my father to the mix was the biggest. The adults around expected me to automatically know how to handle it. Under our roof, any emotional outbursts or meltdowns were treated with steep consequences. It was clear that I was expected to just grow up and handle the problem with maturity.

I tried.

With each letter, holding pages that he'd held, I slipped deeper into a terrifying place inside. Words about it all would come bubbling out, but no adults wanted to listen. At the mention of him, Nora's negativity was louder than ever.

Because my houseparents were so anti my mother, they were instantly on his team. They knew nothing about him but pushed me more and more toward him. They began to tell me I should go live with him, that he was my father, and if I wanted to, I could. The idea of living with my father was way too big for me to process, but I did want to be with him. I'm sure the biggest reason was the thought of getting to leave the Ranch and live a normal life. Despite the romanticizing by Ranch staff, there would have been nothing normal about any of it.

My houseparents continued to push the topic while also making fun of people in Kentucky because "they were all barefoot and inbred." I never really knew what they wanted. *Was it for me to reconnect with my father or just to further mess with my head?* Eventually, my father began talking to me about coming to live with him and his family too. I loved talking to my father on the phone. He was funny and faithful to call on Sundays. The houseparents seldom listened in and never held me to a strict fifteen minutes. There were some calls that lasted well over an hour, and those were the best.

Months passed, and there were only two people I could be open and honest with about the whole ordeal as it continued unfolding so uncomfortably far outside of my control. There was Ryan, of course, but the most surprising was Sherri.

I had been talking one night about how all these people thought I should go live with my father. I don't remember saying it *to* her as much as speaking the words out loud to myself, long after lights-out. From the top bunk came the sound of whimpering. I didn't ask her what was wrong because I was cloaked in my constant annoyance with her, and she cried a lot. After a time, she began shrieking with her tear-strained, annoying voice about how she didn't want me to leave. She didn't want me to go live in Kentucky. She didn't want to be in this place without me. She loved me so much, and all she wanted was for me to love her too, but she wasn't worthy of that.

While she sobbed on and on about what she wanted and didn't want, with Meagy's deep little sleep breaths on the bed next to mine in the background, something Sherri said lingered in my brain: *I love you and just want you to love me, but I'm not enough.* I knew how that felt. While so much of her was foreign to me, I understood that place.

I flipped the internal switch controlling my feelings and responded to her. Did this make Sherri less annoying? Not even close. But it did change everything.

One very sad day in midsummer, Ryan got to go home. It was a time of rejoicing alongside him while once again grieving for me. I had long since identified Ryan as the exact fit for the gaping hole I had all those times when I had begged God for a brother. Long before we met, I spent summers in Phoenix while Ryan was living with his own family just miles away. As I cried those prayers, God had shone down on Ryan, and our paths toward each other were forged. In my forties now, I am sad to say that we are no longer in touch. I believe we might be loosely connected on Facebook, but that just isn't the same. Ryan will always be the closest thing to a real brother I've ever known.

Ryan, true to form, did call regularly. He wrote letters and stayed a very active part of this little sister's life for a very long time. Even though he had gone home to that Arizona sunshine and his real family (complete with real sisters), he did not abandon me.

With the daily absence of Ryan, however, came the most miraculous change—another new girl! Because we couldn't live four to a room, our house kids were rearranged, and suddenly Maegy and I were in one room, while Sherri and the new girl were across the hall, with a Jack and Jill bathroom between.

Though I had already softened toward her, it wasn't until we were no longer in the same room and could steal away to meet in the bathroom—sharing heart-to-heart confessions, talking through heartbreaks, strategizing problems, or just connecting—that I realized the truth that prayers from a lifetime before were still being answered.

Not only had I been lucky enough to get the best brother ever, but I had a sister too.

Even better, just beyond my new bedroom window was a large weeping willow tree. The summer found me spending many afternoons reading beneath its beautiful canopy of tiny tears.

Circle

{To the J of then, from then-M: "Oceans" by Seafret}

The heartbreak of my losing Maegy was life-defining. She was adopted by a family we knew fairly well, and she'd taken with her my beloved Pound Puppy, Spot. Once again, I found a piece of my heart pleading with me to hold on to one of the few things I cherished, and once again I'd given in. That sweet little blonde girl could have asked me for anything, and I would have said yes. In the solace of our joint bathroom, Sherri was my one and only confidant. It was there we talked about her crushes and my heartbreaks. I had become close with a flaky non-Ranch boy I'd known for years. Trevor had become the fill-in big brother, mentor, distraction, and likely a dozen other things I needed him to be. He was several years older, and eventually our friendship became a trusted one where my houseparents were concerned. We'd go to coffee or movies, and eventually he helped me get permission to start attending the youth group he helped lead. Even so, he was unreliable. I knew I couldn't count on him, but I still kept him close. As much as it would infuriate me, there was also a freedom in knowing what to expect with him. Disappointments? Yes, but no surprises.

The undeserved devotion to my mother never wavered. She became little more than a wish, really. I clung to every word she said, into which I infused hope of her love. I saw little to no effort, yet the dialing of a phone or a short note showing up in my mail meant she thought about me sometimes. This felt like everything.

I still spent many afternoons imagining her in my room, surprising me, fingertips caressing the sleeves of my sweaters and the spines of my books. The most important person in my world lived only in my daydreams. The only person I could confide in and trust with all of me had become Sherri. We were well into adulthood before I recognized this because our attachment had formed so organically. Macrofocused in my fishbowl world, I walked the balance beam act of living in the now on one side and dreaming about a practical but better tomorrow on the other. I had a few friends who were girls, but for the most part I was a different (more polished and reserved) version of myself with them. It wasn't that I didn't like girls; I didn't trust them. I could appreciate girl talk, but I was never going to genuinely be me with another girl. Sherri was my one exception.

Sherri knew everything. She knew I was able to be almost myself with the guys I allowed in. She was my confidant during the relationship with Ben. It had been healthy and fun, until one day that changed. I knew I was to blame in many ways. I learned I was able to manipulate the affections of boys, and, though I carried guilt from that, I also had to admit that I liked finally being the one in control of some part of my life. Eventually, we broke up.

I needed to be done with boys for a while.

My small life consisted of flaky Trevor and Sherri, the most unexpected surprise of all. Somehow, as familiar faces left us and new ones came, Mike's former best friend William and I had grown close. Though Mike predicted we'd fall in love, we loved each other (almost codependently) in a different way. Early on in our friendship journey, we were able to realize that not only were our mother wounds similar, but also the ways we felt about our moms. Our hurts identified pieces of themselves in one another. For the first time in my entire life, I felt like I could belong to someone. I felt valued, seen, and understood. We just *fit*.

When he would do stupid things—which he did often because he was a hurting teen boy—I would call him out for his stupidity and speak the truth. Sherri both worshipped William and resented him because he triggered within her a deep sense of rejection. He followed Ricky's footsteps well, becoming the player among our community's girls. He kissed and messed around with most of them, though never me. Sherri wanted to make the cut, but she didn't. She also wanted him to value her the way he valued me, set apart from other girls and holding a piece of him that no one else had access to. When she couldn't get in there either, she jealously resented him. For a long while growing up, the only issue between us was her expectation of me to choose her over him. I can't explain it, but this was something I could never do.

After Ryan left, his best friend Jared moved into our house. I knew Jared well since he was the best friend of my brother. It was a natural transition, and, to my surprise, a brotherly bond formed with him as well. He and Ryan weren't much alike, but I had learned that when you put kids in a confined space day in and day out, deep and intimate relationships happen that probably wouldn't have on the outside. Most of our friendships were like that.

Jared became the second brother I didn't know I needed—my adviser, protector, and confidant when I really needed one. He taught me a lot about stability. I loved him deeply. When he left, the loss only grew the gaping hole Ryan left. I still had Trevor, who I believed was way too good for me and also unreliable. Each time I was with him, I wondered when he'd realize I did not deserve to be there. Spending time with Trevor was my key to life outside the Ranch. We were as close as we could have been, though obviously it couldn't have been the same as with the others in my life as he lived on the outside of our fishbowl. I knew that I would never have another Ryan or Jared. For one, I was older and no longer needed a brother-like figure to swoop in. Two, I knew no one else could ever take their places. I'd been so lucky ...

This was my circle in those days. Aside from two absent brothers and a flaky friend/mentor, I had William and Sherri and the frustrating, competitive battle between them.

The summer I was sixteen, an older boy named James moved into our house. It was bittersweet to hear everyone constantly talk about how nice it was to restore that sense of balance to our Ranch family. Because Ryan (and then Jared) and I had been so close, it was as though this was something the staff expected to happen with James.

One major difference was that James was a few months younger than me, rather than a few years older. In addition, he was angry and full of teenage early-90s angst. He maintained his love of Metallica, even when he was only allowed to listen to soft contemporary Christian music. He held tight to his atheistic beliefs, despite it being a Ranch-punishable offense. He painted canvases and spent hours filling sketch pads and brooding. He had a darker sense of humor, and whatever he did included his artistic touch. He even carved beautiful faces into our government-issued blocks of butter. Clothed in black and dark gray, James was the epitome of everything angry and artistic. He was dark, where I chased the light. He was angry and real, while I was terrified and fake in my quest to make someone find me loveable. James was happy to push my buttons and bait me, and I tried to avoid him as much as possible. This is hard to do when you live in the same house and have the eyes of people watching you, expecting history to repeat itself and an alliance to form. For those first few weeks, it was not uncommon for afternoons to be soiled by heated arguments between the two of us.

It might be that I was angry it wasn't Ryan or Jared there instead. He lived in their room and took their place when it came to palling around with our house dad. Maybe I was tired of change. Somehow, as life transitioned from summer to fall, James and I did manage to establish a civil routine. He could sketch out the way my brain envisioned the poetry pieces I'd begun dabbling with. While each of us almost always had a novel in our hand, we gravitated toward very different genres. Even though I mocked his science fiction and he made fun of my varied taste, we could still sit reading side by side in silence for hours. Every once in a while, one of us would tap the other, jolting them from their fiction-filled escape, to share a well-written line or thought from the book we held. Most evenings this would lead to us dog-earing a page and turning slightly toward each other as deep conversations took shape.

In my memory, it is as though, in a single day, we would be sitting at the long kitchen table debating ethics and then walking away frustrated but also living this synchronized life of sameness. Same stride while walking, same rhythm within the walls of our shared home. A mutual appreciation and respect seemed to appear one day, though his passion for deliberately frustrating me never faded. I never referred to James as my brother. Though she annoyed him, Sherri adored him and would try to convince me that James was far more my best friend than William was. This wasn't true either. The two situations were not comparable.

Neither brother nor best friend, he was simply James.

In those days I was obsessed with music—the "illegal" music that I'd listen to in secret, laying my head on a quiet speaker, in bed, for hours after everyone had gone to sleep. I was mostly into emerging early 90s hip-hop and grunge, even some top-40. When I wasn't hiding and played music at a normal volume, it was usually Elvis Presley or what little Christian music was close enough to trendy, but still allowed. Sherri learned all her best tricks from me, so she, too, would fall asleep with the radio under her pillow, listening to forbidden music. This is something I will tease her about until eternity, because her "rebellion" consisted of a station called K106. It was 1992 and this girl was getting her defiant kicks from slow jams by Air Supply and Barry Manilow, with a scattering of elevator music thrown in.

Other than my love of music and the very rare coffee trip or movie with Trevor, I didn't have many interests. I didn't collect anything, though I had developed a slight obsession of Disney's *Aladdin* ...

My early-Ranch bestie, Tammy, came back to Boise as a freshman at the local Bible college. On occasion, I was allowed to spend the weekend at her dorm. Tammy passionately loved *The Little Mermaid* for as long as I had known her. It had been so much a part of her personality that I'd forgotten how much she loved it until I was spending the night in her dorm room. There she was, dreaming, tucked inside her *Little Mermaid* sheets, while I lay in her absent roommate's bed, wide awake and staring up at a poster board collage of photos. I felt a little jealous, looking at those pictures. There were photos with friends, a smattering of glitter hearts, and the consistent face of one particular boy appearing again and again. It was clear, based on the way they stood in shots together, they were dating. I wanted to hang glittery photos on my wall of my boyfriend and me. I wanted normal things. I wanted to be someone memorable. I hadn't met Tammy's roommate, but those nights I slept in her bed made me feel like I knew her. On photo paper and poster board, she'd become someone. Between Tammy's Ariel bedding and decor and her roommate's evident popularity, I decided that I needed a *thing* that could be mine.

Before it even hit theaters, I decided *Aladdin* would be my thing. I followed Tammy's path and latched on to a Disney movie. Maybe my psychological wiring guaranteed it, but whatever the reason, when I did finally see *Aladdin*, I fell in love. The music, the cutting-edge animation, the various pop-culture references Robin Williams threw in ... it was beyond what I had hoped for. But also, I saw myself within the story. I identified with the trapped and powerless Jasmine and the discarded Aladdin who the world found it impossible to love.

With my babysitting money, I was allowed to take Sherri to see it. We had never been able to do anything like that before, so for the two of us, it was an amazing experience. I don't know if she liked the movie as much as I did, but she loved me spending money on her, going to the movies together, and hanging out like real sisters as we blended in with the normal people milling about around us. She coveted the normal moments, just like me. After the movie, our house dad picked us up, and I treated them both to fried ice cream at a local Mexican place called Maria's. Sherri and I enthusiastically recapped the movie over bites of sugary goodness. It was one of the happiest nights I'd ever had.

This is how *Aladdin* became my thing.

For Christmas, the biggest request on my Christmas list was *Aladdin* sheets. Tammy had her Disney sheets, and, while I was pretty good about making it seem like I was unique and different, deep down I wanted to be just like everyone else. (I didn't get them.)

Despite how very UN-Disney-movie James was, he gave me the most meaningful Christmas gift I could remember receiving—a hardcover children's book with beautiful illustrations of *Aladdin*.

He wrote, "For Misty, Love James."

The movie had released on Thanksgiving of that year. He purchased the book when his family had visited the weekend before, so I had not even seen this movie I had already sworn my eternal love to. I'm still so touched by this boy's ability to look past his own judgment and spend money on something because he knew it mattered to me, even if he didn't understand it.

I'd grown to love James. He loved me too. It hadn't been anything that either of us pursued, it just happened. It wasn't intense like it had been with Mike. Maybe because I was older, different. The feelings had grown so naturally that we just sort of woke up one day and realized it, though to be fair, he was aware well before I was. He never mentioned it or probed me for my feelings. Instead, as our normal routines carried out, he waited. The evening I realized how deep my feelings ran, his response was, "Finally. I love you, too, you know." I hadn't even said a word, he'd just known I'd finally caught up to him.

We lived in the same house and so naturally, these sorts of relationships were not allowed. We'd had the conversation about our feelings, but never really acted on them. There was no sneaking around, no secret letters, nothing that broke the rules save for the knowledge that we had deep feelings for each other.

It all felt very mature.

My first walk on the beach was in conversation with him, in Florence, Oregon. I fell deeper for him there on that shore, having finally made it to the ocean. He had become the person I could share my writing with and was the only other person I knew who could lose himself in deep, intentional conversation. Both of these things felt a bit like life.

He saw me for me, even when half of the world saw only the pretend me that I put out in order to earn their love.

Living under the same roof, he'd seen my teenage mood swings, my bed head, my unwashed morning makeup face, and had been close by for emotional calls with family. He hated so many of the things I loved ...

He saw me and he loved me.

One day after school, as he passed by in the kitchen, he placed his palm on the small of my back and whispered that he loved me. His face lingered for a perfect, hesitant moment at my ear before he continued walking by. Another time, during one of our evening conversations when, books in our laps, we could talk for hours while the rest of the house seemed to tune us out as much as we did them, he told me he was scared he would push me away. I was so macrofocused on how confusing it felt to have these vulnerable conversations that I promised him I wouldn't let him, when he begged me to make sure he didn't.

I flew home to New Mexico for Christmas. I was sixteen and a senior in high school, and everyone in my family took notice of how mature I'd become. It may have been less maturity and more confidence. I was doing things educationally I hadn't imagined myself capable of. I was maintaining a long-distance relationship with my father, and seventeen months in, this had become as much a part of my unique normality as anything else. There, celebrating the Christmas holiday with my birth family, I was proud to prove that not only did I have a real relationship with my father, but I called him *Dad*. This silly thing had changed me. I babysat regularly (happily absorbing as much MTV as I could after the kids were asleep, thank you very much), and made my own money. In all the ways that I could be self-sufficient and independent, I was. When an entire year passed between visits, my gradual growth seemed more sudden to them.

In addition to my growth, that Christmas I had the first big, all-out screaming fight I'd ever had with my grandmother. With years of my mom whispering in my ear about what a devil my grandmother was, it was easy to subconsciously absorb it. When she mentioned one night that I should focus on school and not boys or friends because I was struggling so much, I felt slapped. *What?*

I was on level four of the behavior system, the highest level available. It was difficult to get there and even more difficult to maintain. I stayed on it for as long as I was in touch with my father. I maintained my grades and chores and was allowed to babysit and have certain freedoms with Trevor because my houseparents trusted me. I was never in trouble, and I was completing my junior and senior years of high school within one school year. I was doing *amazingly*, and how dare she say otherwise? I had never seen a Ranch kid thrive as well as I was, and the crushing news that I still wasn't good enough hit me hard.

The screaming match was equally aggressive. Short and tiny, that woman could spar. Of course, she could. I had seen these matches play out at nearly every holiday, though they usually involved my mother, and this was *my* first time in the ring.

It felt like everyone had been waiting for me, as Nora's daughter, to assume the role.

Hours later, both of us tearstained and depleted of anything good, my grandmother came into the bathroom where I'd been hiding. In that gold-accented master bath, she filled in gaps of our story I had never thought to question and showed me a shoebox of letters.

The State of New Mexico (more accurately, Child Protective Services) in the summer of 1988 had deemed the evidence from the investigation of sexual molestation "inconclusive." As a result of their review, they had decided that my mother was neither a fit parent nor was she qualified to provide a safe home for her only daughter. They gave her sixty days to find an alternative living situation for me. Before I told the doctor about the abuse, Melanie told her dad, Ray. Ray, filled with a mixed array of emotions, went to my grandmother. Seeing her worst fears about my mom's boyfriend coming true, my grandmother had gone to the authorities.

My sweet, hard-working, Jesus-loving grandmother had always hated Nora's boyfriend. Why wouldn't she? He had a wife and kids and seemed to enable my mother in the worst ways. At my grandparents' anniversary party just before my grandfather passed away, my family had quietly asked my mom to have her boyfriend leave. He was not a part of our family, nor did anyone know or accept him as such. This was a private family gathering to celebrate something special and to give family members a chance to find closure and make memories with Papa that weren't about cancer, death, and goodbyes. It had been made clear to her well before the actual party that her boyfriend was not invited. There we were, though, the three of us marching in and crashing the event. I was seven and had only wanted to be with Papa and see my family. My mom and her boyfriend had intentionally set out to cause trouble, and after a dramatic scene, they stormed out, taking me with them.

In the years that followed, my mother made it clear that her world revolved around him. When my grandmother would call to see if I wanted to go to Wednesday night church or drive out to get a soda, if he was there, my mother would respond with things like, "He's giving her a bath right now." Or, "They are cuddling and watching a movie." He wasn't my father, and though she didn't know about the pornographic ways he and my mother behaved within our home, she did know something was very wrong. Times were different then, and her biggest fear was that she would open her mouth, no one would help, and she would lose me altogether. Sometimes we have impossible choices, and we do the best we can.

Once she knew for a fact that abuse was really occurring because I began talking about it, she didn't know how to say out loud how she had failed me. She blamed herself in so many ways. When the ultimatum from the state came, she had already petitioned the courts on my behalf. It was denied on the grounds that our small town was just *too small*. I'd have to be placed in foster care elsewhere in the county. Ray and Lorrie also tried to be my new home, but as they lived next door to my mother, their request couldn't be allowed either. It's ironic, really. With how little my mother actually cared about me, I could have lived in either of those places and everything probably would have been OK, save for one thing: Me. I never could have let my mother's disregard for me to exist so close; I would have tried to manipulate her, convince her, and force her to want me, and probably would have died trying.

I had written to my aunt and begged her to let me move to Phoenix with her, but she had never said a word about it to me. My grandmother shared with me that my aunt and uncle had wanted me, but they knew my mother. They knew that, because of how often they came to town and how unstable she could be, this could only happen if my mom would agree to full guardianship. She would not. Her reason? "I don't want her, but I don't want you to have her either."

My grandmother knew about the Christmas family who wanted me several years before. My mother had legally made it so they could no longer contact me when it was all said and done. It had been them, in an effort to fight for me, who had gotten the ball rolling on the second investigation the year before. An investigation that went nowhere because how could it, on the testimony of a foster child, nearly three years after the fact? Still, they tried.

The shoebox full of letters were actually behavior reports, issued nearly every month by the administrator of the Ranch. They described me as a bully, dishonest, and said I spent large amounts of time in trouble. Reading them, penned in the administrator's familiar script, I could not wrap my brain around all the details unfolding.

More than anything, as I read the lies about me, I was devastated that she believed them. I was sad to realize she didn't know me—none of my family knew the first thing about me. They only knew the Misty that was presented to them by way of crafted letters and reports. It was all too much. I couldn't wait to leave and go home. I couldn't wait for the predictable security of William and Sherri; I couldn't wait to be back with James. I wanted to be done with this place, these people. I no longer knew what was true and what was not. I could not begin to reconcile the fact that people had once believed me and fought for me because I had still painfully been kept on the outside, looking in.

I could not fathom that no matter how hard I tried, someone would always believe the worst in me, and my family would take their word over mine.

The years of believing I had not been worth fighting for or worth loving had scarred pieces of me. It felt like no one seemed to notice or care about that.

I'd had my plan for a while. I hashed it over at length with Trevor in the months leading up to Christmas. He was my wise counsel on the outside. I considered every angle I knew to consider and saw the plan as flawless. On my last night in Lordsburg before flying back to Boise, I laid it out. Nora was, outside of Trevor, the first person I'd told. She was, it would seem, always the first person.

Her approval had sealed it as my next step, and being the planner that I have always been, I found myself fortunate to have a lot of alone time to work out the details. My return flight was stranded for two days in Las Vegas due to weather. An airport is an uncomfortable place to stay for any length of time. I was a minor, despite how grown-up I felt, so the airline kept tabs on me and supplied me with meal and beverage vouchers. I called my mom Collect often and worked incessantly on "the plan."

Prior to the start of my junior year, when I learned that my mother would not allow me to go to Kentucky to live with my father, I applied to Kentucky Christian College. I was accepted for the 1994–1995 school year, with an almost-full scholarship. When I originally decided to attempt my junior and senior years together, my houseparents had inquired about being able to attend KCC a year earlier, which they said would be fine ... with my custodial parent's permission because I'd only be seventeen. It was no surprise that at the mention of the word *Kentucky*, Nora's answer was a resounding *NO*. My dilemma had me trapped. I knew graduating early was the key to me no longer being a Ranch kid, and above all things, that was always the top goal.

When I first began to panic, William confided that he wanted me to stay and graduate when I was supposed to. He didn't want to be there without me, and I knew every inch of the place of fear and heartache he was coming from. I also knew I couldn't stay. I had already been there far too long. I knew what it felt like to be discarded and unwanted. I had been chucked in the bin my entire life, over and over again. I had been consistently determined to be easy to leave so my plan would ensure that the people in my circle would never feel that way.

Sherri & Misty 1992

Plans

{To William: "Broken" by Seether, featuring Amy Lee}

The Plan:

- Get a real, full-time job, somehow.

- Save everything I make.

- Have enough money saved to get a small, two-bedroom apartment. (I had a dear friend my age who was emancipated from her parents and living on her own. I saw this as doable.)

- Once I have my own car and apartment, begin visiting William, like the two of us had seen family members visit other kids while we had sat there together, alone.

- Make sure he has the shower soap he loves, spending money for fun things, and new (cool) clothes for school. (All of these things other kids had and took for granted while we watched.)

- When William turns eighteen, bring him home to live with me. We are family.

Two days in Vegas led to a quick detour in Salt Lake City, where we were once again stranded due to weather. In the days of land-line telephones and no cell phones, there was always a lot more hoping than updated knowledge. I had no idea what was going on back in my Ranch world. My biggest hope was that they'd figure it out and meet me at the airport once I finally made it.

I was stranded in Salt Lake City for only one night, and it resulted in me being awarded a hotel room voucher because I was a minor. I had befriended an eighteen-year-old girl who was also Idaho bound, returning to college for her second semester. When the shuttle called me to board, I invited my "seventeen-year-old cousin" to stay in my room as well.

The hot shower and plush bedding of that hotel room held more luxurious comfort than anything I had ever known. I slept like a baby, not wanting to get up and head to the airport the next morning. My flight was right on time, and I landed in Boise before noon. While being stranded in an airport had never been one of my worst fears, getting off a plane with no one there to greet me had been. This is one of the things I miss the most about flying pre-9/11, loved ones waiting for their people as they exited the plane.

Every time I would exit a plane, I was a bundle of nerves. What if I'd scan the crowd and no one would be there? How stupid would I feel? Would everyone know? Would they think no one loved me? My insecurities that I was worth nothing ran deep.

For the first time ever, after being stranded and arriving home four days late, I escaped the belly of the airplane and found no one waiting for me. I phoned the Ranch and waited, fatigue from the journey and crappy airport food setting in fast. As I sat with nothing to do but wait and think, the heaviness of what had happened with my grandmother and all I had learned felt crushing. Eventually, my houseparents showed up, all nine kids in tow, and things went from bad to worse.

It started with James avoiding looking at me. By the time evening came, he'd progressed to exiting a room whenever I was present. It was the sting of the deepest rejection, for reasons I did not understand. A week into this new way of coexistence, chore rotation had him washing dishes while I dried. When he realized this, he got angry and stormed off to his room, leaving me standing there helpless and in tears. My houseparents pulled me into their room, commanding, "Whatever happened between the two of you, whatever is going on, it needs to get better. You need to fix it."

I didn't know how to fix anything. After a week back, I didn't know how to *do* anything. How did this person know me and care about me one day, and then be unable to tolerate my presence the next? I thought about the reports telling my family how horrible I was, and my entire world felt like an illusion. I wondered why it mattered if I finished school. Why did it matter if I did anything at all? Everyone saw only the negative about me anyhow.

That night, James eventually came back to the kitchen. Dishes did not go well. A plate got broken, tears (mine) were cried, anger on both our parts was voiced. It seemed everything I said or did was fuel to his rage. Naturally, my anger was the only one that made any sense.

I longed to blare music that conveyed my feelings and drown out the rest of the world. Because I was at the Ranch, I could not do this. Instead, I lay in the dark of my bedroom blaring Elvis. Elvis because I loved him. Elvis because my father loved him, so we shared something and I needed that. Elvis because it was the closest I could get to rebellious teen music, and I was trying to send a message to anyone who would notice me.

This disconnected life became the new normal, as everything else before it had. I pretended I hadn't read the reports. I chose not to think about the things my grandmother had revealed. James and I settled into an amicable game of pretending the other person didn't exist. It all sucked, and when I needed him the most, I missed my friend. It is horrible to miss someone so much when you are within arm's reach of them every single day.

I couldn't allow myself to add James or any other person I cared about to the long list of losses, so I focused instead on being angry. I focused on my plan. With long evenings suddenly available, I took a full-time nannying position working three full days and one half day each week while doing schoolwork at night. It felt good to be doing something, making progress on my plan. I was confident that things were moving in the right direction.

For two afternoons a week, I was able to go to school. There in our small classroom, I sat next to William, who had become incessantly needy for my attention, and across from James, who seemed to teeter between wanting to murder me and pretending he already had. Those two afternoons each week were hell. The energy between us all was dark.

One afternoon in early March, William asked me to quit my job and come back to school. I thought he was joking, so I played along. As things progressed, he demanded I stop working on my senior year and stay until I was eighteen. I explained to him that I wasn't going to do that, and I finally told him about my plan. The plan that, at the heart of everything, was in motion for him. I was moving my future in a direction that could provide William with all the things that I had ached for. I had known, long before everything had gone south with James, that becoming the advocate, family, and safe place for William to fall was my responsibility. This was the truth that I was most certain about. For the rest of that afternoon, the years of abandonment seemed to fade from him as he accepted the promises I offered. Suddenly, this cad of a teen boy was just a child, wanting deeply to be protected, cared for, and seen as enough.

Because I was still babysitting on the weekends, it wasn't until the following Wednesday afternoon that I saw William again. The moment I walked into the schoolroom, he asked if I had quit my job yet. And then this kid, with whom I'd only ever had one actual fight (which he apologized for eleven minutes later and promised we would never fight again), traded cubbies with my sister and moved across our quad of desks, crossing over to the side of the table that hated me.

By my seventeenth birthday, at the end of the month, my best friend had traded me in for a new best friend: James. Suddenly, these two boys who had nothing in common were together constantly. Hating me seemed enough to bond anyone.

I was under extreme stress. It was clear that, since Christmas, I had become less capable of handling things. Everything was falling apart around me, and the one thing I had left to lose was my early graduation. I was stretched thin, and my grades were suffering. I made the decision to quit my job and focus on school. I kept my head down, retreating in defeat. Any confidence or hope I'd had months before was gone. There was no plan, there was no point. Finish school: this was all I could focus on.

When I had spare time, I usually jumped at any opportunity to hang out with Trevor beyond the Ranch's perimeter. Sometimes he followed through, but a lot of the time he stood me up. I both cared and I didn't. I would get mad, but somewhere deep inside, I knew that I deserved it. Why should he want to show up for me anyway?

As a birthday gift, William stood up and peered over our desk wall, offering the sentiment, "Happy birthday, Bitch." It was the look of hatred in his eyes that carried the hardest blow. I didn't care that James laughed or that their little boys' club spent the rest of the day talking about me in hushed tones and giggles.

I was too inexperienced to know that life plays out in seasons, in periods of ebb and flow. While I'd known healthy, positive, and life-giving minutes along the way, I hadn't ever experienced an honest season of good until the summer and autumn when I was sixteen. For the first time I could remember, I felt seen and valued. I felt like I was doing the right things and achieving something. I felt confident and proud of myself. Of course, I wanted it to last forever and naively believed it could.

When I look back with a grown-up perspective, it is glaringly obvious that the biggest disappointment is not which boys I chose or the choices I made; it is the complete absence of any true adult guidance, save that of a college-aged mentor who was struggling within the sea of his own young adult life stuff. In a world of oppressive rules, constant adult supervision, belittling, and dominance, there wasn't anyone genuinely invested enough in me.

On May 28, 1993, in an obnoxious emerald-green formal dress, I graduated from high school. Every face in the audience belonged to the group-home people I saw every single day, except for one college sophomore, who biked fifteen miles to be there because his car broke down. The dozens of missed movies, coffee dates, and other blown-off plans no longer mattered—at the biggest achievement of my life, when no family members had made the trip, Trevor had shown up.

The other two guys in my life had shown up, too, though they weren't mine anymore. James was going home and had asked not to leave until after my graduation. I was happy for him, but I was tired. Both emotionally and physically, I struggled to find energy for even the simplest tasks. In the two months between my birthday and graduation, James and I had come to a sort of peace, at least when we were in the safety of our house. Sometimes he would get angry again for some unspoken reason, and we would spiral, but we always made it back to this new place of fragile, strained, attempted friendship. It was never the same, but I cared about him enough that I was OK with that. I was happy to have him however I had him.

The afternoon of my graduation, a package came from my mom. At that point, no family members told me for certain whether they would be coming. My grandmother would usually drive out in the spring, and this had been the first year she hadn't. I secretly hoped that meant she'd be at the ceremony, but no. I'd mailed my printed letters of invitation, and no one had responded.

The arrival of Nora's package was the answer I had been waiting for. I sat in my room alone, reading the card and opening the package, which contained a black hills gold ring. I felt a wave of so many things I could not even try to comprehend. When I walked out, I saw James there, sitting on the other side of my bedroom wall.

"Are you OK?"

I wasn't. I cried and he held me, and it no longer mattered anymore. He was leaving, I was on my way out too. None of the obstacles between us existed anymore, except the ones we built ourselves. He told me once that he loved me and would push me away if I let him because that's how he sabotaged things. I hadn't listened; I was so caught up in the moment. He made me swear I wouldn't let him ruin what we had, yet I failed at that too. It had all gone wrong before I even realized it. The very thing he warned me he would do and that I had promised I wouldn't allow, had happened. I had no idea how to repair the damage, so I just allowed myself to sit there in his embrace and cry tears for everything I had lost—this included losing him as well.

After the ceremony, I made sure to be the good girl I wanted everyone to see me as and made the rounds to speak to everyone in attendance. Once that was done, I stole a quiet moment to fall all over myself with gratitude to Trevor for coming.

While the celebration was still high, our Ranch family had to leave. James was riding a bus home to Oregon, and it was leaving that night. As I was saying goodbye to a few friends, I felt a tap on my shoulder. I turned to see William standing there—it was the first time in months there hadn't been hatred in his expression.

"Can we talk?"

I wanted to, but I couldn't. We were leaving. "Later? Can we talk later? I have to go."

Disappointed, he seemed to soften slightly. "Tomorrow?" I couldn't do that either. I was leaving in the morning for a four-day work weekend at our summer camp.

"Tuesday?" I offered. We both knew that, though I was now a high school graduate, I had no real say over what happened Tuesday or any day. I was still a child, still at the mercy of the people in charge.

I felt a hand on the small of my back, and James's voice was in my ear telling me we had to go.

"I'm proud of you. You did it," William said, barely audible, as I walked away.

"Thanks!" I shouted over my shoulder, making sure to catch his eyes as I mouthed, *Tuesday!* William's mouth formed the slightest smile, which I accepted as encouragement that things were getting better. I wore that encouragement as James and I walked in silence toward the van.

I got home from my work weekend late Monday night. On Tuesday morning, I was told to accompany Sherri and our house dad on some errands. As we were getting ready to leave, I noticed William standing by the office with a duffle bag at his feet.

"What's going on?" The gross feeling crept in—the feeling that came when people made decisions about things that concerned me without including me.

"It doesn't matter." It was clear my house dad wanted that answer to be sufficient. My houseparents knew I was close with William, but there was no investment in our personal lives by the majority of Ranch staff and so they had no idea how close we were.

"It does matter. What's going on?" I was seldom defiant. I tried to get William's attention through my front seat window as we passed. His gaze was glued shamefully to the ground.

"He got kicked out. I don't want to talk about it. You needed to be off the property for a while, so we're going. End of discussion."

William 1992

Letters

{To teenage Misty: "Paint" by The Paper Kites}

Nora Jane had a daughter.

There are many milestone days a girl looks forward to. With each birthday, first day of school, and every other meaningful occasion, Nora hovered in the back of my mind. During volleyball games, my eyes stayed trained on the doorway. I did not know how to get through anything without my mother's presence weighing heavily there too. I never lost faith that she would come through for me.

I never doubted her for one second. I believed she would always be there for me, the one person I could count on. She had done nothing to ensure such faith from me, and yet I gave my heart over to her time and again.

On my sixteenth birthday, the mail carrier brought a shoebox wrapped in a brown grocery bag. I recognized her handwriting immediately, but the package contained no note or card. Inside was a pair of purple, pink, and white Reebok Pumps. The kids who sat around the table as I was allowed to open birthday gifts and cards seethed with jealousy.

"Those shoes cost hundreds of dollars!" one shouted.

I had no clue what a Reebok Pump even was. I wasn't one to care about shoes, sports, or brand-name trendiness. I had been living a sheltered existence for four years, with no TV commercials or glossy advertisements. I had no idea what a lot of things were.

The look in their eyes, though, and the sound of awe in their voices ... I made a note of what mattered most. No one noticed my mom hadn't thought to include any form of "Happy Birthday" or communication; they simply decided my mom must be the *best mom ever* because she'd sent me those shoes.

That is kind of how it was, being Nora's daughter. No matter what she did or didn't do, the ideas formed by my peers validated my position. When I had permission to go to church youth rallies or lock-ins, I always found a way to phone Nora collect, and she always accepted. Even she found those stolen, against-the-rule calls invigorating. Ever a rebel, those calls were the moments she was proudest of me.

Her faithful answer and willingness to accept the charges always validated that she was a great mom who loved me very much—I just needed to be a better daughter. When we'd talk, she would mention how jealous she was of my houseparents, how unfair it was that all the Ranch communication went to my grandmother instead of to her. Over the phone, she made a clear case for being the most important person in my life, so she was. She declared herself the biggest victim in our situation, so all my pity and support were directed at her.

I knew beyond any shadow of a doubt that my mother would always be there for me.

I was blind in those days to the big picture—the way she avoided spending any time with me when I was in New Mexico on visits. When I remember her in relation to those trips, I recall the one time she invited me to watch a movie at her house. Her hand was within reach, and mustering all the courage I could, I placed my palm over hers. She sat there, frozen, for a long time. Later that night in my grandmother's guest room, I filled eleven pages of my journal about how *my mom had held my hand. Maybe this meant she'd want to be with me now* ... I was fourteen at the time.

The other thing I'd remember about those visits was how she always cried when we'd say goodbye. I would cry, too, because it was sad. Her tears always triggered mine to flow. I hated, more than anything, to see my mother cry. She was sad and missed me, she'd say; I just wanted my mom.

My mom had always been faithful during those Ranch years with her monthly and special occasion 8:00 a.m. phone calls. The spring break morning of that sixteenth birthday had me rising before the sun because I wanted to be ready for her birthday call, but it didn't come.

All day long, I leaped to my feet every time our phone rang.

After the shoes reaffirmed how great my mom was, I knew her call would come any minute, but it never did.

It was nearly the middle of April when a letter arrived from my mom. It made no mention of my birthday, really. She did clarify that she sent me a pair of shoes that had fallen off the train. It wasn't uncommon for the rails to keep the items when there was a derailment. Nora and her boyfriend had a collection of cool things that had fallen off the train. She went on to tell me that it had actually been about forty pairs, and she'd sold all of them but mine so that she could have a little extra spending money for their trip. She and her boyfriend had spent two weeks in California, going to Disneyland and the beach. They'd always wanted to do that together, and she was grateful the day finally came.

She was thorough to point out that it was the "trip of a lifetime," and she couldn't wait until they went again.

"PS: I'm sure you're mad that I didn't tell you we were going to Disneyland. I just couldn't have you begging me to come to Idaho and see you too. I know you don't realize this, but I'm not made of money."

Misty Mae was a daughter.

Sort of.

On paper anyway.

Dear William,

I wondered how hard it would be to write this letter. In fact, I questioned how to go about it at all, or if I should. What I had to face was that it would be impossible to construct even a fraction of my story without including you.

We were lucky and unlucky to weather the same storm for an unnecessarily painful time. It would have been hard enough being the only two kids in a stifling group home, orphaned, while everyone we loved and grew to trust left us and seldom looked back. To endure such things during the hardest years of our adolescence, with the wreckage of family (specifically our mothers') damage trailing behind us—these were impossible circumstances.

Like yin and yang, we were two opposites who found our way, over time, to being close friends. *The best of friends.* It was not because we had shallow things in common, but because we had the hardest things in common. We never dated, and back then I know there were times I wanted to. I had wanted to be *that girl* to you, for you to love me *that way.* I think, with the luxury of hindsight, this was because you were the only person whose love I could trust, so I believed that might finally make me feel like I was wanted.

In more recent years, we had several discussions where the words *soul mate* came into play. It is true, we have an otherworldly strong connection. We probably always will. While we are not soul-connected in some kismet way, you and I are the sole survivors of a wartime to which no one else can relate. Trauma ties people. You and I, Will, are tied.

When you made choices that cost you your place in that home, I was crushed by the weight of letting you down. I resolved it would be my job to take care of you, to make sure you had a good life and never felt abandoned, alone, or unworthy. For so long, I had constructed this pressure, and then you were gone, and I had no idea how to deal with the loss of the one person in the world who filled the family-shaped canyon of my soul.

Damage upon damage, upon damage ... upon damage. That was me.

When you resurfaced, thanks to the miracle of social media, it was glorious and *almost* healing. I was so relieved and, honestly, quite a lot of mixed things. It was not until years later, when we finally saw each other face-to-face. One of the saddest parts of our story was that our reuniting was the healing thing, and it should have happened decades earlier. If it had, I wonder how our personal hells may have unfolded differently. We needed to heal things. We needed to reconnect with one another. We needed to reconnect with those abandoned places within ourselves. We needed the witness of another person to look back on our youth and verify that it had happened exactly how we remembered it, that it should not have because we deserved better than what we had.

You deserved better than the youth you lived. You were an adorable little boy when we first met, sensitive and impressionable in a place where impressionable people should not go. You also deserved better than the me you reunited with. The timing was the worst possible, for myriad reasons, reasons I held my marriage responsible for, but it was not my marriage's fault. You grew to respect and admire my husband, and I was so glad because he is worthy of that and so much more. I am sorry I wasn't stronger. Between you and me, reconnecting with the feelings of having failed you those years before and having to realize I was likely not going to save you the second time either drove me to nearly kill myself trying to right the wrongs.

I was a kid, and it wasn't my job to save you then. I was a wife and a mother, a daughter and a friend. It wasn't my job to save you the second time, either. I know you never believed I should; it was entirely my own baggage. You aren't off the hook either—you put unfair pressure on me, too, eventually. The truth, though, is you only took the liberty because I paved the path.

Most of all, William, you deserve better than the life you have settled for. I am sad for you. I grieve for you. One day I hope you find your way.

Thank you for being my best friend during the darkest time of my childhood. I would have come out only a shell of something terrible without you. I wish you the best, most courageous, and truth-filled life you can have—but this, my friend, is up to you.

I love you,

M

place is helping me
but its not. It hurts
to wake up in the
morning and know its
real. That you are
truly rejected and un-
wanted I had love reach
out for me. I had it
ask for me, and she
pushed it away. Its
for those reasons that
I fill up with resent
and hatred to her. All

Mom and I had a really
nice time together and she
even held my hand
while we were watching
T.v. It was a great
and once in a life time
experience. Most of the
next day was with her
too. We never fought
and everything was neat.
Then we had presents
and all of that was
fun but love shared
between everyone was
missing. I experienced

Autumn

The Thrill

{To this Misty, the one willing to embrace and look for more: "Breathe Me" by Sia}

The Children's Ranch sat on the edge of the Boise River. Growing up on a river may be the best: lazy summer Saturdays spent tubing, hot evenings spent splashing in its flowing relief. As a naive girl in New Mexico, it may have been the trees I thought I was missing, but it was actually a beautiful, winding river, every dip or gentle splash of my hand beneath its surface healing me somehow.

As we pulled into Winchester, Kansas, we were mesmerized by the forming funnel clouds ornamenting the sky around us. Idaho was not prone to clouds changing shape so quickly or skies of purple and green swirling together. Did I dare wish for Dorothy's fate—a storm to carry me somewhere magically bright and different? One thing was clear: I loved the energy of the storm and of what could happen.

"I love Kansas." I said the words out loud, to no one, really, but that didn't stop me. "I want to become a real adult and live here forever."

Add it to the list: *move to Kansas*.

Despite being a planner by nature, I was done making plans. I had graduated to lists. Wish lists, dream lists, bucket lists ... lists for any and everything. Lists of things to change about me.

Lists for *him* ...

You know him, *the one*, the soul mate you've longed for. The one who will fit perfectly with all your dents and curves; the one who will love you and never leave.

Several years before the film *Practical Magic* came out, I was creating a spell of my own (in list form) for that perfect guy who could not possibly exist. My heart was fractured, and I could feel it laboring, ready for complete surrender with just one more blow. I knew how to put on a good face after a lifetime of practice. Beneath the surface, though, the summer I was seventeen was the most fragile I had ever been.

If you grew up in the early 1990s US Christian church circuit, you may remember a team of group-home kids coming into your church. This is when a group of awkward teens came to sing songs, do skits, and—if you were lucky—perform a puppet show for you, all while telling you about a little Idaho Children's Ranch.

I was involuntarily on a puppet team. When I tell portions of this story at dinner parties or among groups of people, I usually just nutshell it with having been on a "cross-country drama tour." The word *puppet* just opens a whole bag of questions I haven't always wanted to dive into, but now my dirty little secret is out: I am a puppeteer.

Granted, it has been years since I have placed a puppet on my hand (minus socks and children's toys), yet every single day my right thumb still tightens and clicks in an arthritic way to remind me that I am a well-trained (retired), award-winning puppeteer.

A few key things to note:

- Puppeteering is really hard.

- Christian puppeteering can be really embarrassing. (Mainstream songs, with words changed to become preachy, sung in puppet voices—definitely not what a teenager, in any circumstance, was eager to do.)

- Hours are spent on your knees, doing arthritis-guaranteeing tasks with your thumbs. There is no hazard pay.

- It doesn't matter how skilled you become, this is not something that will ever help you further your life, career, or personal path.

As I said, this was not optional for me. Though others may have been manipulated or guilted into signing up for puppets, it felt as though I was the one expected to be a part of this team, and to excel at it. I already felt like a freak, outside of my little fishbowl life, and this didn't help.

It wasn't all bad though. I can honestly say I am glad I did it. The arthritis I've had since I was seventeen says otherwise.

The puppet team opened opportunities that I wouldn't have had otherwise, regarding travel and experiences. Our team was in high demand, and, as Christian puppet teams go, we were actually *really good*. What had begun as a form of our awkward little variety show to solicit donations for

the Ranch became a journey down the path of a very legit-
imate dramatic art form.

For all the things I do not agree with my then-house-
parents on, my house mom was passionate about forging
this road for us. There are no puppeteering scholarships
for college (to my knowledge), and while it may have been
a waste of time for a stressed-out, optionless high schooler,
I learned about teamwork, dedication, and the invaluable
lesson of giving whatever I'm doing my full effort.

As much as it may seem otherwise, I was proud (within the safety of my Ranch bubble) to be a part of this
award-winning team. At competition, when we observed
the performances of the other teams, we critiqued their
methods, hand rod usage, and talked among ourselves. (To
this point, I still do. While I may cringe a little, when I see
a puppet take stage, I also sit up straighter and take notice.)

Probably the most important thing I learned from my
tenure on the puppet stage was that, though passions and
dreams are nice, we need to do our absolute best at whatever task is before us. Whether I wanted it or not, whether
I was embarrassed or not, I was on that path, so it was my
responsibility to give it my all.

This technically makes me an *award-winning dramatic
artist*. Should I put this on my book jacket?

My junior/senior year was spent, amid the James and
William drama, with my extracurricular efforts solely focused on the puppet team. I was not paid for my time,
but our trips to Washington, Oregon, Colorado, and other
states did give me access to new places and different things.
To be on our team, you had to be trustworthy. While we
were on trips, this trustworthiness was awarded with the
privileges which the average Ranch kid was starving for,
things most nineties teens took for granted. We went to

movies and malls unsupervised. We ate fast food. It was glorious!

In those days, deep in the thralls of efforts to control my life however I could, I refused to eat or drink anything with "caramel syrup." This was my own definition of anything sugary and brown. No chocolate, no brown soda. Back then, you could take a 32 oz plastic mug to the gas station and get it filled with soda for twenty-five cents. This one thing was at the top of the Ranch life perk-pyramid. A well-behaved, respectful kid (me) could have this mug filled every day. For a long time, I *did* have this mug filled every day. Our allowance as Ranch kids was based on the behavior-level system. At that time, it was $5/$7/$12/$16 a month. I would wager ninety-five percent of allowance money was used to refill those mugs as often as possible. Entire trips, in non-fuel-efficient vans, were made simply to fill a dozen 32 oz cups with soda after school or for movie nights.

After I decided to avoid the brown devil (the possibly imaginary "caramel syrup"), I became a Skittles and Clearly Canadian girl. My allowance was the highest amount, plus I nannied. What else was I supposed to do with my hard-earned money? Once I'd drained my Clearly Canadian, I would add water and a drop of food coloring to my bottle, then I'd set it on my windowsill. The way the sunlight streamed through those colored bottles fed my soul.

It's the little things ...

While the average Ranch-style road trips involved vans of sweaty kids, cheap and incessant soda refills, and packed lunches that probably weren't worth eating, puppet team road trips involved two adults, four or five girls, Taco Bell, and air conditioning.

This changed everything.

We could spread out and sleep in the van. We could have real, deep conversations. We could eat our paper-wrapped tacos or super value meals from the drive-through. It was a lot like heaven must be, only with lots of trans fat.

The June evening we made it to small-town Kansas was for this kind of trip. While our puppet game was fierce, we had also grown into being professional puppet team travelers. This "drama tour" lasted several weeks, which felt even more special. I was a fresh high school graduate trying hard to live my best life. Whenever the constricting feeling (which I'd later learn was anxiety) would tighten inside of me, I would reassure myself it was only good things coming because there was nothing bad left to happen.

Our crew of storm-focused and weary travelers piled out of the van that evening. The sky grew darker, and the thunder overhead was loud. Internally, I reiterated my goal to live in Kansas. The reunion beneath that stormy Kansas sky was not anything I knew to be prepared for. My first houseparents were hosting our team for the week. We were the missions focus for their VBS and we were staying in their house. Seeing them a little over four years after they'd left Idaho pained me almost instantly. Once again, I found myself blindsided by a wave of deep feelings that I did not understand. It also became apparent that there was some possessiveness and jealousy where my second house mom was concerned, and the whole week carried far more weight than I expected. It was rare that I was given the opportunity to have quiet, private conversations with this first woman I had called *Mom*, but I found myself desperate to seek those opportunities out anyway. I also adored seeing their daughters, Joy and Jennie, again. Four years, measured in the life of a child, really shows. We talked, laughed, and bonded. They were all happy to see me—as if I had actually meant something to them. Sleeping under the roof of that Kansas parsonage felt more like going home than visiting my birth home ever felt. It was overwhelming to reconcile, feeling all at once like I was betraying my real family and like an idiot because these four people were not mine to love like that.

For one such conversation, Julie and I were alone in their kitchen. She shared with me, her voice soft, that they had asked Nora if they could take me with them. They'd been willing to assume all responsibility, leaving her free of any. My mother had, naturally, said no.

How would my life have played out if she hadn't? It was easy to believe my mother was determined to ruin any chance I had of being loved. In any direction, as far as I could remember, this was a common thread within the stitching of my life. *Misty: easy to leave, disposable, not worthy of love, fighting for, or choosing.* I tried not to get swept up in the sadness, but there were times when I felt so tired.

After the week was over, the time came to say goodbye to that first mom and dad and their sweet daughters, Joy and Jennie, all over again. I did call them *Mom and Dad* because they said I could. My new house mom had wanted me to call them *Mr. and Mrs. Thompson*, but I didn't. I was compliant about most things, but this I ignored. It was easy to see that she was glad we were leaving Kansas, moving further along down our puppet path. I'm guessing she wasn't thrilled that we would be seeing this little family of four again at the North American Christian Convention toward the end of our trip. Prior to that summer, I hadn't known there was a gathering of Christians each summer, much like Comic-Con, but with Jesus stuff.

The rest of our trip toward the Jesus convention, where we would be competing with puppet teams from across North America, is a blur. During quiet moments, my mind reeled from the time I'd spent in Kansas. The unearthed emotions, unpacking the plot twist that I had been far more attached to them than I'd realized, and still living deep within the open wounds of everything that had transpired since Christmas kept me spinning.

I'd spoken the words, "I am not OK, I need help," twice, to two different adults in the months since Christmas, but this didn't seem to matter. I was expected to perform, both as the model Ranch kid and as the puppeteer. Within that blur of passing time, the one thing that stands out the brightest is a day spent at Six Flags. I set my fears aside and boarded my first looped rollercoaster. While I was terrified that I might die, I also kind of hoped I would. The anticipation of the rise, the speed of the wind in my face, and the way the people below became specks as the world sped by—I felt *alive*. For the first time, I could feel my lungs doing their job as my heart kept time. It was amazing, and as soon as our ride slowed to the exit, I was out of that car and back in line again. And again. And again.

At one point, a light rain began to fall. It seemed gentle and barely there at all until I was speeding through life on an upside-down rollercoaster, in the front row, with those drops pricking my skin like a thousand needles going a million miles an hour.

To this day, that moment is one of my top ten.

On that trip, I added to my collection of things that I wasn't capable of coping with, but I also learned I could be brave. That June, with the Kansas storms and the upside-down adventure, I learned I wanted to chase the thrill.

Heroes

{To Misty Mae, on the brink of adulthood and yet still such a child: "Reset" by Slumb}

It was decided over my head and all around me, just like everything else usually was. One day we were arriving at a host home in the suburbs of St. Louis, where we'd stay for the duration of the Jesus Conference. The next, I'm being told to dress for a *visit* because my father was taking me to dinner.

A "visit" was Ranch lingo for seeing your family. Maybe you were flying home, or perhaps your family was coming to the Ranch. Trying to cram into the tiny box of "visit," meeting my birth father for the first time—with no one to support me—while staying in a stranger's home isn't accurate. Was I excited to meet my father? Yes and no. I was an absolute disaster, emotionally. I had been unraveling into the mess I was, little by little, since that last New Mexico movie night five years before. My frayed edges had been smoothed in really lovely ways at times, and sometimes the unraveling slowed, but I was still becoming less and less.

Even the most emotionally healthy kid would've needed to approach the situation therapeutically. Instead, having already confessed within the dark moments that I was not OK, I was told I had this *visit*. It was made clear my father was coming "all this way," and I needed to be mature about it. The loudest message I received was that any struggle I was feeling was selfish. That evening, I stood alone in the host home's driveway, waiting for my stranger-father to pick me up.

I both simultaneously prayed he would chicken out and begged him not to stand me up.

There was no right way to be where I was.

Hours later, my father kissed me on the cheek, in that same driveway, and clasped a gold bracelet on my wrist. I did not know how to respond. I had been swallowing the beginnings of my own vomit for hours. Already, with that kiss, I had instinctually locked away the majority of our evening together, deep inside my mind where the hard things lived. That moment, however, in that dark-sky blanketed driveway, I forced myself to remember. I had done it before, willingly etched a moment so deeply into my soul that I would always remember it. And I still do.

The girls clustered around me as I crawled into my sleeping bag, begging for details as girls do. I, too, had done the same after significant moments in their lives. Though I couldn't fault them for their curiosity, I had nothing to offer. Already, I couldn't recall much of what had transpired. *Had the evening even happened at all?* I questioned my sanity, but then the driveway came to mind, and my fingertips found the bracelet safe on my wrist.

It had.

I don't remember getting in their car, but I can remember meeting my two little sisters in a hotel room. They were jumping and playing on the second double bed, and maybe the bedding had hues of reds in it. We ate at Pizza Hut, so perhaps the girls had been there all along, and we only spent time in the room after. I know at some point the hotel swimming pool happened. I sat in a white resin chair off to the side, talking to my dad's wife in the muggy air. My dad splashed and played in the pool with his two tiny daughters. That's the part I see in my mind the clearest—him there, familiar southern drawl from our countless phone conversations, at a safe enough distance from me so I could process. That man was my father—my real-life, flesh-and-blood dad. Those two little girls were his daughters. I was his daughter, and also their sister, but louder than anything was the truth that I did not belong to any of them at all. In that water was my family, and yet *not really* mine. Feet from me splashed everything I had ached for and would never have. I looked at those little, gleeful girls and was so filled with gratitude that they did have their daddy. He loved them so much—it was present in the air all around them—and they reflected that adoration back.

I thought about my mother, my mom's boyfriend, being sent away, and the years of heartbreak and goodbyes. I thought about how my own mother had not only found me unworthy of her love, but of anyone else's as well. Don't they say, "No one's love will ever cover you like your mother's love?"

These were the things flooding, with tsunami force, through my mind as I sat in that resin chair. Periodically, I heard my dad's wife defending him. She talked him up, explaining that he loved me. She encouraged me to talk to him, not ignore him. How could I do that? Only once he was safely in the pool had I even been able to look directly at him.

When the evening "visit" was said and done, my father climbed from the running car and walked me halfway up the driveway belonging to the house our team was staying in. Beneath that star-dotted sky, my father kissed me on the cheek and told me he loved me. His tone was sadder than I'd expected, adding to my awkwardness. The entire evening, against my will, I'd retreated deep inside. It seemed my fear of men had resurfaced, and I had no idea how to be what this stranger wanted me to be. He'd been a safe distance across telephone lines and on the other side of handwritten letters, but kissing my cheek and gently clasping a gold bracelet to my left wrist felt unsafe.

The whole experience had felt terrifying and unsafe.

I knew that he was disappointed in what must have looked like my lack of effort. All evening I'd screamed at myself internally, chided myself for ruining something with the potential of making my dreams come true. Inside of me a war waged, but outside and near him I remained frozen.

As he walked down the drive back to his family's car, I knew I'd ruined it.

Of course, I did.

We went on to win the puppet competition at the Jesus convention. I was shocked we had placed at all, as some of the performances we saw seemed far more "gadgety" and exciting than our low-budget set. In the end, it wasn't black lights or catchy props the judges were after, but skill. We did have that; to this my thumbs can attest.

The trip back to Idaho was uneventful. I felt numb and empty, and even that confused me. I had no appetite and only wanted to sleep. Conversations happened around me, and no one seemed to care that I was less and less available. I had seen Mom, Dad, Joy, and Jennie a few times, but the convention was large and busy, plus my numbness was beginning to set in. To spend time with them was to love them; it was best to close that door.

Back inside the Ranch bubble, the pressure to figure out what I was going to do next began to intensify. My father was no longer writing or calling me, and I was terrified to make the first move and write him. More accurately, I didn't know what to say. His silence only increased the rejection I felt, breaking my thinning thread that much more. Nora had been filled with questions about the meeting, and she utilized her gifts to dig into my head and remind me of all the ways my dad should pay for having thrown me away. It was all too much.

My father never stood a chance, really. I can see the tangled wad of unhealthy issues my teenage self brought to the table, and I feel sad for him. These aren't the types of experiences someone prepares for anyway, but the absolute carelessness with which I was handed over to him guaranteed there was no winning scenario.

Emotional breakdowns are dark and messy. I don't know which exact moment led me there. I'd come home, barely holding it together. I called the only person I had left, and he promised to meet me at the park with all the walking trails. He'd bring me my go-to coffee drink, and we'd walk and talk. Sights set, I knew I just had to hold it together until he showed.

Trevor didn't show. It was so typical and so terrible. And then there I was, just like Alice, tumbling down, farther and farther. I was helpless and lost. It was dark. And then suddenly it was nearing the end of summer, and I was emerging in desperate need of a plan. I was seven months from turning eighteen, and then I wouldn't be allowed to live at the Ranch any longer. I knew I didn't want to be there anyway, but I saw no other options. Kentucky, near my father, wasn't ever going to be my place, and until March I had to rely on my mom's permission anyway. I needed a plan—a plan that would keep me secure forever, a plan which would ensure that I never felt disposable or unlovable again.

I needed a husband.

By that point in my life, I considered myself an "expert" on love. I learned I could be loved if I did the right things. I also had this impossible list that some mystery guy needed to meet, comprised of things I loved, things I hated, and attributes connected to my many heartbreaks along the way. Shattered to my core, willing to lean entirely on my intuition for guidance, I submitted to the plan the Ranch staff had wanted for me all along—I enrolled as a freshman at the local Bible college. On August 28, 1993 (five years and eight days after I first set foot on Ranch soil, and three months after I graduated from high school), I moved into my college dorm. When I look back on the numbers of years and months, it seems inaccurate. The idea of decades having passed felt truer.

Dreams

{For the Misty who stood in that doorway alone, terrified and stepping into her new life: "Hello My Old Heart" by The Oh Hellos}

The List:

- Blue eyes.

- A smile that makes my heart dip.

- Hands big enough to consume mine.

- Taller than me, by at least three inches.

- Plays violin.

- Wants to be a youth pastor or work with hurt kids.

- Hates watching sports.

- Is artistic or will at least sketch or draw.

- Passionate about music. I don't care what kind as long as it isn't country.

- Doesn't like country music. (It's worth mentioning twice.)

- Can play basketball with the guys but won't get super competitive.

- Likes me.

- Thinks I could be pretty.

- Comes from a big family.

- Likes long drives.

- Loves watching movies.

- Is handy and will fix things.

- Muscular arms, like Tom Cruise without sleeves on.

- Not muscular like a body builder. Yuck.

- Can fix his own car problems.

- Likes camping.

- Loves animals.

- Will take me to the beach.

- Loves board games.

- Is funny and appreciates my sarcastic wit.

- Can do almost anything.

- Will live an adventurous life.

- Will hold me when I need that and understand when I don't.

- Will be accepting of my weird family and background situation.

- Someone my family will love so much that I will also have value to them.

- A guy everyone loves.

- A hard worker.

- Someone who can be respectful to girls and know how to be a friend to them.

- Wants kids.

- Likes to dance. (Even though I didn't know how and had only been to a nightclub once.)

- Likes live music.

- Will kiss me in the rain.

- Will also play with me in the rain.

- Will hold my hand during the fireworks.

- Will ask if he can kiss me, before our first kiss.

- Will cup my face when he kisses me for the first time.

- Someone who is kind to me.

- Has a normal, everyday name.

- Doesn't smoke, will never smoke.

- Is at least two years older than me.

My one and only reason for going to Bible college was to get my MRS degree. (It wasn't uncommon for girls to go to Bible college to find a husband, thus the running joke of the MRS degree.) Nothing they offered educationally meant anything to the future I wanted. I was on a mission, and my only two objectives were to meet my husband and have a family. I was dropped off at college, dressed in cutoff shorts and my well-worn Lord's Gym T-shirt, as though I were being left for a week of summer camp. There was no one to help me unpack or settle in; I was once again expected to know what needed to be done, and how not to screw it up. It *was* Bible college after all—a safe and benign transition from my overly sheltered, freak show, fishbowl life, wasn't it?

One day when I was fifteen, I took a nap and had a dream as vivid as the dream I had when I was seven where God came down in overalls and told me Papa was going to die. This dream was in a postapocalyptic world, disarray and destruction everywhere. The air was thick and gray, making the violet-streaked sky behind it blurry, and I was alone. I was calling out for my husband but couldn't find him. I began rubbing my belly and panicking. *Where had my baby gone?* Frantic, I sifted through rubble searching for my family, until I found a cluster of children, huddled, dirty, and afraid. I grabbed their hands and promised to take them home with me.

I woke up gasping for air; all at once, certainty flooded me with dread for what I believed the dream meant. I wasn't much of a napper, which contributed to my intense reaction.

Enraged, I marched into my houseparents' bedroom and exclaimed, "I just had a dream, and now I know that my husband will divorce me, I will never be able to have a baby, and I am going to end up working with foster kids. I'll probably end up working here! I will never get to leave!" Sobs came with the words as the fear over this being my future set in. (I also didn't know that there were women who could not have babies. My sheltered existence hadn't taught me that.)

I'm not sure what I believe about prophecy. I know what I believe about my intuition and what my grandmother believed about hers. I also know my heightened fear of Satanism, which I developed in a crazy legalistic fundamentalist community, told me that these things are of the devil, even though my grandma deeply loved Jesus.

Sometime after my first houseparents, the Thompsons, left the Ranch, a trend set in among the kids. While some would steal used cigarette butts from store fronts and smoke them in secret, most of us didn't. One of the kids introduced us to "passing out." (Perhaps you're nodding your head because you know. Was this a craze sweeping the nation, unbeknownst to the sheltered Ranch kids?)

It was a dangerous game. Once you were skilled enough, you could play alone, but in the early days you'd need a friend. Standing against a wall, you would bend over with your head between your legs and inhale the largest breath you could. Quickly, you'd stand upright, and your friend would place their hands above your windpipe, cutting off air (usually using their entire body weight to do so) until you passed out. *Fun, right?* Once you knew that you loved the high that followed upon coming to and could trust your own strength to get the task done, you were able to follow the same steps on your own. I am amazed when I look back that so many kids with trust issues were so stupid to allow one another to strangle them for fun.

Eventually, the staff caught wind of what was happening and began talking to us about the dangers. *We could lose brain cells; brain cells don't grow back.* They wanted to scare us into behaving, but there wasn't anything they could say that would stop most of us. I did it for the control, and I was happy with the euphoric high that followed.

As with most trends, however, it faded, and life resumed to our odd normal group-home stuff. Time passed, but still on rare occasions, I would find myself so overwhelmed that I would retreat to my room, press my body up against the door and make myself pass out. It would bring me that familiar buzz, and so for a week or so, I'd steal away for those moments of the high, then life would begin to feel more manageable around me, and I wouldn't need to anymore. This was the one stupid, dangerous, and slightly rebellious thing I had in my wheelhouse to mess around with when I needed to feel some control.

The very last time I did this was during the turmoil with James. Sobbing uncontrollably one night, I slammed my body up against my bedroom door, lungs filled with angry air, and pressed my windpipe with a passion-driven force I'd never known before. I needed everything to stop. It wasn't that I wanted to die, but I didn't really want to live either. More than anything, I no longer wanted to feel.

Thousands of times, easily, I had played this stupid game with my life. It went like clockwork every single time. Every time except the last one. This time, I fell to the floor in a vision. A vision of me, dying in a snowy-banked ditch. There was an overturned semitruck on the road before me, a crushed car, and agony all around.

I woke up, convinced that I had seen how I would die.

Every winter road trip, to this day, has me on edge.

I began my freshman year of college knowing I was there to find my husband. I knew that the very second I saw him, I would know to my core he was the one. I knew I'd need to hurry and get pregnant so he would have to stay with me. Babies secure relationships forever, and because I wasn't sure when I would be dying in a snowy ditch, time was of the essence.

Every person I spoke those words to thought I was crazy. Secretly, I also suspected this might be the case.

The first day of school was freshman orientation. The Bible college was small, and I knew all the returning students from the time I'd spent on campus with Trevor the year before, so I knew my husband wouldn't be among them. Freshman orientation, I realized, had to be the key. The nervousness consumed me as I climbed the stairs and filed into the classroom. I was willing, I'd decided, to accept technicalities regarding the list itself, but each and every point had become a firm need based on experience. My brain was milling deep in thought as I scanned the faces of the boys in the room. I looked to my friend, the only other Ranch kid turned Bible college freshman, and told her my husband wasn't there. I was so disappointed. She was annoyed. Aside from our one connection, we'd never really been friends at all.

Shannon and I had very different interests and motivations. She was far more academic than I was, me being more interested in social status and trends. We weren't roommates in the dorms but were together quite a bit in the very early days because we knew each other. In this setting, we no longer stood out as Freak Show Ranch Kids. It was nice to have a familiar face. Being the studious, responsible, and slightly judgmental girl that she was, Shannon hated my life plan of finding a husband. I didn't care about her opinion, but still I mentioned this freshman orientation setback to her because I had no one else to tell.

She said I was stupid and needed to grow up as we parted ways that afternoon. She had gone to her room to pack for the school-wide weekend retreat, organized so students could get to know each other. I, on the other hand, so overwhelmed by all the normal girls who were not train wrecks like me and so sad for my husband's failure to appear according to my plan, went into my room and called my boss. I was working at a local fast-food place and volunteered to work the weekend, even though I'd already requested it off. I then went to my resident assistant and said, "I'm so sorry! I can't go to the retreat because I have to work."

I made some extra cash, which was nice. Trevor and I had dinner and saw a movie one night, which was fun. For the most part, I reveled in the alone time as I attempted to keep the mounting panic at bay. Once again, my life plan was lost, and I had no idea what I was going to do. Without a husband, I didn't want to be a Bible college student, but I had nowhere else to go. I thought I was past the overwhelming feeling of being stuck, yet there I was again. No matter how hard I tried, things didn't seem to work out. All I longed for every day was for some adult to wrap their arms around me and let me rest my head on their shoulder. I wanted them to assure me I was good and that I would be OK. I wanted permission to still be a kid. Try as I might, I couldn't quite figure out how to earn that.

Our school required that all students come together daily for chapel. On Tuesday, during our first chapel, this guy with an ugly baseball hat turned around and said he liked my necklace. The jolt that ripped through me happened in the immeasurable instant between his turning around and the opening of his mouth to speak.

It happened exactly like I had known it would, and I was shocked.

I wasn't looking for it because I had given up. I was, instead, bored and disengaged, having only given the back of him a second of thought because his hat was stupid.

I smiled and, amid the noise of hundreds of kids singing whatever praise chorus was being led, I asked him why he hadn't been at freshman orientation.

"Because I didn't get here until right before the retreat!" He noticed Shannon then, smiled, and said hello. They chatted for a second, and after the normal moment had passed and he was once again facing forward, I asked Shannon how she knew him.

"We hung out a few times at the retreat. Why?"

"Because he's my husband."

She rolled her eyes, but I didn't care. I allowed myself to feel good for a moment about getting something right after all.

Love Story

{To CHW, ALWAYS: "EILEEN'S Song" by Burlap to Cashmere}

The certainty with which I knew that Chris and I would get married came from a place so deep within me I couldn't identify it. Did I know we were meant to be married? I think I probably believed that, but in the years since, I have to wonder if it was more that I simply knew we would be. They might sound like the same thing, but they aren't.

I am pretty sure I don't believe in "meant to be" anymore. Things happen, and most of us do the best we can with the shambles we have.

My grandmother, for instance, when she met Chris, acted like she didn't like him. But when Christmas rolled around, she sent him an afghan that she had begun crocheting the night they met. She knew he'd be her grandson one day. It wasn't that she wanted that; in fact, she was disappointed I had a boyfriend at all and made this clear on her visit.

Shannon had been against my certainty from the beginning. So much so that she giggled and began to aggressively pursue him that very evening. It was a matter of days before they were officially a couple. Chris had met her houseparents (with whom she had more of a relationship than I did with mine), and everyone on campus knew that they were an item. I wasn't worried about it because I knew in my gut what was going to happen, but I'll admit she created some real problems for me. She didn't like him. In fact, after the first few days of their relationship, she was so annoyed by him that she avoided him. Meanwhile, Chris and I hung out from the start. There were a few things about him that made me question why this guy had to be the one (his love of rap music, for one), but most of the time we spent together, we were becoming friends. I had no sense of urgency that anything had to happen right away. Instead, I was filled with so much peace—this hip-hop dancing guy was my future husband, and I could be his friend and live my life, so I did.

While Chris's "girlfriend" continued to blow him off, our friend-duo acquired a super cool third named Joe. Some friendships happen organically, and Joe was that for us. I think the biggest thing, besides a shared sense of humor, that bonded the three of us was that we didn't fit in with the standard Bible college crowd. It wasn't that we weren't liked or didn't love Jesus. It was *us*. Sometimes I would watch those beautiful, conservatively dressed teens, feeling like I was so far removed from being a part of their world. (Also, the truth about Bible college is that many freshmen came from sheltered homes, and in the college environment, a lot of drinking, sex, drugs, and various other "bad" things were happening.) Not a part of the core crowd, the three of us often did our own thing. One of the favorites, because it was cheap, was going to see movies at the dollar theater. We would pool our money for plates of fries at diners afterward, sharing laughs or an occasional deep debate about whatever was relevant in the moment. Sometimes Joe would bring up Shannon, asking Chris what the deal was with his absent girlfriend, and poor Chris just didn't know. He really tried to connect with her. He never badmouthed her. I should have noticed then—I see it now looking back—that he always kept himself chained to the crushing pressures of being the good guy.

Shannon was not Chris's first girlfriend; he had several relationships while he was in high school. Around the middle of his high school career, he was in a serious relationship with an older girl from his church. Their breakup was traumatic, and she'd gone off to college, heartbroken, the year before.

Our college, in fact.

She was still a student there, and, though we weren't friends, I knew her. We were acquainted because she had also been the roommate of my *Little Mermaid*–loving friend, Tammy. On the weekends when the roommate would go home and I'd stay over with Tammy, it was her bed I'd sleep on. I'd lie awake staring up at her poster board collage of friends and this one boyfriend she loved so much that his face was everywhere.

That face I had fallen asleep to so many Saturday nights was Chris's.

As weeks passed, I began to develop feelings for Chris. Though they were the fun and flirty feelings, there was also the underlying sense of security I had about our future. Sometimes, within my head, it played out like I imagine an arranged marriage might. At the same time that I was getting to know him, I knew I was going to be his wife one day. My intuition knew this marriage would happen, whether I developed feelings for him or not.

One afternoon I received a two-hundred-fifty-dollar check from my grandmother to help me with food, the phone bill, and other random expenses. I'd never had a bank account and wasn't able to open one because I was only seventeen. Chris kindly took me from bank to bank, even his own, thinking he could cosign to cash it. The only solution, his bank teller finally told us, was for me to open a joint checking account. When my someday-husband suggested we open one together, I had no idea it was a big deal. Considering we had only known each other for about a month, in hindsight it seems insane. That day, though, he was a friend helping a friend. Why? Because he is the good guy.

I had mentioned to Chris, on two casual occasions, that we were going to get married one day. It was a joke (he thought), and it really was funny. That day at the bank, he joked that "since we were going to get married anyway, why not share a bank account?" As we drove back to campus, it somehow fell into the conversation that I had never been on an actual date. He declared that, since we were going to get married, we should have a classic "first date." It was this fun joke of an evening. He met me at my door with a flower and took me for dinner and paid full price for tickets (no dollar theater!) to see the Stallone movie *Cliffhanger*. He went above and beyond to give me that classic first-date feel. I was a mixed bag of humor, friendship, and in-my-head emotions throughout the evening. We had been to the movies over a dozen times by this point, but that night was different, and it did change things, even if it had been all in fun.

The following Wednesday, a group of us went to see *So I Married an Axe Murderer*. The air was electric as I sat next to Chris. It was clear he wanted to hold my hand, and I was giving every indication that it was OK. Finally, about two minutes before the credits rolled, he took my fingers in his. It was supercharged and also so *normal*. My insides were reeling.

That night, as we talked in his car until curfew, he told me he really liked me. He told me that he wanted me to be his girlfriend. He continued holding my hand and asked me, beneath that beaming streetlight, if he could kiss me, cupping my face with his palm as he did. Little by little, this guy checked off each and every point on my list. While it wouldn't have mattered even if he didn't—because I was so certain I was destined to be his wife—I still took notice when things about him lined up with the silly list.

He asked me to break up with Shannon for him, which sounds like a jerk move, I know. He never saw her, and when he would, she'd quickly dart in the opposite direction. This was well before cell phones or email, so his options were a handwritten note passed through various sources or me. I marched straight to her room and very kindly told her he wanted to break up. She had told me numerous times before that she didn't like him and wished he'd end it. It just didn't seem like a big deal.

By lunch the next day, when Chris and I walked into the cafeteria together, it was clear that the majority of the school thought I'd stolen this poor girl's boyfriend and I was a terrible person. I was used to being the one on the outside, so it didn't affect me except there were a few people who made a point of letting me know what a whore I was. Not surprisingly, one of them was Tammy's old roommate.

School wasn't for me. Not then, and not *that* school. This was clear to me in the first week. My academic adviser stated he did not like Ranch kids and personally believed they should not be allowed to go to this Bible college. By my second meeting with him, he indicated he was going to make it as hard as possible for me. As wrong as he was about my right to be there, I didn't have the heart to fight for it. I'd been desperate to leave the Ranch and knew the key to my future was marriage; there was nothing beyond those benefits that I hoped to gain from Bible college. I had no motivation. There was another reason that I was failing from the start: my health.

I had my first period at thirteen and never found a regularity to my cycle. From the beginning, I had such heavy, painful flows that it was common for me to ruin clothes and bedding, writhing in immense pain for days. When I was sixteen, I had an abnormal period three weeks in a row, and my houseparents finally listened to my pleas for help. Because I did not have health insurance or anyone who would have candid conversations with me about my body, I had to see the local charitable doctor. His house was close to the Ranch, so this physician offered up advice and gave quick exams on occasion. For my inaugural visit with the good doctor, I was naked from the waist down on the Ranch administrator's desk in a dimly lit office. The director's wife was there, too, looking off to the side, pretending she wasn't uncomfortable. This was the first time I met the doctor everyone raved about, though he did not say two words to me. I had no idea what he was doing, only that it was uncomfortable. It was communicated to me several weeks later, when I began violently bleeding and cramping again, that the doctor had seen nothing wrong. They told me I was *lying.*

Week five of college found my inconsistent period violently visiting. My RA was mortified by the amount of blood. Since I was on my own at college, I was able to wear tampons. It didn't help—they would fall right out after an hour, full. I couldn't attend most of my classes that week, and my academic adviser demanded a letter from my doctor in order to avoid expulsion. Since I didn't have a doctor, someone took pity on me and got me in to see their gynecologist. Nora gave them her credit card over the phone for the bill. No one told me I could have applied for Medicaid. In fact, no one was offering up any helpful information at all. This was added to the long list of things I was simply expected to know, then ridiculed for when I didn't.

Due to the emergent need, they fit me in with a nurse practitioner. After a lengthy appointment and several tests, we learned I had a uterine infection. She said that, though she couldn't be sure, the infection seemed advanced and had possibly been in my body for years.

I was given a prescription for a strong medication that rang in at nearly fifty dollars a dose. My mother was not impressed with me and held me responsible for the situation being so advanced. This is how I learned no one had ever communicated with her or my grandmother that I'd complained of problems. My grandmother scoffed, saying that the Ranch wouldn't have made a mistake, so this doctor was probably not telling the truth. And my mom was furious. *How dare they neglect her precious daughter?*

I suspect it was a combination of how hard my body was working to heal, the medication, and depression that had me sleeping almost constantly. I was given leave from work and was granted permission to make up assignments without having to attend class. It probably wasn't a good idea to tell someone who already didn't want to be in class that they didn't have to go. When I was able to spend time with Chris, I was able to be present and enjoy him and our blossoming relationship. When I wasn't, I was numb. I was terrified of losing anything else, burrowing myself so deep inside that I wouldn't have to feel when it happened again.

The day I moved out, my houseparents became mostly hands-off. Other kids were going home on the weekends to eat good (free) food or do laundry, and they'd bring their new out-of-town friends with them to do the same. This was even Shannon's college weekend experience with her houseparents, while things like laundry and weekends became additional items on the growing list of stuff I was expected to figure out on my own. I was surrounded by kids missing their families and was reminded that the "family" I had close by had moved on as though I were nothing more than a checked box on their task list. This caused me to lean into Nora even more. Her rising credit card balance from the doctor's bills and medication was causing her stress, so it wasn't long before she began encouraging me to get pregnant so that Chris would have to marry me now. The more she insisted every conversation go in this direction, the more I knew that this was finally something I could do to make her happy.

One afternoon, in pajama pants and my trusty, worn Lord's Gym T-shirt, I made it to the cafeteria for lunch. My sweet boyfriend was happy to see me. He was a good guy attempting to handle this college thing despite his girlfriend's slacker ways. The rest of the group at our table gave me a hard time about finally making an appearance, saying, "The princess life must be nice."

I piped up, "Hey, how would you like it if you had an infection in *your* uterus?" My defensive words had been aimed at Chris's roommate, and an uncomfortable silence settled over the table. A few odd laughs escaped the mouths of friends before Chris piped up with the only logical response: "I couldn't imagine that because I don't have a uterus."

I was instantly overcome with sympathy, "Oh my gosh, I'm so sorry! What happened?"

I was seventeen, and it was the long cafeteria table of that Bible college where I learned, for the first time, what a uterus was, what a period was, and how babies were made. My brain, over the years, had pieced together things here and there, but the specifics of it all had never seemed quite right. It wasn't that I was dumb as much as I was the product of extreme neglect. It's true, my basic human needs had been met, but I had been wired to thrive on behavior-based rewards, never being worth the time to teach or guide.

I had decided to love Chris before I started to actually develop strong feelings for him. I knew this guy was my only shot at "happily ever after," and in my ear was Nora's continual push for him to plant his seed within my belly so I could finally be loveable. Most of that life season was me going through the motions and doing what I thought I needed to. Turning in the late homework, saving my energy (or faking it) for when Chris wasn't at work or in class. He held a full-time job and actually made it to his classes, so it could be tough. I had developed real, albeit heavily guarded, feelings for him. Also, eventually the sex helped.

The making out in his parked car or at the back of the dollar movie theater had been nice. Then, late one night, I thought back to when I had taken charge with my first kiss in that YMCA closet. I was tired of having my mom's boyfriend pop into my head at the worst moments when I was close to Chris. It made sense that to go all the way with him would mean new thoughts of Chris would replace the dark and terrible other ones.

We began dating in late September, and it was the third week in October when my grandmother came up to visit. Even though Chris and I had been dating for only about a month, I'd known I was going to marry him for two. Combined with the way my broken brain was incapable of measuring time, I was convinced we were in a long-term, serious relationship. My grandmother was not happy I had a boyfriend, but she was willing to have dinner with him during her visit. It went OK. While she was a lovely, brave, and strong woman, at barely over four feet tall, she could also be a force of intimidation—this is who Chris met that Saturday. I don't remember the full conversation, but my grandmother did bring up my mom's boyfriend and what he'd done. The last she'd known, some five and a half years before, I was speaking openly about it, so I guess she believed I still did. In truth, I didn't talk about it with anyone, save the time I fell apart on Ryan and the second investigation ruined my life for a while. Outside of James, William, and Sherri, no other friend or boyfriend had ever known.

On the way back to campus, Chris asked about what my grandmother had said, and I told him the truth. A truth I hadn't even considered I might one day have to share with him. He listened intently and, with a tone so full of support and adoration, said, "I love you so much."

I soared.

This was the first time that he told me he loved me, and for so long the details seemed framed in such a lovely and romantic setting. This amazing boy did not see me as the ball of shame that everyone else saw. He knew about the Ranch, and now he knew why. He saw me with my physical flaws and these even bigger things stacked against me, and even so, *he loved me*.

The mental images from the abuse started not long after that, so I pushed for him to go all the way. The plan worked at chasing the monsters away, for a while.

When Chris and I started dating, I encouraged him to mend fences with his family. He was estranged from them and had been for quite some time. He finished out the last two years of high school living in homes other than his own. He was used to taking care of himself, too, which I found attractive. Despite my overall ignorance regarding reproductive health, I was far more mature than a lot of the freshman around us. The silly drama and gossip were things I had lost patience or interest in years before.

Chris was adamant he did not want a life with his family in it, but I pushed. I was being one hundred percent selfish. I wanted a family and here was this guy I knew I was going to spend my life with, refusing to be involved with his. I did not always utilize my sway for good where Chris was concerned. Should he have healed things with his family? Maybe. Should I have forced him into it because I had this imaginary idea of what it would be like for me? No.

Chris met Nora in early November, just after he proposed to me. I knew we would get married, and it wasn't long before he realized he liked me a lot, and I was sexually abused and damaged, so he needed to love me too. One afternoon he took me to the mall to choose a ring, and a few days later, in the parking lot outside of the dollar theater where our relationship had blossomed, he asked me to marry him. It was sweet and fun, but also it hurt my feelings. While I was exhibiting control wherever I could over my own life, I had only known an aching for someone to come in and do something bold for me. I was consumed with a festering sense of shame over being a dirty Ranch kid, whom everyone easily threw away, and having to choose my own ring and being given it in the seedy parking lot of a dollar theater felt like the sort of garbage I deserved.

My head knew how sweet it was. He was so thoughtful, sentimental, and considerate, and I am not proud of feeling the way I did. I faked my way through a surprised yes and acted happy, while inside I cried. I longed for this knight of mine to come in with bold gestures of love, sweeping away all the pain-filled moments with new, beautiful, love-filled ones. Chris has always been an amazing guy, but there is no man in the world capable of meeting the expectations I had tucked away.

Things became strained between us, but the sex was spontaneous and fun, so we focused on that. When I had first gone to Chris, explaining that I missed my mom terribly and needed to see her, I was sure he would say no. Instead, he made a way for us to drive down to New Mexico because his fiancée was *deeply missing her mom*. How do you explain to a nineteen-year-old boy that you've never known anything other than feelings of deeply missing your mother? It didn't matter. I hoped that coming home with someone who loved me would finally be enough, but I was no longer sure *why* I wanted to be enough.

Chris & Misty Engagement 1993

Spontaneity

{To the lost ones, forever in my heart: "To Build a Home" by The Cinematic Orchestra}

My mom wanted to see the ring and told Chris I should be wearing the wedding band with the engagement part of the set. "Is she going to be your wife?"

"Of course, she is."

"Then she should be wearing the whole ring. The engagement ring alone looks dumb."

The time with my mom was rough. She only allowed us a quick visit to my grandmother's house, deciding that, since my grandmother had just been in Idaho weeks before, it was her turn. She didn't want to know anything about college, my friends, or my life; she only cared about Chris. She was her fun and flirty self, and because she was so personable, he liked her. Due to a death in his family, however, we had to cut our trip short and drive back. All in all, the twenty-seven-hour drive gave us one night in Phoenix at my aunt's house and eighteen hours with my mom before climbing back in the car for another twenty-seven-hour drive back.

We broke up a week later. There were many factors. My mother in person and the effect she had on my head among them. In the years since I'd been sent to Idaho, I had not slept in her house. With every difficult moment of that brief visit, my inner self scolded me for being stupid. In every critical way, my mother made it clear I would never measure up. My inner voice took her side every time: *If you weren't such a failure ... If you weren't so ugly ... If you'd been a better kid ...* Both Chris and I were damaged in different ways, and we were so young. The most painful part of the breakup, other than that I truly cared for him, was that I felt like my intuition had betrayed me too.

Being a Ranch kid in such a well-connected nondenominational Christian area meant that I was familiar with the affiliated churches. I fell in love with one particular historic church, in downtown Boise on Ninth Street, the very first time I walked through its doors. It is, as old churches go, stunning. At the time it was called Central Christian Church, and I knew the day I met that building I would someday be married there. The feeling never faded. When I first took Chris there, he seemed unimpressed. In hindsight, it was probably the awkward moment when a seventeen-year-old girl introduced you to the church she one day planned to marry you in.

The Sunday before Thanksgiving, there was a gathering at Central Christian Church, so a large number of Bible college kids filed into those wooden pews. Things between Chris and I were civil, but not great. He'd broken up with me, and I was grieving the pain of every loss and rejection through the lens of this break up. Among the peers who had once deemed me a boyfriend stealer, I was now a dumped fiancée. Even my own mother, when I called her in tears, said I'd "really screwed up" and had "missed my last chance."

Beneath those stained-glass windows depicting a loving shepherd, I was feeling anything but loved. For the first time I could recall, I allowed myself to accept I was alone. No Ryan, Jared, Sherri, William, or James to fall back on. No family and no real friends. There were other students and quad mates who were friendly, but we weren't close. Everyone had their own dramas, and I was a fortress of inner tension and self-protection.

During that uninteresting presentation, a folded-over slip of white paper made its way down our pew to me.

"I'm sorry. I love you."

My eyes traveled along our row until they landed on Chris looking my way, his expression both broken and hopeful.

"It's OK. Me too." I passed it back, not sure what anything meant but knowing that it was true: I was sorry.

By the time the piece of paper made it back to me, I had resolved to that glass shepherd that I would do better. I would become a better person. I would make up my schoolwork after Thanksgiving break. I would meet with my adviser, even though he wasn't supportive, and have him help me make a plan. I would be good and do good. When I set my mind to something, it always got done.

The note was back in my hand. Unfolding it, I saw a drawing of the engagement ring, two boxes, and a simple "Check Yes or No."

When people ask me how Chris proposed, this is the story I tell. When people ask Chris how he proposed, he talks about the parking lot of the Plaza Twin dollar theater off of Overland. It used to be embarrassing—the idea of it made me feel worthless and cheap for a long time. Now, though, I find it funny. Either story told, I knew the instant I saw this man that he would be my husband, and I agreed to do it—twice. I would do it a hundred thousand times, as long as it led me to him.

I had given my adviser far more credit than he deserved when I resolved to do better. He wanted me to fail, expected me to fail, and, though I couldn't hold him responsible for the poor student I had become, I do believe I could have done better if he'd cared a little.

To the best of my ability, I met with my professors after Thanksgiving break and began the task of making amends. Granted, I didn't want to be there, but I accepted that I was there because at one point I chose to be, and it was my responsibility to make things right. For about a week, I was doing the work. I was feeling better, had sustained energy, and was making it to class while tackling missing assignments in the classes where grace allowed. On December 8, Chris drove me to a follow-up appointment with my NP. I invited a friend along, and we were all going to go see a dollar movie afterward—a reward to myself for how great I was doing.

I had to pause and take a deep sigh as I began to write this out. There have been many of those moments throughout the sharing of my story within these pages, but this one felt different. Even as I move to type, there is a jagged rock in my chest.

A reminder that this life has never been easy...

It turned out I was seven weeks pregnant. I got pregnant when my mother told me to. I got pregnant when I believed that a baby would solve everything. I got pregnant when it made sense, even though it hadn't made any sense at all.

There I sat, ashamed because my sweet Christian friend was sitting beside me. I was terrified because I had finally allowed myself to feel encouraged about the future, and there was a real future within my reach. I felt sick because I knew this would change everything, and not in the happy ways I once hoped it might.

Still stunned, as we pulled into the Ranch to drop my friend off, I told Chris I needed to talk to Brittany's mom. My houseparents hadn't been very supportive since I'd left, and I was terrified. I knew that I needed an adult I could trust to confide in, and Brittany's mom had always been loving and supportive to me.

Just as I'd expected, she was so comforting—exactly how a mom should have been, in my mind. As I left her house, she enveloped me in a warm hug. Climbing in the passenger side of Chris's car, I felt loved and capable—forgiven, even.

I carried out the remaining days of the semester unsure. Chris was angry and stressed. Guys deal with things differently. While I, too, worried about the future and admitted that, outside of Chris, I literally had no other option, he was crippled with the fears of what fatherhood meant. He hadn't had the best experience with fathers, and he'd barely been sure he wanted to marry me someday. He had no idea how to speed all of that up, alleviate the Christian-induced shame of his immorality, and make enough money to support a family. He held fast to dreams of being a youth pastor, and all of a sudden that dream couldn't exist within his reality anymore.

When the school administration finally learned about the pregnancy, I was asked to leave. While their official reason was that I was on academic probation, everyone knew the real reason. Chris was permitted to stay. It was sexist. However they chose to justify it, I'd enrolled as a "dirty Ranch kid" and left as shamefully as they'd expected. So many felt I had made them look bad or found it their privilege to focus on how my situation affected them. Within the well-networked system of churches, the news traveled like wildfire.

I was treated unforgivably by Brittany's parents in tandem with my houseparents. While it had seemed as though

Brittany's mom would be supportive, it became clear that she was a driving force behind much of the negativity and shaming. My grandmother was devastated, and the words she said over those telephone lines took me back to that argument the December before—back to those reports I'd read. I knew she hadn't believed me when I told her they weren't true, and it was clear she never would. She'd crocheted my husband the blanket for Christmas and sent me a dorm fridge. It was such a supportive gift. Its arrival, right before I was asked to leave the school, reminded me of when I was little, of the times my mom would dangle the things I could have gotten to do, if only I'd been good enough. When I moved out of my dorm, my entire world fit into a suitcase, two shopping bags, and my mini fridge of shame.

I was ten weeks along when I woke up on Trevor's couch and knew that something was wrong. Chris was asleep on the floor beside me. Trevor and his roommate had originally asked me to move in with them, but word traveled fast, and before I'd decided one way or the other, the Bible college and their church affiliations made certain that wouldn't be happening due to the position Trevor's roommate held in both.

In the blink of an eye, I was seventeen, pregnant, and homeless. We'd tried staying with Chris's parents, but their one-bedroom trailer and his dad's alcoholic rages assured two weeks of that was enough. The desperate call to Trevor the night before was intended to get us through the winter cold to morning, when we could figure out a solution.

What I found instead was spotting. Spotting led to the emergency room, and the words *Spontaneous Abortion* were diagnosed.

To my naive, seventeen-year-old self, I was both terrified and confused. *Abortion?* No. The clinical term for miscarriage felt as unkind as every other handling of my health had been. Added bonus, the doctor on call was the charitable Ranch neighbor-doctor. The only other time I'd seen him up close had been my nightmare cervical exam on the office desk. As his monotone told me that I was losing the baby, two things became clear: he did not approve of teen pregnancy, and he did not recognize me from our previous time together. He wore mismatched socks on his feet and disdain in his eyes. All I could think about this awkward doctor and his horrible bedside manner was how he'd paid an obscene amount of money to have trees imported in from some other country to use as decorative beams in his fancy house. I knew this because, in exchange for his occasional medical assistance, Dr. Charity had allowed our teen boys to do countless hours of uncompensated work on the construction of his home and landscaping.

Boys like William, who were told how grateful they should be for the experience.

I was referred to a male obstetrician, who chastised me for not drinking enough water, not eating healthily enough, and not taking my pregnancy seriously. He told me half a dozen times that my uterus was the size of a grapefruit, and that my baby was dead. The ultrasound showed no heartbeat, and he assured me it was only a matter of time before the fetus passed.

Once again, I was expected to just know these things. When I didn't, the people willing to hurl judgment lined up, while the only real grown-up showing up (sometimes) was Trevor.

No one, except maybe Chris, understood how dire the circumstances surrounding this pregnancy were. It shocked me how cold people could be when they didn't agree. There was no empathy for a seventeen-year-old girl being forced to spend fourteen days catching "everything down there" with a plastic ladle because the hospital needed to test the fetus. There was no kindness when the cramping was so severe that a nurse had to help this child get into a hospital gown, and midway, a tennis ball–sized blood clot splatted on the tile floor, splashing said nurse's white shoe. *It's the girl's fault*—she was to blame for having sex. Me. I was to blame for having sex, but that didn't mean I deserved the horrible things that came after.

But didn't it? This is how legalism works. This is the rhythm of the religion I'd been taught. The love and support I *could* receive were merit badges to be earned.

We found a basement to stay in. It belonged to a retired schoolteacher named Ilene, who had multiple sclerosis. Chris had several friends who rented space from her. I was on day one of my fourteen-day miscarriage when we settled in. Anything either of us owned was in the backseat of Chris's car. We were grateful for a pull-out couch to sleep on; it was early January, and I was glad to be somewhere warm. I got to know Ilene from afar—she, trapped in a wheelchair on the main floor of her home, and me, bleeding and sobbing on the underground level below. She knew of me, and I of her, but circumstance mostly kept us apart.

My nineteen-year-old fiancé would rise early and leave for work at a glass factory about an hour away. After work, he would make the tiring drive home. The last thing he wanted to do after a few days was hang around the basement with me. I was a heartbroken, emotional mess. I spent every waking moment sifting through bowls of tissue and blood, as instructed. He found the idea of hanging out with friends far more appealing, so that's what he did. When I explained that I didn't want to be alone, he decided to invite his friends over to hang out upstairs and watch movies. Ilene made the boys snacks while I lived downstairs, between bathroom and bed, faithful ladle in hand.

The night I finally passed the baby, that is where Chris was. They were watching a movie about people who eat each other when they are trapped (after a plane crash maybe) in the snow. He really liked that movie, I guess, and has asked me to watch it a few times since, but I've always said no.

He didn't care that the miscarriage was finally over. On my twelfth trip to the emergency room, while he flirted with the nurse on the other side of the curtain, I was told to rest and drink lots of fluids for the next ten to fourteen days. Before that rest period had passed, he'd broken up with me. Ever the good guy, he assured me I could stay there for a few weeks, until I found a place.

I know this makes him sound like a jerk. He was.

While I was a broken, emotional basket case dealing with tissue, blood-stained nail beds, and the pain of my insides wringing out, he was only a nineteen-year-old kid who had no clue how to cope with any of the things happening. There wasn't anyone lining up in his camp either. He hadn't signed up for any of it, and he didn't deserve the mess we were in. Sometimes it was easier to check out and be a nineteen-year-old kid.

The truth is you just can't *always* be the good guy. He was also a clueless kid, in over his head, just like I was. When I'd seen my houseparents, they did not hide their disgust for me.

"When will you stop lying, Misty? We know you didn't have a miscarriage. This is just like all the times you lied about irregular periods and cramping. The doctor confirmed there was nothing wrong with you. Is this not the kind of attention you were after?"

We didn't talk for a long time after that. We had never been close, but even so, the loss of anyone felt devastating.

Nightshirt

{For the young woman expected to figure it all out: "Surrender" by Natalie Taylor}

From the moment I met Chris, he was proud of his car. With the credit he had worked so hard to build, he'd financed this flashy car he loved. I never really liked that car. I found it unattractive and imagined our future playing out with a different vehicle carrying us there. Even so, in February when his car was repossessed, my heart broke for him. He blamed me. Here was this kid who had made it all work out on his own, but then I entered the picture, complicating everything with my pregnancy and the many hospital trips resulting in his missed work. I blamed me too.

He mostly stayed upstairs. I rested, cried, slept, starved myself, and attempted to watch all the TV that had happened since I'd left home at twelve. One Sunday afternoon that early February, Chris came downstairs and asked me when I'd be moving out.

"Where is it you think I'm going to go? I'm here in this tiny town with no job, no money, no friends, and no family."

"You have Trevor." I did, but Chris and I both knew why that wasn't a real option.

I had been even more of an emotional mess since the miscarriage started. It had been two weeks since I'd passed the baby, and even I was annoyed with myself. *Why couldn't I get over it?*

I had no idea what to do. No one in my family would allow me to live with them, and the Ranch had forbidden me from setting foot on their property because I'd shamed them.

Chris and I talked for hours, our conversation somehow going from my lack of options to him being willing to marry me because he blamed himself for this position that I was in. He didn't believe I deserved to be on the streets. I accepted his very reluctant offer because I had nothing else. In those days, shattered and lonely, I entertained the thought of suicide more than I'd like to admit. I knew Chris would have been so relieved.

The way I saw it, everyone would be.

For Valentine's Day, Chris bought me a comforter and a VHS copy of *Untamed Heart* with Christian Slater. He had mean-girl friends who were always at Ilene's. One of them rented a room upstairs, and the other just hung out often. One of them had gotten beautiful flowers from her boyfriend. Later, when Chris and I went to the store, he offered to buy me the movie because he felt bad that we were going to get married and he hadn't even thought to get me a Valentine's gift. I then fell in love with the comforter, so he agreed to spend the twenty dollars on it, too, even though we couldn't afford it. It was my first Valentine's Day with a real relationship, and the gifts confirmed, to me, the worthless piece of garbage that I was.

Halfway through the movie, he reached over and pulled me into his arms. "I'm so sorry I hurt you. I'm so sorry I kept hurting you. I really do love you so much." The words were warm against my cheek, and I wanted to believe him.

I loved the moment and how safe and nurturing it felt. I wanted to be loved like he claimed, at every moment and not just on Valentine's Day as we're watching a movie about a dying love. The truth was that I couldn't trust him, at least not that he would take care of my heart. It wasn't because he kept breaking up with me, but because losing our baby had been the closest to hell I had ever been, and he hadn't cared. I was dying, at my core, before his very eyes, and all he could think about was hanging out with his friends. This included his mean-girl friends who hated me, and he allowed space for their unkindness. He couldn't give me room to exist as he took up all the space with his truths—that he didn't want me, but he'd agree to marry me anyway because he was a nice guy.

I forgave him and moved forward toward our wedding because I knew I didn't have any other options. It was my ugly truth.

The weight of the obligation can overshadow any beauty.

I turned eighteen four days before our wedding. With my mother's insistence that I get pregnant so we could get married, she'd promised to sign for us if I actually did. With a positive test, however, she told me that I was a whore and had to clean up my own mess. So, we waited. We were poor, and hospital bills were flooding in. Still, no one had talked to me about Medicaid, food stamps, or any type of assistance. My health was still declining, and while I wasn't recovering the way I should have, a lack of money dictated I couldn't go to a doctor to find out why. In addition to consistent bleeding, regular migraines had set in.

Chris had to take my birthday off work so he could ride around in the back of a friend's pickup truck in search of junkyard parts to fix the total clunker of a car he'd been driving since the repossession of his dream car. When you live an hour from your minimum-wage job, a reliable car is a must—and it needs to start.

I spent my eighteenth birthday alone, which I knew I deserved. It was long-distance to call Trevor, and what would I say to him anyway? I reflected on all the things that had happened in the span of the year and that I would be a wife by the week's end. The last birthday, shut out and hated by James and William, had seemed so painful then—and also about a hundred years earlier.

I wanted to be a wife, but more than that, I wanted my husband to *want me*. I knew that Chris was there, attending cummerbund fittings and going through the motions, because he had internally resolved that I was some consequence to mistakes he needed to see through.

I had called and asked Brittany to be my maid of honor. She was, in my mind, the closest girlfriend I had.

"I really wish I could." She paused before dropping her voice, almost whispering, "My parents heard about what happened with Chris's youth pastor."

"What happened with Chris's youth pastor?"

"You know, when he came to visit you at the house you're staying at. He told my parents that he knocked on the door, and you both yelled for him to come in. And when he did, you guys were having sex, and you told him he could stay."

What?! An iciness flooded me from head to toe. His youth pastor would pop by from time to time, and he did come over the week before. But I was making a box of macaroni and cheese on the hotplate, so I yelled for him to come in—Chris had still been on his way home from work. I assumed he hadn't heard me because he never opened the door.

"Brittany, that never happened. If he told your parents that, he lied." Why would he lie about something so terrible?

"I'm not allowed to be your friend anymore. I'm not supposed to talk to you or anything."

I was crying by this point. No matter how hard I tried to fix the bad things I'd done, they just kept getting worse.

I saw Brittany a few times before she left for college the following fall, but she'd never look my way. I may as well have been dead to her, but I never blamed her. She was obeying her parents. She was a good kid.

On April 2, 1994, I became Mrs. Chris Wagner. Our wedding was a low-budget event with contributions from family and a few friends. Aesthetically I loved everything about the day. The attendees on my side of the church were scant. My brave, beautiful friend, Sarah, was a bridesmaid, and even her disdain for the hideous pink dresses is something we cherish now—it added to the depth of the day's story. I did love my husband, and I was happy to be his wife.

Minutes before our rehearsal the night before, my grand-mother had shouted across the sanctuary that she'd enjoyed her visit with the Ranch that day. "Everyone there is so disappointed in the mistakes you've made, but they are still willing to wish you their best."

By "everyone," she meant Brittany's parents. She'd never cared for my second set of houseparents, but after the Thompsons had left, Brittany's father had become the ad-ministrator, and she thought the sun rose and set with him. This, of course, was the very same person who had sent her the lie-filled reports. He was the reason there weren't more people at my wedding. He had scheduled a choir tour for the weekend of my wedding. Most of the people who cared about me were sent on that trip. The few who remained were forbidden from coming to the wedding at all.

Three people from the Ranch came anyway. My once-boyfriend Ben's dad performed our ceremony, and his mom played piano for the service. They told the administration that it was a commitment they weren't willing to break and even managed to get the beautiful and historic Central Christian Church to agree to let us be married there, despite my shame.

"I'm sure they do, Mommy. You would think they would be happy that I am here trying to fix my mistakes."

"You just had the potential for so much more, but you're ruining your life with your choices. They are just so disappointed."

My grandmother didn't intend to hurt me with her declaration, but it also wasn't quite what I needed to be hearing the night before what was meant to be the happiest day of my life. She also didn't intend to hurt me as Chris and I were leaving, everyone tossing bird seed in our hair and sending us off with congratulations, when she yelled, "STOP! You're wearing my pearls, and if you leave this church with them, I know I'll never see them again. Also, give me the veil! It's your cousin's, and we need it kept safe."

It's fair to say that she also didn't mean any harm when she phoned the hotel that we'd barely been able to cover for our wedding night to demand our presence at dinner because I'd "already had a honeymoon," and I owed it to my family to be there, since they had come all this way.

I did owe it to them, didn't I? Eleven months earlier, I'd ached for them to be in the audience at my graduation. I wanted them to be proud of me. Here it was, my wedding, and while it may not have seemed like anyone was actually celebrating our marriage, they had shown up, and I knew I was indebted to them.

We went to dinner because she had tapped into my sense of shame, multiple times. I believed that I didn't deserve a beautiful wedding night with my husband because I was garbage, so I dressed in normal clothes and ate an undercooked steak with my family at a restaurant near the airport.

My wedding night reminded me a lot of that first proposal, which wasn't Chris's fault. I was the consistent theme, the mediocre obligation, the garbage. Me.

There had been two bridal showers before the wedding. One was in New Mexico among my grandmother's church friends, and the other in Idaho. I did not attend the New Mexico one but heard many stories about the way my grandmother responded to the gifts she opened on my behalf. Many of them had been intimate wear, and my poor grandmother simply could not reconcile that her immoral little granddaughter might use things of that sort.

After the party was over, she phoned to tell me that our family friend Petra had given the best gift. "It is the most beautiful purple nightie I've ever seen, and you should definitely wear it first!"

I was mortified, some 2000 miles away, that my grandmother had opened those kinds of gifts. It was also embarrassing to think of these sweet old women giving me such things. I had assumed the gifts would consist only of things like mixing bowls and spice racks. (There were those things, too, and several crock pots. Because it was 1994.)

Meanwhile, in Idaho, my bridal shower for twenty-six became a party of five. It was embarrassing and one of those classic worst-fears-come-to-life moments. The hostess chose to skip the party games and instead we ate cake and talked. I rotated through embarrassment, nausea, and an overwhelming sadness at the nearly two dozen ignored invitations while my beloved was out jean shopping with our college buddy Joe. This would constitute his bachelor night. They found a pair for work at Kmart. We were shameful outcasts, and I knew the only reason for Chris was his association with me.

When my family arrived for the wedding, I was given the opened gifts from New Mexico. Petra's gift was a heavy purple satin nightshirt, with long sleeves and buttons, resembling an oversized men's pajama top and was easily the most modest of the bunch. It wasn't hard to see why it was my grandmother's favorite. While I didn't think it was very cute, it was the most comfortable thing I'd ever worn. I wore that nightshirt for years.

While it felt like my grandmother was being so unreasonable and mean, she was human. She was disappointed.

I kept thinking about that nightshirt as I wrote this. While these little old small-town ladies were living out their wilder sides through my bridal shower gifts, my grandmother was embarrassed, but also thinking practically. She knew that sex may be great, but life and marriage aren't sex. They are hard nights, stress, fights, struggles, loss, and real life. Having a faithful, comfortable nightshirt can make all the difference sometimes.

I believe this is true in the ways she inadvertently hurt me at the wedding too. She had been told I was a bad kid by "good, Christian adults," and because of distance, this is all she knew. The information was coming from people she trusted, and why would they lie?

Indeed, why did they?

My family *had* taken the time and spent money to help me with a wedding. Everyone had done their best. Their entire short visit had been filled with the wedding, and they wanted to have dinner with us. It's really not so bad.

My mom came to my wedding. Her trip to the wedding was her gift to me. I took the only birthday gift I received, which was twenty-five dollars, and I bought my mom the Disney release of *The Fox and the Hound*. Nora had an unhealthy obsession with Disney movies and told me she really wanted to buy that one but couldn't because of the cost of the wedding trip. I was so beside myself with excitement that my mother was finally coming to Idaho that I surprised her with it when she arrived at her motel. She never said, "Thank you," but I didn't care. I made excuses for her, just as I always had. I was filled with a million emotions because my mother had finally come to see me.

It would be years before I would learn from another family member that my mom's boyfriend was the reason she came. That he bought her a new dress, handed her a wad of cash for the trip, and told her to have an amazing time with her daughter. She hadn't wanted to be there, but he insisted and compensated her well in order to convince her.

My mom struggled through the entire wedding, making the usual snide comments, and causing friction with my grandmother.

After we had dinner with my grandmother, aunt, uncle, and cousin near the airport, I felt overcome with guilt. "If my mom finds out," I cried, "she will be devastated that she got left out. She always gets left out."

We drove the hour out to where she was staying.

{To Chris, my love}

"Always" by Bon Jovi
"Bloom" by The Paper Kites
"Gone, Gone, Gone" by Phillip Phillips
"Mess is Mine" by Vance Joy

And every other song that makes my heart swell with immeasurable feelings of love for you.

April 2, 1994 Misty (18) & Chris (19)

with Nora

Mommy & Misty

Motherhood

{To an aching mother-heart: "Elastic Heart" by Sia}

It began with two daughters.

Two beautiful little baby girls. They weren't mine, but they felt like they could have been—like they should have been. Then, the day they would have been, a courtroom technicality took them away.

Callie and Rheagan, beautiful twin girls. One was full of energy, all giggles and smiles. The other lay listless, failing to thrive, needing reminders to breathe, lest she die in her sleep.

I poured myself into those two girls in the rawest way I knew. Months in, the pediatrician assured me I had saved Rheagan's life. She giggled and gurgled and even dared to play with her toes.

"It's a miracle," the doctor said, smiling. *Did doctors believe in miracles?*

The rushed packing of their sweet-scented sleepers, hair bows, and tiny socks did not feel unlike the sobbing messes I'd known on icy tile floors, with yet another miscarried baby dead in the palm of my hand. *They were never yours,* the mantra I would forever tell myself.

None of them had been.

Not those dying inside of me, and not these squirmy, mashed-banana-loving ones birthed by someone else.

Between our wedding day and our divorce five and a half years later, we experienced a lot of loss and likely learned nothing healthy in the process. Seven miscarriages fell within that space. With each pregnancy (six—one had been twins), I found myself taken right back to that fourteen-day torture from my first motherhood loss. Along the way, with a faulty medical system and no justification for this hell wreaking havoc on me—body and soul—we ventured into foster care.

I could write an entire book on the seasons of pregnancy and loss. On the heart and the death of those days. When I first started writing this book, I thought I was going to be penning more words about that time. I'm not. Someday ...

The second time I learned I was pregnant, I hoped beyond hope the baby would live. Finally on Medicaid, the doctor I'd been assigned assured me I wouldn't miscarry again. I lived a fearful life of overcaution, and the day the spotting started, Chris rushed home, and off to the doctor we went.

We had made it further together, my baby boy and me. An ultrasound revealed a strong heartbeat and his gender. Again, the doctor assured us this baby wasn't going anywhere. I hung onto every dry, clinical word he said. He was the doctor, after all, so this baby would live. He told me to go straight home and to bed, that everything should be back to normal in a few days.

We had our own place by this time, no longer living in a basement. Married nearly half a year, I wondered if God was giving us a second chance since we were doing things the right way this time. We belonged to a quiet church; we didn't live frivolously. We hadn't gotten pregnant on purpose. I was offering daycare for neighbors during the day, and Chris was still at the glass factory. Things were good. We were cautious but moving forward.

After the doctor promised me my world, I went next door to call my mom **collect**. We didn't have a phone because we were young and poor. I stood in my neighbor Heather's kitchen, at her wall-mounted phone. I was re-assuring Nora—because that somehow made me feel like everything was OK—when I felt the sensation of a heavy egg cracking on the top of my head. Whatever had been in this invisible egg ran right through the center of me, like a flood. Head to toe, the rush. My mind dipped for just a moment as my eyes trailed down my body, following the feeling.

There was blood everywhere. Not menstrual cycle blood, but murder victim blood. With the contrast of my white maternity pants and my neighbor's tan kitchen carpet, she and I both screamed.

Chris had been next door, getting the bed ready. He'd wanted me to go straight to bed, but I argued that I had to tell my mom.

It wasn't real until I told my mom!

He heard our screams and bolted over.

I guess my neighbor told my mom; I don't really remember.

I rushed to my house, into the safety of our bathroom, Chris on my heels. As I ripped my pants off, our son was there, lifeless, in the padding of my Hanes Her Way.

Just like that.

No days, no ladles. It had been so quick.

The wailing and earth-shattering sobs of that afternoon did not belong to me. As if possessed by the pent-up intensity of everything I had gone through ten months earlier, my husband lost his mind. He screamed, he writhed. He thrashed about on the floor, intermittently with the slamming of his head into the wall. Eventually, after some days passed, his state of grief prompted him to run out our back door and into the highway's oncoming traffic.

In the bathroom of our first place, that October day, I saw the way this man-boy had never been taught to express deep emotion—to grieve. I watched my husband react in ways that could end his own life because he had no idea how to handle the overwhelming loss of our son. The only tears I cried that day were because of what I'd done to him.

It had to be my fault. I hadn't gone to bed like I'd been told.

The nurse asked us to bring the fetus into the hospital in a container. I cleaned out a yogurt cup and delivered my baby to the hands of our monotone doctor who met us there. He examined me, giving only that, "These things happen."

The physical pain didn't come until later that night. Though my experiences with miscarriage hadn't made me an expert, I knew something was wrong. Back to the hospital we went.

My memory of these moments is so saturated with the loud and colorful pain I was in. I can still see the beige of the waiting room walls and how blinding the triage lights were. I was placed on a gurney in the ER hallway. Surrounding me were the curtain-clad cubicles that normally give patients some privacy, but I wasn't in one.

A doctor rushed over to take a look *down there*. In my mind, he is young and has glasses. Memory tells me he looked a lot like Chris, which may not be true at all. Maybe I'm only seeing Chris because everything else was chaos.

The doctor told me to hold my husband's hand, and I did. At one point, Chris was crying, too, as the volume of sound and light exploded around me. There was pain slashing itself through my insides, and I wanted to pull away, but there was a woman holding one foot, and the doctor yelled for me to stop moving.

It was too much, the hurt and the bright. I looked still at Chris, and the fear in his eyes did me in. I tried to summon up that faithful dark place I have been known to surrender to, but I could not find it.

We were sent home in the early morning hours. I'd had an emergency D&C procedure. They had assured Chris that this procedure of scraping my uterus had been medically necessary. We were the responsible adults in our lives, so we didn't know any different. There had been no anesthesia, no painkiller, no numbing. It wasn't until two years later (when I miscarried the second twin, thirty-seven days after its sibling) that a doctor informed me I'd need to schedule a D&C. I jumped out of the chair across from his desk and told him, "Absolutely NOT!"

My reaction could not have surprised him more. When he asked, I told him about that hospital hallway. I explained the pain and being sent home only to end up back there three additional times, finally having a procedure (on the tenth day) to relax the uterine muscles that had been in a "contracted state of trauma."

In those days, Medicaid dictated who my doctor would be. I had the same uncaring experiences time and again, except for this second D&C doctor. A friend had taken me to her doctor, appalled at how my situation was being handled. While it may be true that some miscarriages unfold in textbook ways, mine involved ambulance rides and hospitalizations, each one separating itself from the others. This friend paid for this appointment, and hearing about my first D&C, this doctor wrote off the rest.

"The rest" ended up being a hospital room and a two-day stay, an unlimited supply of 7UP, anesthesia, a reserved slot in the operating room, pain killers, and actual follow-up care. He even brought flowers to my bedside as I was recovering. His reaction, hearing of that first experience, had been a horrified expression and one word: *barbaric*.

After that second miscarriage, it seemed I was never able to emotionally connect with pregnancy. I knew that I'd lose the babies. Deep down, I recalled the dream resulting in a certainty—at fifteen—that I'd never have a baby. I ached desperately to be a mother, and to have a family, so I kept trying ...

And failing.

With each loss I grew more consumed with being someone's mama, and with making it right for Chris. Time passed, and though he wasn't the shattered man of that afternoon, I couldn't forget when he had been. I could not erase what I had done to him.

Women have babies. This was what our bodies were designed to do. When I couldn't make that work either and added it to the long list of unlovable things about me, it seemed both fitting and unfair.

In high school, my creative obsession with decorating my space had begun with sunlight streaming through Clearly Canadian bottles of colored water along my windowsill. The very first time I was given the liberty to decorate my own space, a fire was lit inside of me. By the time those bottles were casting rainbows across my bedroom floor, I learned I could create spaces that meant something. This had been cemented as a part of my DNA one afternoon when I'd been crying on my bed when I was around fifteen or sixteen. The administrator and his wife were watching us while our houseparents were gone. His wife came into my room to comfort me, but she was distracted by my room itself.

"Did you decorate in here?" I had. "Did you paint this dresser yourself?" I did. She continued asking questions, pointing out small details here and there. Finally, she sat beside me, "I know you're hurting right now, but I want you to know that you have a true gift for decorating and creating a space."

This woman was one of the sweetest and kindest people I'd met before I realized how two-faced people are more viper than kindness. The lesson she subtly taught me that day was that it didn't matter how sad or horrible something was, I could create a beautiful space and other people would never know that anything was wrong. She had reaffirmed that *I* didn't matter as much as what I could do.

We became licensed foster parents in 1996. Our brief stint with state foster care was equal parts cathartic, heartbreaking, and enlightening. In the spring of 1997, we received a phone call from a foster mother in California. It seemed my Ranch sister Sherri, seventeen at the time, was in her care. This woman told me that Sherri was set to be moved into a dangerous group home where girls were often raped and several had been stabbed.

She was calling us because there wasn't anyone else to call.

Sherri went home to her real family when I graduated. We hung out here and there since her family lived in the area. Life happened, and this was before cell phones or the internet. With my moving around, we fell out of touch.

I had been out at Chris's parents' new house one day about a year after I'd last seen her, and as I was leaving, I saw his younger brother talking to a neighbor and her friend. The friend happened to be my little Ranch sister Sherri. In a rural subdivision, nearly an hour away from where our relationship began, she stood before me. It was almost impossible to believe, but there she was.

Four months later, Sherri's mother decided Sherri would come to live with me. She was sixteen and acting out—a lot. She'd dropped out of school, was doing drugs, and while multiple people had tried to help her, Sherri would only respond to me.

I was nineteen years old and Chris barely twenty-one when we got our first foster placement—a sixteen-year-old, wild, defiant, and manically depressed girl.

She was with us for a good chunk of time, and though it was HARD (and I was conceiving and miscarrying through-out it), it was so good. She ended up having a great-aunt in Washington who wanted her, so she eventually moved up with her.

Then, almost a year of random postcards and scattered calls later, this California woman called.

We learned that Sherri had gravitated down to California to be with her dad. There had been some abuse, and she ended up in foster care. The foster woman had taken it

upon herself to save Sherri from further trauma and decided she needed to come live with us. By Sherri's own
admission, the happiest place she had ever been was in our
home. We were licensed foster parents, but at the time,
there were no state-to-state exchanges.

It was reckless and illegal, but we bought a plane ticket
for Sherri, and she ran away, home to Idaho. Because this
was before a lot of flight regulations, it was easy. For four
months, we laid low. We turned down real foster place-
ments and hid this seventeen-year-old. There hadn't been
a plan, other than to protect her. Sherri has always been
excitable and easily scared, so when this California woman
told her of the group-home horrors ahead, she was terrified. If we could keep her hidden until she was eighteen,
we'd all be in the clear. If we got caught, she would be
returned to California and kept in the system until she was
twenty-one. We would be facing prison. It was an intense
time.

One afternoon while I was at the supermarket, Sherri called her grandmother and told her everything. Her
grandmother called the police. In the end, we chose to surrender our foster care license, though they hadn't required
us to. It turned out, there had been instances of girls being
trafficked, and our situation led investigators back to that
foster mother. We were thanked, a lot, for our help. No one
faulted us, except for Sherri's grandmother, and I get it.
Her grandparents had been scared for months. Chris and
I lucked our way through what could have been a horror
story. The downside was Sherri had to return to California.
Her social worker flew to Boise to escort her back. She wove
into Sherri's placement that we were to be involved, in place
of her parents, for the duration of her time in care.

Sherri would be with us several more times as the
years passed. Sometimes long visits, sometimes more. Even

when she wasn't living under our roof, our home was always home base for her. She struggled with addiction, and on one near-fatal overdose, I had to face my personal demons, years after burying them. It was Sherri's nineteenth birthday, and less than a week after our twin foster girls returned to their birth mother.

On that terrible afternoon, days before, we'd returned home from a pediatric appointment to find their great-aunt on our steps, and my mother-aching heart was dealt its worst blow. We had begun doing privatized foster care, feeling a lot more comfortable with the personal ways in which the cases were handled. We had several truly rewarding experiences, the last being Callie and Rheagan. They'd come to us at three months old. It had been a long and hard road to that afternoon. We hadn't expected to adopt them initially, but as things had transpired, this became the plan. In a state of sheer exhaustion with two babies turned near toddlers, I had allowed myself to truly love them. It may have been Rheagan first—with her failure to thrive, she needed so much of me all the time.

I lived my life by the mantra that good things never worked out for me, so self-protection was essential. Even so, by that day, I was wholly theirs. That afternoon their birth mother was meeting with the aunt and her attorney to sign over her rights. The entire day had felt like this swarm of butterflies inside. For the first time, good was happening.

And then it didn't. A technicality had charges against the biological mother dropped, and the aunt was on our step to get the girls. She was emotional, devastated. Devastated for us, and for the babies.

I was dead. It sounds dramatic, but it is no less true.

After the immediate reaction of complete shock, my beautifully constructed world in rubble all around me, I was gone. I went through the motions, though only the necessary ones. We ate a lot of ramen. On the step that day, as I shattered, I heard Chris say, "Never again. No more kids. No more babies, no more pregnancies. Nothing, unless someone can guarantee us that it will end well."

He said it *for* me. I knew this. He was scared for me, and he was unable to process any of those complicated emotions boiling more and more aggressively to his surface.

Glue

{Song: "White Blank Page" by Mumford & Sons}

Chris had conceded to try fertility therapy. He wasn't on board so much as he just slipped on his good guy cape and wanted to make me happy. Emotionally, he was somewhere else. It would turn out, actually, he was *with* someone else too. Long before that revelation, though, was Sherri's overdose.

I had to come face-to-face with whom I'd become. Losing the girls had done me in, a thousand times more severely than any loss before them had. I finally saw that my relationship with Sherri was complicated. By this point, she was far more than foster sister. She relied heavily on me and often said I was the only mother she had. But I wasn't her mom, either. I was only three years older. She would cry and tell me I was her best friend, but I knew she could never be mine. She was an addict. Though I loved her beyond comprehension, and the thought of a life without her was unthinkable, our relationship would always consist of me giving to Sherri. In small ways, she could reciprocate, but in the end, she would always need to be the one to lean. I've always called her sister, though we are the only two people in the world to understand it as something somehow bigger than that.

In a complicated chain of events, I found myself in the hospital for an operation in early 1999. I had a uterine tumor the size of a Nerf football removed, along with one ovary. The doctor knew my desperation for a baby, so when my body was ready, he strongly encouraged fertility therapy. "Time is of the essence," he'd flatly stated. It was not a matter of *if* tumors would take over my uterus and remaining ovary, but it was a small window of time *until* they did.

Nora flew out to stay for six weeks and help while I recovered. It was her boyfriend threatening to cut her off financially if she didn't that inspired the trip. A friend picked her up from the airport, and when my mom saw me answer my apartment door, she was livid. "Why the hell did I fly up here if you're fine?" The six weeks went pretty much just like that. She was mad at me, constantly. She was intrusive. She was patronizing. She was also really funny. We had deep conversations, ate lots of delicious food, and played hours and hours of Yahtzee. I both couldn't wait for her to leave—this had been the longest we'd been around each other since I was twelve—and wished she'd move to Boise.

It wasn't her first visit to see us. It was as though, with her trip to the wedding, she had conquered some invisible barrier. After that, she never minded coming to see us. She'd flown up several times before that six-week stay, and those visits had always been great. Nora was my best friend in those days. She was such a great long-distance mom. Chris and I would travel down to New Mexico as well, so it wasn't like we never saw each other, but in the decade between me going to the Ranch and that six-week trip, our visits had been in small doses. We talked on the phone every morning, and she held all my secrets. I saw my mom as the source of my stability and support, while everything else around me had become a barren wasteland. If anyone saw us together and didn't know how our journey together had gone, they'd have thought we had the best relationship and were very close. She told me I was her best friend and the light of her life. When she'd answer my phone calls it was, "Hi, baby girl!" And when we'd hang up after hours of conversation she'd tear up and tell me she missed me.

This version is the mother I'll always remember. The long-distance mom who was free to be whatever she could because she was void of all responsibility since I was now grown. Our short-dose visits were always heavy on the fun and laughter, so this was the Nora that Chris got to know and fall in love with too. She felt like my confidant and stability because these calls and visits where how I saw her now—I had nothing to compare it to. On the surface it looked and sounded like the ideal mother-daughter rela-tionships that appeared on TV and in movies, so it had to be right.

But also, I believed she was those things because that's all I ever wanted. It's easy to lie to ourselves and filter our perceptions.

By that summer, Sherri had gotten clean and was married and pregnant. That's the miracle of being the one with infertility and miscarriages in your circle—you become a magnet of luck for the people around you. It is possible to be so happy for them, jealous of them, broken for you, and still be a decent human being. I didn't know that then, so I felt buried under the weight of shame because of the self-centered person I was, because I couldn't be happy for them without feeling sad for me.

Nora flew home a few days before my twenty-third birth-day. Chris had planned an amazing celebration with my closest friends. Ten of us had gathered at our favorite Japanese steakhouse. We lingered long after the entertainment of our chef was finished, savoring the incredible food and laughing. A gorgeous, glistening chocolate cake was wheeled out, and those beautiful people sang "Happy Birthday" to me. My husband kept touching my hand and telling me he was happy I was alive, and everything about the moment felt significant.

I could have been dead.

While no one had actually said that, the truth was not lost on us that I'd been lucky.

Months before, I had my first positive pregnancy test in two years. I was nauseated all the time, a feeling I'd never had with any of my pregnancies, which I took as a positive sign. By this point I knew all the teas, all the vitamins, and all the things that specialists claimed would strengthen uteruses and help babies grow healthily. I knew that this baby had better odds of sticking around if I just rested, ate well, prayed, and waited. I had learned the hard way not to trust doctors, so I would just wait.

Time passed, and with tender breasts and other on-track symptoms filling my days, I did everything I could to ensure success. This time would be different.

We estimated that I was about a week into my third trimester when Chris finally convinced me to see a new obstetrician. My firm belly was showing a healthy pregnancy, and hand in hand with my husband, I went to our first appointment feeling none of the complicated fears and optimism I'd felt with past pregnancies.

They tried to convince me I wasn't growing a baby, but instead a tumor. Up until the surgery date, the following week in late January, I was terrified the doctor would cut me open to find he'd been wrong. Instead, he found the largest uterine teratoma he'd ever encountered. He found it fascinating, he shared in my hospital room while I was re-covering, that it was filled with teeth, hair, and tissue. While he seemed overjoyed by the situation, he was emphatic that my window for having a baby had gotten significantly smaller. "But hey, at least it wasn't cancer!" he beamed as he left the room.

The September after that procedure, my husband chose to begin a life with his girlfriend of seven months. He had "never been more in love." Our fights around that time were the worst. We were stopped at a red light, following a nice Saturday together, when he told me about her. I felt blindsided. For nearly six months I'd been in the best place I could remember. We'd bought our first home. We were in fertility therapy. I had allowed myself to accept and believe in the love I received on my birthday, and this deeply impacted the way I saw my circle of people afterward.

For the five years we'd been married, I'd begged Chris for a puppy, and now that we finally had a place of our own, we'd adopted a little black lab from the shelter. She was a roly-poly of clumsy affection, and I named her Laney after one of the main characters from my favorite movie *She's All That*.

We were painting, wallpapering, and making the home ours. Sometimes when Chris would walk in the door from his third-shift job, at 3:30 a.m., he'd hold me while looking around our living room and sigh, "I love our home. This is ours."

He sounded so proud. I was proud of us—of him and of me. We'd been through hell and back, numerous times, and yet we'd done it. The very last thing I had expected him to confess on that sunny afternoon was an affair. As though a switch flipped in him, he became violent and cruel. Many things he said to confirm the awful things he knew I believed about myself. He called out my closeness with my mother. He mentioned a long list of ways in which she had failed me and told me I was ignorant for loving her. Prior to this moment, he had never said one negative word about my mother. In fact, he praised her often—they'd always had a great relationship. It wasn't lost on me that this was probably what led to my mom and I being close.

The other thing he mentioned often was that he loved this woman not only because she *could* have children (she had two), but because she wasn't a "complete waste of life." He made it clear that he was grateful we'd played out our five years without children because no child deserved the fate of me as their mother.

Marriage is kind of the worst, sometimes. Within such an intimate relationship, we learn the deepest, darkest things about one another and ourselves. He knew what would do me in, and in that moment, Chris was consumed with using any effective tactic he could. It became war.

Of course, I blamed him then. What an awful man he'd turned out to be! I lost almost everything because of him. I lost friends I loved, many people I cared about, my sweet little Laney, and most of the beautiful things I'd acquired for our home. There was no longer a well-manicured life to hide behind; I couldn't make others believe it was perfect, so in turn, I could no longer lie to myself. Looming heavily over all of it was the knowledge that there was only a small window of time before I would lose any chance of ever having a baby.

After a few weeks at the mercy of dear friends, I ended up moving home, to New Mexico, and into the house of Nora and her boyfriend. My options were null.

After I'd gone to the Ranch, my grandmother had flown me home every year for a visit. Each visit was so layered. Beneath my debilitating hope that someone in my family would find me valuable enough to want me, there was the growing chasm between them and me.

Well into adulthood, it became clear that my birth family had this idea of the sort of life I was living, and it was nothing like the life I actually lived. Over several phone calls, my grandmother referenced my "wild lifestyle." Neither of us drank, smoked, or anything of that nature. Most of our friends were from church, and the most consistent things we did were play pinochle once a week with Ben's parents and have Sunday night taco night at Chris's aunt and uncle's house. While she felt we had our home open to all sorts of hooligans, it was true we almost always had someone living with us. Down and out people who needed help, or the eighteen months that we acted as a shelter home for pregnant teens. We had decided before we even married that our home would always be open to anyone who needed it, and this is a practice we have always stood by.

As an adult, when I would visit family, it was always clear that beyond a few childhood memories and some DNA, there wasn't a lot of connection there. Their lives had all gone on together, and I'd become the outcast my mother had so desperately believed she was, while ironically, she was there, a part of the fold. I wasn't included in reunions, weddings, anniversary parties, or events. Whenever "family" things happened, I learned about them after the fact. Whether it was that I wasn't wanted as a part of the family, or that I was merely an afterthought, it didn't really matter.

The general consensus of my family was that Chris was such a great guy, and I'd screwed it up. I'd gotten too fat. I hadn't been the kind of wife he needed. I'd had too many issues. I was too lazy … The list was endless. I was twenty-three years old, and the way it was told to me, my life was over. My mother was my conspirator—she told me all the hateful things my grandmother and aunt were saying behind my back. However, I would overhear her saying terrible things in hushed phone conversations when she didn't know I'd walked into the room.

My aunt told me, in one heated discussion, that I needed to move in with my grandmother.

"Terry has a family. I'm in Phoenix and I work full time. You have no family of your own, you have no career. You've really messed up your own life, Misty. It falls on you to be the caretaker."

I was stunned.

I loved my grandmother, and as much as I wanted to help her, I felt too young to resolve myself to living out my days in that way. Instead, I attempted to set boundaries and compromise. I would visit her every day and help her out and spend the night a few times a week. This seemed to ease tensions a bit, though my aunt had decided she wasn't speaking to me. My grandmother was upset that I would not be sleeping in my grandfather's twin bed like I did when I was younger.

Maybe I was in the wrong, but I felt I needed some privacy, so I took to one of the guest rooms at the other end of the house.

That first night a couple weeks after Thanksgiving, my grandmother fell in her bedroom doorway. I found her in the morning. She was livid, claiming she'd screamed her voice raw, and I'd just ignored her.

I hadn't heard a thing.

I felt terrible and tried to make it up to her, but she didn't want any part of that. My mother relayed to me the even more hateful things my grandmother and aunt had progressed to saying. I'm not going to say she loved the negative attention I was getting, but there was an underlying smugness there I couldn't quite figure out.

That Christmas I ran away with a guy I'd met online. These were the early days of online community, and feeling like I was completely alone, this was where I had retreated. It wasn't a romantic relationship. Brad was one of many friends I'd made in a Christian chat room. We were the same age, only at twenty-three, he wasn't going through a divorce and life crisis. Instead, he was a third-year at Arizona State and in an odd love triangle with his high school best friend. As he was heading to his hometown for Christmas, he asked if I might want to escape my predicament for a while and be his buffer. It was, all at once, the dumbest and most age-appropriate decision I'd ever made. That road trip led to another one, where I was at the mercy of family friends over the actual holiday. The situation at Brad's family hadn't been one I was comfortable with, so tail between my legs, I called Nora and she bailed me out by calling a good friend back in Phoenix.

As a totally humiliated cramp on their holiday plans, I crashed on their couch. In the three months since Chris had left me, my life had managed to sink lower and lower. Though their couch was opened for me, their holiday plans were not. I understood and was willing to spend the time curled in a ball, listening to my Sony Discman, passing the time until my mom could come to Phoenix and get me. That was until I had dinner with Ryan and his girlfriend (now wife). He'd been the first person I had called when I learned about Chris's affair. It had been years, and though we'd talked on the phone as time had passed, it was the first time we'd seen each other since the day this brother of mine had left the Ranch.

He and his girlfriend took me to dinner and then we saw a funny movie. The three of us sat talking in his tricked-out

SUV, bass booming to a mix of Beck and hip-hop on the high-end stereo, until late into the night. Hugging good-night on that Phoenix doorstep reminded me of how this giant of a boy-man would forever be my brother, and yet never really be. In some complicated way, I realized how everything made sense within the chaos of *not*.

Compartments ... baggage ... steamer trunks busting at the seams with their pieces of my life. My New Mexico childhood, my Idaho adolescence. My friends there never mixing with my birth family. My marriage to Chris and how he wasn't really a part of either of those things either—simply another piece of luggage housing another time.

It was freeing, and for the first time, I was able to see the many things I'd chosen to carry with me, things I needed to put down.

I craved a life of wholeness.

Sometimes I wonder if that Arizona front step still holds the baggage I shed that night.

Back in Lordsburg, I was ready to make a plan for my life. Y2K came, and society survived. It had been a complete mind wreck living with my mother and her boyfriend again. While only eleven years had passed since I'd been sent to Idaho, I could have sworn it was lifetimes.

When my houseparents reached out in support, having heard I'd gotten divorced, they told me of an opportunity at a facility they were working at in Kentucky. Even though we'd never been close, I felt there were family ties with them, and I knew I needed to place supportive people in my life while I rebuilt it. I took the job and relocated to the same state my father lived, though we weren't in touch. I was damn good at that job. The downside of that particular life season was that I'd gone to work for an employer who valued legalism, not the actual kids they housed. While I was forging beautiful connections with those kids, it became clear that this closeness was somehow threatening. When the job turned out to be less about impact and more about discipline and demoralization, I knew it was time to move on.

Incidentally, at the same time, the school accused me of ringleading an underground gang of girls into a seedy life of vandalism and scandalous behavior. The allegations were ridiculous, and as I emphatically denied them, they called my former house dad in for a meeting as to my character. While he and his wife had been happy to vouch for my character to help me land the position, suddenly they felt it pertinent to tell the facility's administration about the one time I had lied about not having sex with a boy and how I'd clung to my lie for weeks. That one time nine years before, when they had all but forced me to lie after weeks of telling the truth.

This told me more about their character than it shed any truth-based light on mine. My former houseparents were kind enough to drive me to Vail, Colorado, where I stayed in a hotel until my other former house dad Vic Thompson could pick me up. They hadn't allowed me to bring my dog, and they'd spent a lot of the trip pointing out my many disappointments and lies (about the miscarriages and health issues, in addition to the big Jim scandal from nine years before) and driving home that I was destined for an eternity in hell because I hoped to remarry someday.

It seemed they agreed with my family, that even though I'd just turned twenty-four, I had ruined my life, and any chance at a future was over.

Empowered and more confident, I ended up going home to Idaho. While I wasn't any more put together than the girl I'd been when I'd left a year before, I was learning who I was. I hadn't ever known that luxury before, and this made me very different, even if I was still at the mercy of crashing with friends.

Sherri's marriage had ended, and she'd relapsed into addiction. While that was all so heartbreaking, I was daily falling more in love with my beautiful niece, her daughter. I took a job in retail and was willing to do the hard work of building a life that I was proud of, on my own terms.

Around the time that my sickness came back, in August of 2000, word made its way to me that a group home was seeking me out. Everyone in my immediate circle could feel the gravity of the choice I had to make. I had no health insurance and needed another surgery. I couldn't keep my brand-new retail job. They specialized in designer, name-brand things, and one lunch hour when I nearly bled out in the break room, they reconsidered my ability to do that position. I was a burden on friends. The group-home job not only offered health benefits, but also the promise of setting me up with a doctor and paying the co-pays while giving me housing and a paycheck while I recovered. For me, it seemed like a no-brainer. The best bonus of all was that Kentucky had shown me how much I loved working in similar settings to where I'd grown up. In the dinner interview, I had been honest about the events leading to my leaving the Kentucky job, and this director assured me that connection between staff and the kids was her goal.

It all sounded like the most responsible decision.

No one else, however, agreed. Not Sherri, not the friends I was staying with—there was not one person who supported my decision. Due to their disapproval, some people pulled away, but thankfully there were others who stood beside me anyway.

On October 28, I went in for surgery and woke to find I'd had a full hysterectomy. True to my new boss's word, she had set me up with a gynecologist. When the doctor had seen the state of my mangled uterus while I lay on his operating table, he made the judgment call to remove everything. I'd been warned at my last appointment that if he saw any signs of cancer, this could happen. While he hadn't seen definitive cancer, he'd seen no other option.

I awoke to the news that I would never be able to have a baby. The last dangling piece of baggage that had been weighing me down left by way of that only-ever-faulty womb. I had already shed lifetimes of tears over no babies. For the first time, I was overcome with relief. That chapter was finally over.

During the days that I was in the hospital, I wondered if this had been how Chris had felt. Had the relief of never having to feel the anguish of my miscarriages again driven him into the arms of someone else? We'd stayed in touch loosely, but I doubted I'd ever really know. That relationship hadn't lasted long, and he'd packed it all up in exchange for a brand-new life in Michigan. When we talked, it was clear he was the happiest he'd ever been, and I was happy for him. While I still believed he was a great guy, I didn't particularly like him. I'd seen the man he could be—both the fun, jovial guy and the resentful jerk. I believed we both stood our best chances at good lives far away from one another.

My communication with my former second set of house-parents, after they left me in Vail, was minimal. There were a few months of the occasional email. When I had my emergency hysterectomy just three months later, their response was that it was embarrassing how I would still stoop so low as to lie about my health. They wrote in that email, "What you are claiming happened isn't even possible. It's probably best that you don't write again. We pray you find the Lord." Thus, concluding the very minimal relationship we had.

A perk of my new group-home job—which I loved—was counseling. I'd told the director when I'd interviewed, that I needed counseling. She was more than willing to set me up with a therapist and cover the cost. She had pursued me because she knew I was great at my job. She also had a soft spot for me because she'd become associated with the Christian Children's Ranch where I'd grown up.

Twelve years earlier, I had moved to Idaho. I went through so many impossible things and had never seen a therapist. Not once. I identified my need and knew it would help, and it did. In those sessions, we unpacked and dissected years of life. I was challenged regarding beliefs I had. While I was doing a good job of casting aside the wishes of others in pursuit of owning my own life, it really was those hours with my counselor that made the biggest impact.

One day I'll share the story of Chris and me and how we came to remarry. During our time apart we each went through a lot of therapy, a lot of healing, and a lot of growth. In November of 2001—almost exactly two months after the planes hit the Twin Towers—we remarried. It was beautiful, simple, and drama free. This time it wasn't because I had no other options or because he felt obligated to be the good guy.

We chose each other and would continue to, again and again.

These pages aren't meant for that story though. This moment is about my daughterhood and motherhood, and in order to get to this moment, you needed to see how I fell apart and eventually came back together.

I asked Chris what things he felt uncomfortable about me sharing as I told pieces of my story, and he said there was nothing. His exact words were, "The times I was an asshole, I have to own. I trust you, and I know you'll say what needs to be said."

For a long time, I wondered if it was a betrayal to tell the stories of the boys who came before him, since I am now his wife—my anxiety over it was sometimes quite intense. As I began to process through my deconstruction from legalistic and oppressive religion, sifting out the patriarchal garbage that did not fit in with the nature of the God I'd always known, it became clear that this was where the language of my shame and anxiety were written. The truth is that none of these stories were secrets from my husband, and every single person mentioned in this book is here because they were important in the shaping of me, in some way. As flawed as the brothers, boyfriends, and boy–best friends could be, they were also among the brightest spots through the formative parts of my journey.

Of course, where boys are concerned, none of them come close to the places in my heart where my husband and son live.

Chris, Misty & Nora
during Nora's
six-weeks in Idaho.
February 1111

Surrender

{For the two girls I love most in this world: "To Love Forever" by William Fitzsimmons}

As an adult woman I have known my share of hospitals. Over the years, I have had a dozen procedures, spent many nights, and it would be fair to speculate close to a hundred emergency room visits. I have been tired of hospitals for a long time. As an eleven-year-old girl, though, it seemed really exciting.

My mom and grandmother had driven me to the hospital for admitting. The psychiatrist was willing to play along with my mother's insistence that I was suicidal, if only to get me in care. Silver City, New Mexico, is a small city, and although it stood several stories high, the Gila Regional Medical Center itself was unexceptional. During admittance, the doctor hovered close by, insisting I be placed in the pediatric unit, not the psych ward. Nora was argumentative and had an instant response for every reason he provided. She insisted the psych ward was where I belonged.

I don't know if he succeeded in convincing her, or if the hospital simply didn't care about her opinion, but eventually, my private room was in the pediatric unit.

For the first few days, it was an adjustment, but eventually a routine set in. I had a physical therapist who came to get me once a day. We'd go down to the occupational therapy room and exercise a little. We'd do some balance games, and on the best days, we'd grab an ice cream sandwich on the way back.

The dietitian would deliver daily menus, and I loved that I could eat whatever I wanted. I spent most evenings in my room, watching MTV or HBO. Sometimes the nurses would come in to check on me and give me a hard time if it was past ten o'clock. There was one nurse who would leave books on my nightstand for me to curl up and read in the afternoons. I was free to roam and wander wherever I wanted to go. If I popped into the gift shop and the candy stripers were nearby, they'd always buy me soda. Except for the afternoons when my pediatrician would come in and question me about sexual abuse, I was living an unparented dream life any eleven-year-old would envy.

The doctor took me on a walk down to the psych ward one afternoon. She wanted to explain to me why I wasn't staying there, even though it was what my family thought was necessary. We went down in the elevator, and as we entered the ward, the big metal doors locked behind us. The hallway was dingy yellow with artificial light, and there didn't seem to be any windows anywhere.

"There is only one patient here." Her tone was measured, informative. I wondered if she could hear him screaming from down the hall, or if it was just me.

I thought it was a scary place, and as we walked back to our hall, I was so relieved to see the plants and windows bringing forth sunshine. One of the reasons the psychiatrist had given Nora for why I needed to be on the children's floor was loneliness. He wanted me to be near other kids because the isolation could make things worse. Nora responded that I wasn't there to make friends, I was there to "stop being so bad." I thought about his words often because I'd spent the first few days wondering when all the other kids were going to show up. On that particular day, though, I could feel how unsettling and empty the ward downstairs had felt. There were no happy nurses, no teenage or elderly volunteers. There was no laughter coming from the nurse's station. Even at my young age I could see how life existed where my room was, and down there felt like something else.

Ice cream sandwiches, MTV, unlimited pudding cups, and people always there to give me kindness and positive attention aside, none of these things was why I loved the hospital so much. My doctor was a pediatrician, so every morning when she came to the hospital, she would tend to the babies. The first time she took me to help her give baths and stamp their feet, I think she hoped it would help me let my guard down and I would open up to her. When, instead, I fell in love with the measuring and the exams and all the things that kept me near the babies, she began to include me. She gave me the title of her helper, and sometimes, when I walked the halls, I would get invited into a room where a mom I had met that morning would talk with me. Sometimes they would come find me in my room to say goodbye as they left. A few times they even left their flowers and balloons.

I don't specifically remember any of these moms, their babies, or the nurses. What I can still feel is this constant sense of awe over how so many people actually wanted to talk with me or go out of their way to bring me small bits of joy.

Upon leaving an "It's a Boy" balloon, one mom winked, saying she had an idea just what I would do with it, and she was right. The second she was gone, I took it around the corner to Gabriel's room and tied it to his bed.

Gabriel...

How is it that well over three decades later, I can still remember his smell?

My doctor introduced me to Gabriel as soon as she saw how I responded to the babies. "You both need each other," she'd said, and she was right. Gabriel had been born early because his mom had been on drugs. She was in jail, and he wasn't very healthy, so he was going to be in the hospital for a long time. I don't remember how old he was on that first day, but he was so tiny. His breathing was rattly, and he wore an oxygen cannula in his nose.

Because there was no family to visit him, Gabriel spent the days mostly alone. Sometimes candy stripers would rock him for a moment, but everyone had a task to do.

Everyone but me.

The day I was discharged, leaving that baby boy hurt the most. I cried myself to sleep for days, my arms achingly empty from the hours I'd spent rocking him. He loved it when I sang to him and always reached out to wrap his tiny fingers tight around my thumb.

I had never really been around a baby, and then, for five weeks, my days revolved around him. By the end of my first week there, I would assist in his baths and do the majority of his daytime feedings. The nurses would bring him to my room in the evening, because they said he missed me, and everyone else made him cry.

I hated his mother, whoever she was. I hated everyone he belonged to because no one ever came. They just left him alone. By the time I was discharged, he needed oxygen only when he was sleeping.

Maybe it was that sweet, innocent baby who awoke my inner advocate. Had I learned something by loving him that had inspired me to fight for myself in the months following my release? However it happened, Gabriel became a piece of me. At least that version of him, etching into the core of my soul—someday I wanted to be a mother.

While I do not believe an eleven-year-old girl would make a great mom, my time with Gabriel connected me with my inner mother. All the things that a mother feels and does out of instinct for her child, I did for him. I wouldn't tap into that source again for several years—not until Maegy.

With her, there had been the nurturing, the love, and then the loss. I was fifteen, and there is no way I could've been the best "mother" for that little blonde ball of energy. I also knew I gave her all I could. I protected her, and for the second time, I was loving and mothering when the actual mother couldn't be. Right or wrong, it was a pattern—one that would continue.

On the night of my adopted daughter's ninth birthday party, a cluster of my very favorite people fell asleep lounging on our oversized leather sectional. We were all worn out from the festivities, and the comfort and quiet of togetherness had hit just right. When I awoke and took in the scene, my heart felt like it exploded into a million little pieces. While, leading up to that moment, life and motherhood had held some really beautiful moments causing me to pause and take stock, this particular one earned the brightest of gold stars.

Later that night as we crawled into bed, Chris remarked that the nights we were all under the same roof were his favorite.

"MINE TOO!" I exclaimed. After everything we had been through, we found ourselves in this place of shared love and a united front that only the two of us could understand. There were many conversations when we talked in depth about how every single terrible moment we'd endured on our path to parenthood had been worth knowing and loving the four young humans who made up the sum of our shared heart.

The oldest of the four found someone else to fill the role of mom in her life. It hurt me at first, but I realized I loved her all the same anyway, and it didn't matter. I didn't have to be the one she called "mom" to love her or to believe in her. With the other three, it was a little different. I was the only mom our youngest had ever known. After broken years of trauma and abuse, she'd come to us at four and a half. I went to hell and back for her. Early childhood trauma is an ugly beast, and I'd proven there wasn't anything I would not try, buy, learn, or explore if it meant that she had a better chance at a whole and healthy life one day.

With the middle two, one boy and one girl, it was weightier. More complicated. They could tell others I was their mom, but not call me such. They could love and trust me, but also not really at all. They could need to reach out for my connection, but also dispose of me as though I'd never meant a thing. They were teenagers by the time life finally opened a door for us to sleep under the same roof sometimes, but when my heart committed to loving them, they were children, and I never gave up that pursuit.

Motherhood feels less like victory and more like being cracked open, your everything spilling out onto the floor. After the pain and loss that I'd gone through, I expected this moment to show up—where I felt like I finally belonged, bonded to my child—but it never did. I waited for some spark or zap to signal my motherhood was officially valid, but none came. This didn't impact how much I loved our kids or how grateful I was for this family we had. Against insurmountable odds, Chris and I had found our way to this beautiful, flawed masterpiece. These three kids known as ours were the most beautiful, bright, hilarious, and inspiring balls of life either of us had ever known.

Every time more than three of us existed in that Idaho house on Wiltshire Court, I thanked God. The memories and moments within those walls were restorative and, hands down, the best ones of my life. One Saturday morning, as the five of us sat around our kitchen table eating brunch, I saw where life was headed. It was less of a vision, more feeling, and I knew those moments filling my motherhood chasm up were going to slow.

Still, I moved forward. This is all I have ever done, really. Move forward, keep going. My determination was the one reason the five of us ever made our way together in the first place. It was never easy. The easiest part of the whole mess was loving those kids. Everything else was hard. Every step we took as parents involved calculated measures. We had to hold back our hearts and dance our lives atop eggshells, ensuring that we didn't do something to send one of them running. It was exhausting, but they were worth it.

As humans, we adapt.

Many of our family members believed we were "playing house" and that these weren't our "real kids." I was angry they felt this way, and resentful they'd said it, but deep down I was terrified they were right.

Meanwhile, well-meaning friends who were parents of their biological, non-ECT (early childhood trauma) kids encouraged us to be stricter, less graceful, clearer. They couldn't comprehend the liberties we simply did not have. This wasn't a bad thing, but it was isolating. Even so, for a long time it unified Chris and me even more. Many days felt like it was us against the world.

I fear that it may feel as though I shared so many intimate details from earlier in my life, only to gloss over two decades of motherhood. I promised from the beginning, to share *my* truths. Beyond the scope of my motherhood, the stories of these three souls are not mine to tell. For the most beautiful period of time, I allowed myself to pretend I was a real mother. The very first time I had surrendered my fortress to embrace the beliefs and the hopes that came with finally being a mother involved two baby girls.

It all came tumbling down to rubble with two sisters too.

A time came when the girls who were the daughters of my heart no longer saw a place for me in their lives or future, and as much as the whole ordeal sucked the breath from my lungs, that was their choice to make.

Marriages where two consenting adults dissolve their union are deemed socially acceptable. We need to allow a space to accept that adopted and heart-parent loves can break apart too. Unrequited love is not exclusive to romance. A baby bonds with a mother because they grew in her womb. Her body literally gave them life, and they develop into a human being set to the soundtrack of her heartbeat, the sound of her voice. When a child who has been hurt, abandoned, or neglected meets a stranger who calls herself mama, there is no magic button that guarantees attachment. There is no natural course of organic growth guaranteed, and this is something I have witnessed that more adoptive parents need to be educated on. Though these types of things are labeled "failed adoptions" or "failure to bond," this isn't failure. Sometimes life is hard and there is so much damage and hurt, and no one can win.

Though it will feel like the worst of all failures to an aching mama-heart.

Trauma affects us each in different ways, and those are beyond our control. Sometimes, years and years show that no matter what great measure of love and sacrifice a mother may give, the child simply can't reciprocate. A child is not obligated to love an adoptive parent. Sometimes relationships just don't work out. It isn't fair for these kids to grow up in a world where people expect this of them. The truth is, when it comes to attachment disorders, the primary parental figure almost always becomes the target of significant villainization and resentment. In many instances, mine included, no matter how hard that parent tries, they won't be able to exist beyond that.

It is psychological.

It isn't deliberate, but it does hurt.

It is tragic for everyone involved—parent and child. Quite often, the only outcome available is one where no one wins.

For a long time, I believed if I could just love enough, try a bit harder, and give even more, I could finally be enough. I chased that moment so fervently, and in doing so allowed myself to unfairly expect these kids to love me back, to *want* me back. In truth, while I stood up and chose them, that doesn't obligate them to choose me in return. *Because* I love them, I have to be honest and admit that I don't want them to be obligated to me. They deserve better than that.

It took a lot of time in the trenches, along with wise counsel, to help me accept that I am allowed to be sad for what could have been. I am allowed to remember the beautiful times, to miss them. I am allowed to grieve the family that isn't. There is nothing "meant to be" about situations where children come to be a part of nonbiological families just because they went through hell to end up there.

I did not lose my babies because God knew these kids would someday need a childless mother. A lot of people believe this way, and it is wrong. It depicts a heartless God. These girls who I will always carry in my heart were *never meant to be mine*. They were knit in the womb of their birth mothers, and those mothers hurt them.

Though we may have been good at pretending for a while, they were never able to accept my love. I can't blame them for that. The world felt full, and my cup overflowed as the mom of two beautiful daughters and one brave son. My heart burst with some unnamable magic over being loved as Mimi (grandma), by the next generation of these beautiful souls I'd loved as my own. One day this was life, and then on another day it wasn't.

I learned the world is full of wonder and ever-changing beauty outside of motherhood too. Once upon a time, deep in that jungle, I didn't think it could be.

I am the daughter of a mentally ill woman who is now lost to a disease inside of herself. Some days she knows my face and sees me, others she does not. Nora was not a perfect mother, but at least she got to be one, and I am forever grateful she was mine. For all the awful things that unfolded between us, Nora was an exceptionally beautiful soul and a lot of people loved her.

Some of those people knew only the parts she showed them, but more than anyone else, I saw the truth.

I saw the real, full, shattered her.

I love her.

Not because I have to, but because I can't imagine not.

She deserved better than what her mental illness and insecurity gave her. I grieve that for a woman my world was truly better for having known.

The very small chapter of time when pages from the girls' stories overlapped with mine is among my favorites. I am so grateful I had the foreshadowing then to live in the moment and realize the gifts I had in two beautiful daughters who grew into two incredible women. We were not meant to be a family, but, for a minute, we sort of were. I'll store that minute with my life treasures and carry it with me until I am no more. My entire life has been about trying to make others accept my love, accept me, find me worthy.

And the truth is I am tired.

After a hundred lifetimes of this heart-wrenching chase of my mother's love, and then for my own motherhood, when it finally ended at the request of these beautiful girls, it was time for me to allow the door to gently close.

It was time to extend myself the grace to be done.

Soldier On

{To LBT: "Never Alone" by Jim Brickman, Lady A}

There once was a little boy dressed in camouflage who played army with his friends. He grew from the sweetest, most tender heart to a teenage athlete, and from there to a real-life soldier in the military.

As a boy, he found the courage he needed to ask me to be his mom. Though my association with the word itself has known such complication, I answered *yes* that day and every single day since. This boy has chosen me time and again. I never sought in him perfection, and he chose to love me as I've always been. It hasn't always been easy because life is hard, and traumatic things bring with them complications. Even so, this soldier will always be my son, one-third of my mother-heart. The one reason I can't declare the whole motherhood venture a fruitless effort.

These pages are not a collection of my losses and failures, but of my darkest points becoming flooded with the brightest of light. Sometimes high school crushes did that, and sometimes my high school best friend William did. A thousand times over the years, Chris has. Marriage can be tough, and, while honest stories make us uncomfortable, we should be willing to embrace them over the polished, curated ones.

Always, always, always the kids I loved as my own became the brightest and warmest of light, beyond any other. Even in our darkest moments, that light was why I lived. Eventually their children added to the light, and not one single day passed without my heart feeling it could burst from the gratitude consuming me.

When my son's light was far away, seldom seen, and the girls turned theirs away from me, I had no choice but to reflect on the status of my own illumination. I once again stared down at my own Vegas Strip collection of neon signs displaying how I hadn't been enough and I'd been easy to leave. I have lived in that dark space so many times.

At the hand of my mother, my husband, my kids, but most often, myself.

There are so many things about this life that did not end up as I'd hoped.

I never found that belonging with others.

I never did find a forever family.

Though I know my husband loves me, I'll likely always feel like something to fall back into rather than his pursuit or choice.

I didn't know I could survive the hurt attached to any of these things, but I have. It turns out I had it in me all along. It was here when I realized it was time for me to tear my internal neon signage of lies down.

Girls, Assassins & Other Bad Ideas is a glimpse into the differing variations of me—me and the women and girls throughout my journey. Both the givers of life as well as many of my deepest wounds. The female heroes who sometimes, me especially, are also the villains.

The only unfailing embrace to hold me was that of an overall-wearing God and his faceless son.

These were not the deities introduced to me through manipulation, purity culture, and legalistic oppression. These were not the same God and Jesus associated with shaming me into submission.

These were the source of light every time. In the redeeming of two people's broken journey and their shared life.

Light from the moments of radiant smiles in children who had known such hurt before.

Light from the way the orange sun paints the Pacific tide, as it crashes into the sand in which I stand, sinking, feeling at home in the water as it rushes my feet.

Light—it is everywhere.

This God-light lives in me. Where bitterness could have set in like a cancer, his light warmed me to act in love.

Love—the riskiest decision of all, and still, I'll choose it a thousand times more. Loving means seeing another soul as they are and embracing them anyway, believing in them and fighting for them. It looks like pouring out all that loving light.

Sometimes I may get hurt, but eventually I'll get up and I will love again. It isn't because I'm better than anyone.

It is because God scattered people to act as lanterns throughout my life, when I was my most broken, so I could one day find my own way to understanding the value of being a beacon for someone else.

2001

Misty with Lucas 2019

Sherri & Misty

2013

Alzheimer's Walk for Nora

Winter

Luminaries

{Song: "Winter" by Mree}

The first time I remember ever feeling whole, I was knee deep in the Pacific Ocean the summer I was seventeen. It was an average, overcast Oregon coast kind of day, but my memory of that first ocean tide inhale is illuminated beyond any other memory. Every visit to a continental coast has this same effect on me—salt air cleansing me, sea sounds centering me. If I go too long between visits to sink my toes in that sand, it can really start to take its toll.

When Chris and I first dated, I would go out to the Ranch to pick up my mail or check in with the people I was missing. It wasn't often I felt welcome out there, but I went because it was the only home I had.

One such afternoon, as we were climbing into Chris's car, the sight of someone toward the back of the property caught my eye. She looked exactly like my first houseparents' oldest daughter, Joy. Had I not seen them just months before on my trip to Kansas, I probably wouldn't have recognized her. People were carrying boxes and items into a small apartment, and curiously, I followed them.

There, smiling while she directed where things should go, was my first house mom Julie.

Julie was beautiful. She had the voice of an angel and a smile that could literally shift the energy of a room.

I don't know why they moved back to the Ranch. I know that, for their little family of four, it was a hard season. Not everyone benefited, but adoption grew them into a beautiful family of five, and we were all thankful for that. My mom Julie told me once that seeing me those months before inspired their return. *Had it?* I don't know. It doesn't matter. In the years that would unfold, those two people became my parents. Dad would continue being the only actual dad I have had, and I wouldn't trade that for anything.

Julie was my mom. She had not birthed me, but she had been the one to truly love me the way that only a mom can. It took a lot of time and a lot of hard conversations, but eventually, I could accept this.

Thanksgivings and birthdays were celebrated with them as family during those early years of our marriage. Eventually they relocated to a house up in the mountains, and long weekends away usually had us going to "my parents." Chris had a mostly long-distance relationship with Nora, so these two people were his "in-laws." They were the ones he built a solid relationship with, and his connection to them surpassed even the bond he had with his own family.

That kind of love mesmerizes me.

For all the ways Nora hurt me, I am fine. There is no gaping wound in my life from a lack of mothering. Somehow, over time (and well into my adulthood), Julie's mothering filled those gaps. She sat and cried with me when Callie and Rheagan were taken. She loved me, from right beside me, through the hardest, ugliest, and scariest parts of my journey, even when those things happened as a result my own stupidity.

When my attempt at motherhood left me so lost, attachment disorder issues taking me down at every curve, she would answer the phone and know all the right things to say. We were living long-distance by this point, but our connection had not wavered.

She was my mom.

The reality that Julie also wasn't my mom never went away. While we were close, there was a whole portion of their family life I would forever be on the outside of. He was my dad, and those girls were like my sisters—and then, also, they weren't.

As I came down the aisle a new bride, it was Dad Thompson, hiding in the back beaming with his perfect gap-tooth smile, who made my day. I hadn't expected them to come, and in fact, Julie was among the people sent on the choir trip, but there he was.

Six and a half years later, my dad sat drinking coffee and filled with worry while I lay on an operating table down the hall. With tears in his eyes, after I woke up, it was him who spoke softly to me the news of my hysterectomy—that I would never have a baby.

These are the things that make them my parents. It was never about genetics or age, but about the accepting, the loving, and the being there.

Julie died unexpectedly in August of 2006. She'd been wrapping up some tasks before she was going to come up to Michigan to visit us. The phone call came—she was barely hanging on. In a rush we packed our car instead to drive down to Kansas. As we got near the interstate to head out, my cell phone rang. It was Nora.

"Put Chris on the phone." She sounded angry. I passed her over to him but knew instantly that my grandmother had died.

We turned around and bought airline tickets to New Mexico instead.

I thought about my grandmother's phone call the Sunday before. I heard her uncharacteristic words as the goodbye they were, when I'd been too busy to notice.

We flew to Phoenix and rented a car for Lordsburg. We were all exhausted, but I had grown to find solace on the road, so I took the wheel that desert night. The passing of the shadows and the silhouetted landscape soothed my weary spirit. Deep in heart and thoughts that evening, I allowed myself the reassurance of only one lie—*Julie would be fine*. I knew, to my core, that God would never take both of these women at the same time. I knew, despite any terrible things I had ever been through, that death was the biggest loss of all, and God loved me, so he would not allow me to be hurt that way.

The call came about my mom Julie's death during the reading of my grandmother's will. In that moment I assumed that God didn't really love me enough to spare me such heartache after all.

When I was fifteen, I met Donna. Donna had been coming to the Ranch in her black BMW to take William on outings every couple of weeks. In the same way a random family had taken me home for Christmas, she'd adopted the opportunity to take William out for some normal fun. They would go to the movies or the arcade. I knew *of* her, and knew he really loved her, but hadn't met her.

One afternoon as I was walking to my house from the barn, her BMW approached me. As her window rolled down, she asked if I was Misty. "I just got back from a trip to New York City, and I brought you a little something. I hope you like it, and I hope I get the chance to know you better someday because our William really loves you."

She'd bought me a shirt from *The Phantom of the Opera* musical.

A few months later, my camp friend and pen pal came to Boise with her family. She was school shopping and visiting her grandmother and wondered if I'd be allowed to spend the weekend with them. My houseparents agreed, so she and her mom picked me up. We went to the mall, we ate lunch at a restaurant, and then we pulled into her grandmother's tiny duplex in Meridian.

Family coming into town meant the extended family who lived locally would be gathering too. There was a lot of family crammed into that little duplex, but they accepted me with open arms, no weird *Ranch kid* vibes at all. After a while, my friend mentioned that her aunt would be coming by, and we'd be going with her because we'd be sleeping at her house.

Her aunt was William's Donna.

After that weekend, when my schedule allowed, she and William included me in their outings. We saw the movie *Benny & Joon* once, ate Blimpie subs a few times, and played at the arcade too. In those days, the biggest gift was the opportunity for my best friend and I to have some normal teen experiences, and she gave us that.

Donna came to my graduation, and so did her mom. She was still very much the aunt of my friend and belonging to William, in my eyes. On the storming night I learned I was kicked out of college, no longer allowed at the Ranch and without anyone in my corner, I showed up at her door.

Maybe I had done it because I still missed William. For so long he had been my person, and since then I'd not belonged to anyone at all. Maybe it was because she missed him, too, that she let me in. I don't know. What I am sure of is that Donna became someone special to me.

This amazing woman was my maid of honor, hosted my poorly attended bridal shower, and acted as my confidant during that dark season of my life when no one else showed up. It was her house where I recovered from several miscarriages and where I spent the first ten post-hysterectomy days before being well enough to make the road trip to my parents' mountain home for the rest of my recovery. It was her tiny, spirited mother who defended me to my husband when he ended our marriage. She stood, shouting at him, in her driveway. (She may be small, but Donna's mom is the strongest woman I have ever known.)

Through the years, Donna's husband has been the inspiration for so much of my growth and of Chris's courage to face his own demons and heal.

The three of them have stood by my side, without condition, opened their arms to the kids I loved, and faithfully welcomed Chris back—no questions asked—when we reconciled. I have known no better, more gracious, accepting people than Donna, her husband, and her mother.

When I take stock of my heart and who I am, I hope that there are some pieces of them within the mosaic of me.

My mom Julie taught me the basics of playing the piano. After she left the Ranch when I was fourteen, I continued to try and teach myself. My eyes had always been trained on the prize of mastering "Für Elise" because this was Nora's favorite. The summer I was fifteen, I had gone home to New Mexico for a visit. My grandmother took me to the little yellow church every day so that I could practice for the evening that I had invited Nora to come too. I had planned to surprise her with the song; she had no idea I'd been learning piano for three years.

In the weeks leading up to my visit, I'd told my mom about this special gift I had for her. I was all nerves that evening when the time had finally come.

As it turned out, Nora was disappointed that I didn't have an actual gift for her. She said she loved it, but also mentioned the time I hit two keys accidentally and made sure to point out that if I would just practice more, I might sound good one day.

That was the closest my two moms ever came to connecting.

One of the hardest years I've known was 2019. My chosen word for the year had been *Faith*. I had been hesitant to settle on that word, fearful of where it would lead. In so many ways, the first half of the year looked a lot like facing loss. My Aunt Gloria's husband, Phil, passed away in February. My Uncle Phil had always been special to me. As a small girl, after Papa had died, he'd been the male presence in my family. Since I spent so much time with them in Arizona, he filled that space. When Chris and I got married, it was Uncle Phil who walked me down aisle.

It was unfair that I was so set apart from my family after I was sent to Idaho. Distance consumed the spaces between all of us, and so much was left unspoken. It isn't anyone's fault. As I traveled to the funeral, my thoughts were overcome with this man, my Uncle Phil, with whom I had shared a significant portion of my life, to a point. At that dividing line, he and my aunt had become grandparents of four incredible kids, who grew to be a part of a family to which I no longer belonged. There's a "Before Idaho" and "After Idaho" timeline that divided my family, and there's been very little crossover.

Traveling to Uncle Phil's funeral, I questioned where I belonged, a lot. *Was I intruding on their family? Did I really belong?* When I arrived. It was awkward, comprised of moments that were connecting, moments that exposed distance, happy memories, and astounding grief. In this way I suspect it may have been pretty normal. There is always some drama, some angst, some unspoken vibes, and a hodge-podge of varying energies. I hadn't been in Lordsburg in years. It was overwhelming, having lived the journey I have, to travel back and come face-to-face with my soul—the soul parts that lived in that trailer on Zinc Street, with those fence posts that held the foundation of the most defining friendship of my girlhood.

Before the funeral however, I flew into Tucson. Melanie's dad, Ray, had been the one to meet my plane. Whenever I visited New Mexico as an adult, Nora would make it nearly impossible for me to see Ray and Lorrie. On rare occasions I could sneak over but had to keep it short. In the years since my last visit, they'd moved to Tucson to be closer to the VA hospital. I was nervous to see them; I had no idea what to expect. I carried so much guilt for loving this family so deeply and yet having spent such a small amount of time visiting them over the years.

Suddenly, there we were, an adult me and this man I have adored forever, alone in a pickup truck. As he drove toward the house they now live in, he unpacked over thirty years of stuff he has carried. He told me another perspective of the times I'd lived next door to them—what they saw and knew, what they feared, and apologies for things I don't even remember. Forgiveness is an amazing concept, and I have learned that there are so many people who believe they need it when the opposite is true. Ray and Lorrie owed me nothing and had given me everything. I, too, had carried guilt over not spending more time with them, not being more present in their lives. Not ... So many *nots*.

For days, as a very abnormal winter blizzard blanketed the Southwest, I sat inside their home absorbing. Melanie and I looked at photos, watched TV, and talked about normal things like makeup. There was an abundance of conversation and gap-filling, heart-mending smiles, laughter, and a generous amount of my soul food—tacos.

The time with them felt like my own personal stream in the desert. With every moment, my spirit knew these were *my people*, and in the oddest, most unexplainable ways, a piece of me was more at home in that house I'd never been in than I had felt in a very long time.

On the last evening, Joseph and his lovely wife came over.

I wondered what that would be like for me. I hadn't seen him since I was twelve. I had been such a stupid child then, why would he care to come say hello? (I'm pretty sure it was less that he should care, and more that his parents thought he should.)

Sometimes in movies, people can touch another human and see visions of things that reveal certain truths. When I hugged Joseph Martinez that February night, this is exactly what happened. It was less science fiction and more the connecting of something deep within my spirit. It was a healing—I was able to see a fraction of safe and normal that each member of their family had provided little-girl me. It was everything. It was in that *normal* that they had protected me.

During the grieving days in New Mexico that followed, I came face-to-face with many things. I saw beloved places. My mom's old house and the street I learned to ride my bike on. I walked the aisles of the tiny grocery store and drove past my elementary schools. I visited with some familiar people and listened to nearly everyone I encountered speak such beautiful things about my mother. People genuinely loved Nora, and I love them for that.

I saw the small town I'd resented for so long with fresh eyes—no longer filtered with my mother's expectations of me or what I'd been through when I'd lived there.

At some point in the middle of those days, my foster sister Joy (Julie's daughter) stood on my grandmother's porch next to me. In the most bizarre twist, she had moved not too far from this little town where I lived my life up until the day I met her—the dividing line of *Before* and *After*. My entire life felt like train tracks of division, perforated lines of my fragmented pieces. I was forty-two years old when those two pieces of my life collided on that patio in Lordsburg, New Mexico. It felt both small and monumental.

Just two months after the passing of my uncle, my biological father died. I found myself once again traveling, deep in thought, to a funeral. This time, Chris was by my side, and I was grateful. This amazing Kentucky family is another example of a fragmented piece of my life where I don't really belong. I can see commonalities I have with my siblings, just as I'd had with my father. We hadn't been strangers, per se, after that odd day when we met in 1993.

We each had tried, in various ways, to have relationships. The distance had always been far more significant than anything we could cover in a car. It's sad, but also another thing that folds neatly into *it is what it is*.

It was a sad day. I have a deep, genuine love for my father. I love his wife. I love their daughters and my older brother and sister. They all fit nicely bonded into the parts that truly make a family, and the piece that is me just doesn't have a spot there. I am so grateful to see these beautiful human beings and know that they are a reflection of our father. When I see how incredible these siblings are, I can't feel sorry for myself that I didn't really have him because they did.

Our lives consist of patterns. Yours does, and mine does too. Toward the core of my own personal patterns, there is loss and breakage, but these patterns do not equal my whole.

Nora would never be the mother she should have been.

I never did have a child or that family I tried so hard to force.

We are not more valuable because people love us, just as our worth does not diminish when they do not.

In the midst of our life storms, it is easy to lose sight of the horizon. It is the most natural reaction—as we are being beaten by such raging rain and wind—to be consumed by the ways we fear we may not measure up. The truth is we can face our deepest fears, weather our biggest losses, and still be alive.

Sometimes we survive the unimaginable.

When I was six years old, I sat cross-legged on my bedroom floor, surrounded by books. I looked around at those picture books and thought about how happy they made me feel. To the same God who would come to me in a dream, I prayed, "God, please let me do this. I want to grow up and write books that make people not be sad anymore."

And that desire never went away.

With the faith of a child, I prayed and believed in a God who would answer. As the years passed, I prayed for a brother and a sister when reality made those things impossible. I prayed to remember hard things and then for the strength to make it through them. I prayed for the love of parents because mine didn't love me. And I prayed so incomprehensibly for a family, for belonging, and for love.

The details in these pages are not evidence of a girl kept down by injustice. The dark parts are not ways in which that same God looked the other way. The patterns within these pages show that when people messed up, God still showed up for me. He showed up in the faces of a mom and dad, brothers and sisters, and Donna and her husband and sweet mom. With the faithful love of Ray and Lorrie and the gifts of Anjanette, Melanie, and Joseph, God gave me more answered prayers than I could ever add up.

In the no-questions-asked first kiss from a boy to his unyielding concern and heart for me. With the boys that followed who showed me pieces of myself and shaped me into the best parts of myself, God SHOWED UP.

My prayers for a baby gave me several amazing children to love, complete with a treasure trove of memories to hold on to.

The paired losing of Julie and my grandmother did not mean God's love was not for me, but that I needed to see how lucky I'd been to see God's love in them both.

This life has taught me the courage to hold tight, fight hard, *and* to let go.

I once heard that nothing would fit perfectly until I fit. It wasn't in the places I thought I should or in the spaces I longed it to be. In this process of truly seeing me, my mother, my journey—in the clarity of seeing the things I hadn't quite seen before, I found my fit.

I was able to belong to me.

Spring

(again)

Ends and Beginnings

{For Nora's daughter and for Misty's mom:
"Sad Dream" by Sky Ferreira}

In the early hours of October 24, 2021, Nora Jane took her last breaths and left this life. Awkwardly, I sat by her bedside not knowing what to do or how to be. I'd like to think she knew I was there, but with Alzheimer's you never know.

It had been roughly eighteen months of pandemic life, battling state and nursing facility restrictions. We'd moved a few hours away from her facility in 2018, so my three to four times per week visits had gone down to one to two every couple of months. Sometimes she realized, and sometimes she hadn't. Leaving her had been much harder than I'd expected, and if too much time elapsed between visits, it started to get to me. I had decided I wanted to spend my late-March birthday with her and even planned a small friend get-together for the weekend. I'd been on this lifelong journey not to hate my birthday so much and thought long and hard about how I wanted to spend it: Mom, friends, coffee, tacos, and cake. Perfection.

A couple of weeks before, however, the 2020 "two-week lockdown" was put in place.

I hadn't seen her since Christmas as it was, but these were the early COVID days and fears were high. We were disrobing in our mudroom and disinfecting everything that crossed our threshold. More than anything, I wanted my mom to be safe.

When we were finally permitted to see her, we had twenty minutes to sit outside of a tent while she was inside. She had no idea what was happening or why we had to wear face masks. She couldn't understand most of what we said, but the gift of all gifts was that she knew my face. She knew I was her daughter. It had been nine months since I'd seen her, and the fear that I'd missed her last recognition plagued me. We recorded the visit for my Aunt Gloria. My mom was childlike and funny, and I knew in the deepest part of me that I likely would not see her that way again.

Several months passed, with restrictions once again in place. She refused video visits. Of course, she did—she had no idea what was happening.

In the spring of 2021, we were permitted a window visit, which I didn't love. My mother sat by the window completely catatonic while I stood in the sweltering Michigan humidity watching her. Chris would tap on the window, trying to get her attention. Perhaps she couldn't see us; she certainly couldn't hear us. The State of Michigan wanted me to write a report answering how I thought her quality of life and care seemed. She looked vegetative. How was I supposed to answer that?

There had been many planned visits, scheduled at the facility's request and then canceled by them due to positive cases and campus lockdowns. Then late September came, and they called to tell me my mom had fallen and was in the hospital. Seven hours later I was told she was being put on hospice and we needed to make the trip over as soon as possible because she didn't have long to live.

What does one expect to be greeted with when dealing with Alzheimer's and so much time passing? Which mom would I see? Would she even know she was a mom, or worse—*my* mom?

Chris and I drove separately because his employer wouldn't grant him permission to work remotely, and I was determined to be there until the end.

For the first several days, she rallied and it was wonderful. She regressed through stages of knowing I was her daughter, telling me about her daughter, and being a child waiting for her mom to come pick her up. The consistent things in each scenario were her upbeat spirit and that there was a Pharaoh in the corner watching her. Those days were the very best days.

The hospice nurse believed Nora's Pharaoh was the angel of death; I was just happy to have real face-to-face time with my mom. I brushed her hair every day, massaged her hands and feet, and we laughed so much. We kept all her favorite songs looping on repeat, and she still knew all the words, even if life beyond those lyrics was a bit confusing.

Chris finally left for home, and I temporarily moved in with a friend and waited. The staff assured me she really was dying, even though she had seemed to come alive.

During her nap times, I tried to read but couldn't focus. I researched the effects of isolation on the elderly and began to wonder if that was all that had actually been wrong with her. I marveled at the COVID risk we'd been deemed before, and yet had free range of the facility now that my mother was in hospice.

So much time brought on a flood of memories. Like a slideshow of a life lived, I recounted the dozens and dozens of times my mom had visited Chris and me. She was always spending excess money on me, and when I'd try to decline her generosity, she would say, "Don't tell me what to do. I owe you more than I can ever spend. You deserved a better mother. You deserved a better life. Buying you this one thing is the least I can do."

And I'd let her. I didn't love it, but I wouldn't argue. She was trying, and in a lot of ways, she was right. In the earlier days, of course, the endless supply of money came from her boyfriend, and I could justify it because he kind of owed me too—even though he really didn't. Neither of them owed me anything beyond taking responsibility for what they had done.

Their relationship ended in 2002, and in 2008, my mom had a stroke. Those six years were the happiest and most stable any of us had ever seen her. It was also the longest period of time she hadn't been in a relationship. After her stroke, it all changed. She was placed on permanent disability, and ever so slowly, when she couldn't afford things, like the power bill, her property taxes, or the significant amount of consistent overdraft fees she incurred due to severe depression shopping, I absorbed them. She was embarrassed and always "hated to ask," but this never stopped her doing so, nor from making me promise I wouldn't tell my aunt.

After her stroke she underwent several procedures. She had rods placed in her back, a foot surgery, and a double mastectomy due to breast cancer. Jolly Nora was around far less than ever. Bitterness had always been a struggle for her, but as time passed and her will to live shrank, the resentments grew worse. As did the shopping—coin collections, Blair catalog clothes she couldn't actually wear, Disney Movie Club, Fingerhut. Her "convenient monthly payments" far exceeded her social security allowance, and there I was, stepping in. I felt like it was my responsibility, like I owed her because she was my mom. It caused a lot of resentment to grow in my husband and drove a wedge between us.

The truth was that we couldn't afford to support her, yet I left us no choice.

In the summer of 2014, she was told that she wouldn't likely be able to live alone for much longer. She made me swear I wouldn't let her go to a nursing home but would instead bring her to live with us when the time came. With the same obsessive behavior that she developed for shopping, she immediately began preparing to come live with me. She was giving away possessions and selling things left and right. Her shopping had made her a hoarder, and she'd always been a collector. She pulled out her will and gave my two cousins everything she'd plan to give them. The plan consumed her, until she woke up one day no longer remembering that perspective. Suddenly it was me forcing her to part with everything and move to Michigan. Me. She didn't want it. Her exact words were, "The thought of living with you and seeing you every day sounds like hell. I didn't want you when you were a kid, why would I want you now?"

And there it was.

It had been years of believing she was my best friend, years of burying those long-ago aches deep down as I validated her love for me because she'd call me, buy things, and visit. With one sentence she broke me open and split me right in two. I knew that I would never be the same again, and I was right.

She no longer wanted to come, and I no longer wanted her. Our phone conversations were briefer, with days in between. She'd still reach out when property taxes or homeowner's insurance bills were due. She had a credit card maxed out that we'd already been covering the minimum $380-a-month payment on for seven years, which of course primarily went to interest and not the principal. Chris put his foot down in the spring of 2015 and said we weren't paying the credit card bills anymore. I was in therapy for strictly mom stuff, layers and layers of mom stuff. My counselor saw his actions as controlling, but I knew he was right.

I'd made it clear to my mother and aunt that she wasn't welcome to come live with us. I felt so good about that. I still loved her, but with my therapist I was working on putting boundaries in place. Chris was growing more distant and justifying that distance by zeroing in on my shortcomings. I was willing to take it because I believed I deserved it. My therapist helped me see the decades of poor choices I'd made regarding Nora. Chris and I went away for a weekend, and I talked to him about all of these things. Our conversation was so good, so honest, and it felt like a turning point ... and then my life blew up.

My aunt had grown tired of dealing with my mother. She'd taken over my grandmother's house and was building a life in Lordsburg. She'd chosen to stay to be a support for my mentally ill mom, but as time progressed, my mother was becoming more and more hateful and difficult. We all assumed this was because she was prone to bitterness—this made sense.

"She's coming to live with you. I'll have movers bring her stuff. I bought her a plane ticket. She's coming on August first. She will be happier there. She's home alone, all the time, and it's just not helping her."

"I understand that, but I'm in therapy, and honestly, this is not the best time. This is actually the worst time."

"Misty, it doesn't matter. It's done. It's happening. She is your mother, and she is your responsibility. I've done all I can with her, it's your turn."

And there it was ... my lifelong belief. Months and months of therapy undone.

In mid-June of that same year, I emailed William a "Happy Father's Day" note. Our Facebook connection had been hit or miss for several years. When he replied, he shared he'd just gotten out of jail from drug charges and was struggling with addiction.

And there it was ... twenty-two years after he left the Ranch, I was called to the plate to step up and claim what I'd always believed was my responsibility.

It started with adding him to our phone plan so he could find work and check in with his parole officer. I was in Michigan, and he was all the way in Idaho. It felt safe, and Chris was trying so hard to be supportive even though I suspect he felt I was going a little crazy.

He would have been right.

I wasn't handling Nora's impending arrival well at all. My counselor seemed to be unclear of how I'd allowed my aunt to make that decision and decided to home in on Chris. She didn't like how "controlling" he seemed. Not in his favor was that he'd call or text me during sessions, which were the same time every week.

"Classic narcissistic behavior," she decried, shaking her head.

In late August, I bought an airline ticket to go see William and my sister Sherri. It had been a while since I'd been home to Idaho. I was sure that by late August we'd have some home health care aid lined up to help my mom and even more certain that I'd be ready for the break.

It turned out, I'd never use that ticket.

William absconded from Idaho and, after a couple of weeks hiding out in Oregon, came to Michigan. He'd made it clear that he would never be able to stay clean out west because he had too many triggers, too many connections. He made it double clear that I'd been the only person who saw him as better than he was and that I was his one shot at a better life.

Me ... and it was so ingrained in me that he was my responsibility, I agreed.

My counselor was in complete support of this decision, which didn't help. She was very eager to see how our reconnecting in person would affect my emotional health, how my mother and William would get along, since I wasn't used to people from different times of my life overlapping, and if having another male's perspective would finally get through to me on how terrible my husband was.

It was all bad. All of it. The two months Nora was in my home before she was diagnosed with advanced Alzheimer's and placed in a home had been an absolute nightmare. In all the ways I'd feared she hated me as a child, she exhibited actual hatred every day. I began to avoid her. She loved William. Ironically, he was the only one who would defend me to her. (She didn't love that part.)

Chris had taken me to the airport to pick up William but waited for us at baggage claim. As we came down the escalator toward Chris, I watched something about his face change. Much later he told me that he'd never seen me radiate the way I did when I was with William. He decided I should be with William in whatever capacity of relationship we'd one day have and wanted out of our marriage.

Again.

This was the farthest thing from what I wanted, but my counselor was ecstatic. It was true that I felt more whole connected to William than I remembered feeling before, but I was also pouring myself empty (and bleeding myself financially dry) trying to help him.

And there it was ... I was empty. I was done. I moved out; William relapsed. I had nothing left.

I was thirty-nine years old and facing lessons I should have learned when I was fifteen. Neither William nor Nora had been my responsibility, yet I would jump through hoops and sacrifice myself for them to no end. This pattern played out, in smaller ways, in my enabling Sherri when she was younger, in attempting motherhood, in various jobs I took on over the years. I gave and gave of myself because I believed this was what love required.

Part of this was misconstrued beliefs at the hands of a legalistic, evangelical upbringing, and part of it was my own ache for someone to find me worth fighting for.

I loved others in the way I wanted to be loved.

The only person I'd been ever been truly responsible for was me, and I was the most crumbled variation of discarded garbage I'd ever been, but most of this was because of my own actions.

At thirty-nine years old I took the painful examination of my life. Despite actively loving and prioritizing people, I was alone and at my lowest point. I had to ask myself how was I responsible for getting there, and where did I want to go from there?

It was all terrifying. It was extremely uncomfortable.

I cut ties with anyone who wasn't aligned with the me I wanted to be: a confident woman who felt whole. A woman who loved herself and continued to advocate for herself because she believed in herself. A woman who valued the stories she'd lived as purposeful and important.

I juggled three jobs and slept in my car sometimes or in the homes of friends. I surrounded myself with women who emulated the sort of woman I wanted to be. Some of these women loved Jesus and some of them read tarot and believed in the healing power of crystals. I began to fine-tune the voice in my head against the truths I knew.

Did the idea of God loving me bring me comfort when the gospel I'd been told was that God loved everyone the same? It did not.

Did the "voice of God" I'd spent my life adhering to belong to a loving creator? Or was it the accumulative patriarchal voice of white men subtly ensuring that I believed I was worthless and had to earn God's favor? And if that wasn't God's voice, then what was God saying to me anyway?

So, I began to listen ...

I began to listen to the lyrics of random songs I'd hear and pause to notice the rhythm beneath the surface of the rustling leaves on windy days. When I was working, I would encounter random women who would open up to me about their struggles and insecurities. Again, and again, the things I was learning about myself, about God's voice, and about life were showing up.

I started taking classes and working my way through a coaching program to one day work with women who had struggled to embrace the dark parts of their own story. I worked alone to rebuild my marriage because I realized that in the same ways I had placed "loving" my mother and William above myself, I'd done this with Chris too. One day he took the leap, slowly reflecting on his own mistakes, and we grew together.

It would be years before I'd realize the secret to life, to healing: It is the intentionally doing.

It is the intentionally listening—and trusting intuition. It is the intentionally seeing and accepting the things that won't always feel uncomfortable. It is the intentionally prioritizing oneself, and then loving others gently. Loving gently does not enable but supports.

Walking through hard things with others, once my own oxygen mask was in place, healed me. I have the strongest

relationships I've ever had and genuinely love myself because I embraced the intentional doing.

Eventually my mom's rallying did come to an end. Mostly she slept, so mostly I sat beside her in that dark,
urine-scented room, reliving my entire adulthood where
she (and succinctly William) was concerned. Replaying it all
and seeing more clearly than ever how I'd grown. I relived
all I'd lost out on because I didn't know that I could let
either of them go be responsible for themselves. I loved
them both so much. All I had ever wanted was someone
to advocate for me and find me worth fighting for ... wasn't
that what love was?

I sat in that uncomfortable chair mourning for the girl
turned woman I had been.

In her awake times after the rally, my mother had no
idea who I was. She didn't have a daughter, she insisted.
She knew I was trying to trick her. She'd hit. She'd hurl
insults. She'd grab the stuffed bunny I'd sent her for her last
birthday, hold it tightly, and tell me she'd kill me if I took
it. All of that was fine. I could take it—if it hadn't been for
the one expression: The way she'd glare her hate-filled eyes
at me, purse her lips, and click her tongue. Each time she
did that I would go straight back to when I was a little girl.
Abuses I'd long ago buried came rushing back.

I could feel my emotional stability slipping. I needed to
go home. I needed to sleep in my own bed, binge watch
my own TV, cuddle my dog, and spend time breathing easy
next to my husband.

The old me would have ridiculed my weakness and stayed with her anyway. The old me meant well, but the old me was wrong.

Ten days later, we drove back. There hadn't been much change other than that she mostly slept now, was on consistent morphine, and seldom responded.

I'd been scared to hold her hand or touch her for fear of waking that terrified and broken girl inside of me again. Instead, I'd occasionally caress her forehead or her shoulder atop the ratty quilt spread over her. Her favorite songs were still looping on repeat. I'd gently sing the lyrics or talk to her about things she might like to know.

"I signed a book contract, Mom. Someone wants to publish my book, my story. You know, in a lot of ways, it's your story too. I don't think you'd love it, though," I laughed a little.

She was gone twelve hours later.

I had not shed one tear during those five weeks, but as we waited for the funeral home, I cried those weeks of pent-up tears.

Maybe she'd waited for me. Maybe somewhere, deep down she had still been there somehow. Maybe she'd be proud of me and who I am now. She never saw this me before. I laugh to myself a little at the thought because, honestly, I don't care if she'd be proud or not. I can love her anyway, in a pure and gentle way, even if she felt I'd been her biggest disappointment.

I've known since I was six years old that I wanted to be a writer. While I knew I'd someday write out these stories to share with you, at various points in time I dabbled with children's stories, a novel, and lots of poetry.

After my mom died, I took a day to go through a collection of pages she had, of things I'd sent her when I was still a kid living in Idaho. While most of them were in my writing, I came across a very worn page printed from an old computer. The margins of the lines were adorned with clip art roses, dating the whole thing to the early 90s.

As I read the very poorly written prose, I transitioned from cringing to full-on heartbreak. It wasn't until my eyes scanned my middle school signature at the bottom that I accepted these as my words. These words feel so foreign, though the resolutions behind them do not, and I cannot read them without crying.

I remember this girl ... *this* me. The fourteen-year-old me who was in the care of people who supported these feelings, these self-beliefs, and found them worthy of adornment and framing.

More than a mother who has gone on from this life, and more than people who should have cared more, it is this girl for whom I grieve.

I am no longer her, though I carry her with me always.

I fight for her.

I love her.

With the following piece was a note, written in my handwriting, introducing this gift I'd made my mother:

Dear Mom,

I'm sorry that I don't have any money to buy a frame for this poem I wrote for you.

I hope you love it. I hope it helps you love me, Mom. I worked really hard on it. My house dad helped me with the rose art on the computer because roses are your favorite. I'm sorry they look a little weird. I hope you like it. Happy birthday Mom, I love you so much!

    Misty

It seems like only yesterday,
I was a growing little girl.
But since that day I have changed,
so much in my special little ways.

The nights I needed a mother,
You were always by my side.
One to guide my direction,
You, my mother and no other.

All I've left you is a scar,
Not physical, but mental memories.
For years & years I put you through hell,
But yet you've come so far.

I'm sorry can't you see,
I have felt the guilt along with fear.
Then made the same mistake,
Yes, the blame is all on me.

All these years of your poor life,
Have died from misery.
All the sleepless nights you saw
From all the hell and all the strife.

The unforgivable pain and misery,
All the hatred and the strife.
And yet you wait with open arms,
For this selfish little girl to say
                    "I'm sorry"

I Love You Mom!

I hope that you have a great 26th birthday. By the way, the little angels on the front of your card are you. I am so proud of you that I can't really find the words to say and I'm glad that you are my daughter. I also hope that this gets to you in time for your BIG day.

I Love You,
Mom

Letter from Nora, 2002

Acknowledgments

I recently read that it takes a village to write a book, and, in my case, this feels so true. While I personally typed these pages, I could never have gotten this far without my village. I couldn't begin this section without writing out my immense love and gratitude for the Martinez family: Ray and Lorrie, there are no words yet breathed into existence to convey what you've meant to me. From the very beginning, your presence in my life provided me a constant source of love, even today as you've supported this author journey and the writing of this book. Melanie, I'll love you forever and am so grateful that, despite so many odds, we are forever friends. Anjanette, thank you for becoming a beautiful, supportive friend I've been able to share some truly dark days with.

For my Peterson family, I love you each so much. While you had your "real" family, and rightly so, you loved me and chose me into your fold when I needed it the most. So much of my healing came from that.

Ryan Caviness and Joe Haynes, time has passed and life's circumstances took us in very different directions, but my gratitude and admiration for you as *brothers* have never wavered. I heard this line in a movie once: "I would kill tigers for you." I've always loved the sentiment behind it. Where you and yours are concerned, I'd like to think it's true ... but also, you're both far more capable of fending off a wildcat attack. Even so, even after all these years, if you ever needed me, I would do anything I could to be there. In addition to these two brothers of mine, I'd like to thank Will Gates, Leon Rothauge, Justin Krahn, and especially Vic Peterson for showing me that men could be good. At different times you were validating voices of my worth, and I've never forgotten that.

Sherri Perkins, my sister in heart, soul, and life moments, I cannot imagine a deeper bond with another human. This connection vines its way to your K-babies and their babies. This radiant family tree growing from you gives me so much life.

I don't know who I would have become if it hadn't been for the friendships of Donna Nelson, her mom Joan Oldham, DeAndra Everist, Sarah Hall, Leon and Carol Rothauge, Kaylynne Keen, Debra Weasonforth, Angel O'Brien, Karen Harrison, Breanna Chud, and Laura Todd. Though various chapters of this life held these relationships dear in different seasons, I'm eternally grateful for those precious, life-sustaining journeys.

Matt and Kozzette Bennett, you are simply the best of the best people in the universe! I cannot imagine this life without you in it—Thank God that I don't have to.

I always knew this book would come. I am so grateful for Lauren Eckhardt! Lauren, your vision for Burning Soul Press is the sort of thing that sets my own soul on fire. Thank you for making a space for me and my story inside of your dream. Thank you for assembling my beautiful success team who have made this journey incredible. Claire Coffey, Taylor Harvey, and Julie Navickas, thank you each for being brilliant, motivated women who have empowered me along this journey in the best of ways! To my editor, Deborah Clark, thank you! As my editor, please feel free to insert all of the affirming adjectives here because you deserve them! You journeyed with me through many of the most intimate parts of my life and did so with love, grace, and encouragement.

Robin Chapman, this book would not be in anyone's hands right now if it wasn't for you! Your hand and heart through these pages, your compassion around these words ... thank you, though that barely touches the surface ...

My Carpe Diem powerhouse, BADASS women—you motivate and inspire me in a bazillion ways. Leisa, Cami, Willow, Rachel W., Alisa, Ashley, Habby, Kara, Lindsey, Rachel (and by beautiful extension Everly)—what beams of solid love and sunlight you have been! This book was quilted together with you by my side. Speaking of rays of light—Nikki Johnson, Chantal Roaché, and Veronica Hummel ... How did a girl get as lucky as I am to support the power and magic of story, womanhood, and community with the most amazing humans??? Thank you!

Thank you to my first "friend" Tom, who gave this weird Gen X girl My Space, rocked my outdated ideas of what community could look like, and gave me the beautiful gift of Maggie Friedenberg. What an adventure it's been! My friend, you've been there through the darkest parts of this adult journey while being a source of light for many of the best. From the birth of The Collective and Carpe Diem, you've been by my side. I love you, friend, so much!

Rabekah, Lucas, Amanda, and Gennica, thank you for the most "dream come true" seasons of my life. No matter what has happened, not a day has passed where I wasn't the most grateful for the moments, memories, and time with you. May you always know, wherever your lives take you, that you are worthy, so loved, and the very best parts of everything. *Love* cannot convey what my heart will hold for you until the day I leave this earth.

Austin, thank you for the beautiful babies. Their Mimi loves them an infinite amount. Thank you for your friendship, witchy-sisterhood, and deep love. You'll forever be one of my favorite women!

CHW, my adventure partner and love of my life, you are the best and most incredible man I have ever known. You are my favorite! It has been a real journey. Through it we've each been our own versions of children, monsters, heroes, broken messes, loves, and the deepest of friends. There is LITERALLY (said as only Rob could) no one else I could imagine building a life with. You promised me old and gray for always, I'm going to hold you to it.

Lastly, thank you God for each and every one of these people and the moments that fill not only these pages, but this heart of mine. Thank you for the ones no longer with us; even in the hard parts you taught me so much through them. Thank you for healing, wholeness, divine femininity, valuing me, guiding me, and being the God of full circles.

Also, God, thank you for letting me coexist with Tyler Joseph and Josh Dunn because their music brings me life and fueled the penning of these pages.

One last thing ... Thank you for dogs.

About the Author

Mae Wagner is a strong advocate of women, community, and connection. She is an author of fiction, personal essay, memoir, and personal growth strategies. A gypsy soul, having lived all over the continental United States, Mae currently lives on the coast of Lake Erie with her husband, their adoring golden retriever, and their spicy rescue cat.

You can find her on Instagram and Twitter @rainydayin-may and at www.rainydayinmay.com. Accompanying Spotify playlist can be found here: https://cutt.ly/aLwMtfs

Lightning Source UK Ltd.
Milton Keynes UK
UKHW041808110922
408396UK00016BA/220/J